THE CHICAGO PUBLIC LIBRARY

FORM 19

COOK'S TOUR

COOK'S TOUR

A HAPHAZARD JOURNEY FROM GUANGZHOU TO DUBLIN AND BACK AGAIN

PAUL CULLEN

ALLEN & UNWIN

This book is dedicated to Dorcas Cullen—traveller, companion, editor and friend.

First published in 1995
Allen & Unwin Pty Ltd
9 Atchison Street, St Leonards, NSW 2066 Australia

National Library of Australia
Cataloguing-in-Publication entry

Cullen, Paul, 1954– .
Cook's tour: a haphazard journey from Guangzhou to
Dublin and back again.

Includes index.
ISBN 1 86373 910 6.

1. Cullen, Paul, 1954— . Journeys. 2. Voyages and travels.
3. China—Description and travel. I. Title.

910.4

Set in 10.5/12.5pt Goudy Old Style by DOCUPRO, Sydney
Printed by McPherson's Printing Group, Maryborough

Cover design by Seymour Designs
Map and illustrations by Diane Bradley

10 9 8 7 6 5 4 3 2 1

CONTENTS

With Intourist out of the way, there's no longer any obstacle to completing a journey from Asia to Europe and back again by public transport, so we set out to do it. Rumour of a new rail route through Central Asia. Packing up the house, the bags and the children, and the first step—by air to New Guinea.

Two weeks in Hong Kong. Chinese New Year. Preparations for winter travel in China and Russia. Cantonese cooking and the cult of *yum cha*. A trip to the oyster farms at Laufaushan. We visit Macau and discover why Buddhists eat oysters, too.

Taking the plunge into China. Up the Pearl River by boat. Shamian Island and the White Swan Hotel. A cast of thousands at Guangzhou Railway Station. Qinping Market and the edible zoo. The girls star in a television show and we get an introduction to Chinese trains.

Lost in Changsha, a very long way from home. A bleak arrival in the dark, and Chinese hotel clerks. Hunan cuisine and the

Doggy Café. Chinese museums and the cult of ancient corpses. The Shanghai Express and our first meeting with Dr Peng.

class into the Gobi, and the gate at the end of the world. The high desert and the Mountains of God. Arrival in Ürümqi, and Kerry gets arrested.

PREFACE

This book is an account of a rather haphazard journey across Asia and Europe which I took with my family in the early part of 1993. We set off with the idea of tracing the old Silk Road, which once connected China with the Mediterranean, through the Gobi Desert and Central Asia. Owing to the continuing political changes in China and the republics of the former Soviet Union, the route was uncertain, but it seemed reasonable to suppose that if there was a train going from one place to another, we ought to be able to get on it. It was not a journey we could have planned in any detail, since information about public transport in very remote places is hard to come by, unless you happen to be there. Generally, there are few places on the planet you can't get to, if you are willing to travel by whatever means local people use. Asia and Europe, in particular, are well served by a network of railway lines which will take you great distances if you simply get on at one end and keep going.

I am indebted to my friend Joel Becker, who asked me to write a journal while we travelled, and encouraged me to make a book of it when we returned. He was also indispensible in persuading my publishers, Allen & Unwin, to accept a manuscript from an unknown author.

This is neither a work of scholarship nor a guide book, but rather a story told as well as I can manage it, based on my own recollection of what happened, and on lengthy notes written at the time. I have tried to weed out the more grievous errors of fact or chronology. Those that remain are all my own. I am indebted to the authors of the following books for numerous bits of geographical, historical and technical detail: Mildred Cable, *The Gobi Desert*, Hodder & Stoughton, 1942, London, reprinted 1984 by Virago Press, London; Storey Cummings et al., *China—a travel survival kit*, Lonely Planet Productions, 1991, Hawthorn, Victoria; Norma Martin, *The Silk Road*, Methuen Australia, 1987, North Ryde, NSW; Reay Tannahill, *The Fine Art of Food*, The Folio Society, Alpha Books, 1968, Sydney; P.I. Tremlett (ed.), *Thomas Cook Overseas Timetable*, Thomas Cook Publishing, 1993, London.

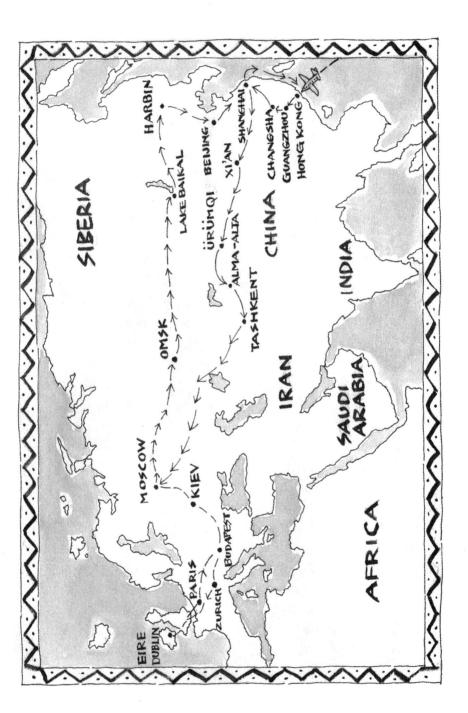

ONE

In the pre-dawn darkness, the toot of a taxi's horn told us it was time to go. Our three girls hoisted their light packs, while Dorcas and I did a last-minute check to see that everything in the house was locked and the gas turned off. We carried our bags down the stairs and clambered into the taxi for the short run to the airport. We were setting off on a journey that was to take more than five months, and cover some 45 000 kilometres, travelling overland from Hong Kong to Dublin and back again by public transport. We'd worked out a general idea of the route. The details were still a little hazy.

The trip had been prompted by a brief morning radio item, two months before, from Monica Attard, the Australian Broadcasting Corporation's correspondent in Moscow. She reported that the foreign press corps in the former Soviet Union was enjoying much more freedom to travel about, since Intourist had lost its monopoly on internal travel in what was now the Commonwealth of Independent States (CIS). This, to us, was an important bit of news. If Intourist had released its strangle-hold on Russian tourism, then it might be possible to travel independently in that country.

Although western tourists had, for years, been allowed to visit the Soviet Union on government-organised tours, they wouldn't let you just wander around on your own. It was necessary to pre-book everything from hotel rooms to taxis in advance, at rates that Intourist considered suitable for fat-cat capitalists with more money than sense. Without a Gold Amex Card and a suitcase full of cash, the largest country in the world was effectively out of bounds for the independent

1

traveller. But if Intourist had changed its spots, then another piece of news we'd heard became important, too.

The rumour was that the Chinese government, after 30 years of painfully slow progress, had finally completed the rail connection between Xinjiang province in the far west of China and the Soviet railhead at Aktogay in Kazakhstan. If that were true, it would mean that a new route was open between China and Europe, a route that followed the ancient Silk Road through the Gobi Desert and into Central Asia.

I telephoned the China International Travel Service (CITS) in Hong Kong:

'Can you tell me if the rail line is now open from Xinjiang through to the Russian border?'

'You want to go on the Siberian Express?'

'No, I want to know if we can go from Xinjiang to Russia.'

'Everybody go Siberian Express, very good train.'

'I'm sure it is, but what about the Xinjiang railway line?'

'No, not possible, we never hear about that one.'

'Could you find out, perhaps ask the China National Railways?'

'You call back, next month, maybe we have information.'

This was a rare gesture of co-operation from the CITS, an organisation that many independent travellers to the People's Republic of China have come to know and loathe. CITS is the official government bureau dedicated to preventing foreign travellers from going anywhere inside China, unless it's on a hugely over-priced bus tour full of rich American tourists named Chuck.

Three weeks later, I called the Hong Kong office again.

'Have you any information about the train from Ürümqi to the Russian border?'

'Yes, we hear something about that one.'

'Great! Is the line open? Can we cross the Russian border?'

'We got no details, just hear about it.'

'But it is open?'

'Don't know that, just somebody tell us about it.'

'Where did you hear about it? Can I call someone else?'

'No, maybe just somebody mention it.'

My heart sank. I had an idea what was coming next.

'Who mentioned it?'

'Somebody call, Australian, I think.'

'I think that was me.'

'Yeah, no problem.'

That booking anything in advance in China is next to impossible came as no surprise. The country just doesn't work on western expectations. With more than 1000 million people to look after, the Chinese government does not put the requirements of a few thousand tourists high on their list of priorities, which is understandable. On the other hand, China has one of the longest railway systems in the world, a lattice of clattering rails and tatty rolling stock that carries several million passengers every day, and goes just about everywhere. We decided to take the punt. Public transport had always worked reasonably well when we'd travelled in Asia, and we supposed it might do so again.

The idea was to travel by train from Hong Kong, up the east coast of China, and then west to the ancient city of Xi'an, and on to remote Ürümqi, the last outpost in China's western Xinjiang province. From there, we hoped to cross the Russian border into Kazakhstan by rail, and continue up the line to Moscow.

On the Kowloon side of Hong Kong harbour, just where you get off the Star Ferry, there's a small brick tower, standing off to the right. The old-fashioned clock on the face of the tower still works perfectly, and serves as a hurried time-check for the crowds of commuters piling on and off the ferries. The tower is all that remains of the original Kowloon–Canton Railway Station, long since demolished to make way for the soaring architecture of Nathan Road and the Hong Kong Cultural Centre.

In the years between World Wars I and II, it was still possible to board a train in Hong Kong that would take you to London, if you had the price of a ticket and several weeks to spare. In the intervening years, the revolution in China, border disputes with the Soviet Union and the heavy chill of the Cold War made this trip impossible, and the expansion of commercial air travel made it unnecessary. The route, when it operated, was the longest continuous rail journey in the world, connecting Hong Kong with Canton, Shanghai, Peking, Moscow, Berlin and finally, London.

Although the rail lines still existed, and were in fact much modernised and improved during the 1950s and 1960s, this particular journey had been impracticable for more than 30 years, until the thaw in relations between China and the West began with Richard Nixon's visit to China in 1972. Individual travellers had to wait another ten years before it became possible to make limited trips into the People's Republic of China. A handful of foreign tourists began to make the Trans-Siberian trip, under the watchful eyes of Intourist and the CITS. We had contacted several tour companies in Hong Kong who offered group tickets on the Trans-Siberian, but none of them had heard of the alternative route through Ürümqi. It was too recent a development to have trickled down into the tour brochures. But a call to the Russian Embassy in Canberra confirmed that it was, in theory, possible:

'Is it true that we can now enter the CIS independently?'

'Yes, that's true.'

'Across the border at Alma-Ata, for instance?'

'Why not?'

'And we can travel by train up to Moscow?'

'If you have visa, you can travel.'

'You're being very good about this.'

'This is nothing. Last week, we had man who wants to ride bicycle from Vladivostok.'

'Really, what did you say?'

'In winter, Russia is very cold.'

'Good point.'

There was, then, no particular reason why the journey couldn't be done, so we set about doing it. The only real uncertainty was the rail line into Central Asia. We decided that we'd keep asking as we got closer, and would, with any luck, hear news of it along the road. At worst, it would be possible to backtrack from Ürümqi to Beijing, and catch the Trans-Siberian after all.

My wife, Dorcas, had a long-standing fascination with the Central Asian cities of Tashkent and Samarkand, and I'd been promising us a thorough tour of China for years.

I am a professional chef, and for years had been intensely interested in traditional Chinese cooking. As an under-funded student in New York, I had haunted the cheap noodle shops and *yum cha* houses of Chinatown. Living some years later in London, the superb Cantonese restaurants in and around Wardour Street got my (almost) undivided attention. As I gained experience in large hotel kitchens and rose through the ranks, preparing the 'international' cuisine demanded by international hotels, I nursed a private obsession with the Chinese repertoire. Practising at home, reading everything I could find on the

4

subject and occasionally presenting Chinese dishes on hotel buffets and menus, I had begun to master some of the basic dishes. The more I learnt, the more I became aware of how complex the subject was. To understand more, I'd have to go to China.

Our three children were game travellers, so we saw no reason why they shouldn't come along. We found that travelling was actually more fun with our kids than without them. The presence of children often breaks the ice with local people who may otherwise distrust the 'foreign devils' wandering through their village. Besides, train travel is probably the easiest means of transportation with kids. There's none of the cramped boredom of aeroplanes and buses, and as long as you're careful to round up the little beggars from the platform when the train starts moving, you're unlikely to lose them.

Getting ready for the trip was a matter of about six weeks' work, organising passports for all of us, finding someone to rent our house while we were away, farming out the cats and the budgies to friends, and tracking down the cheapest flight out of Australia that would put us in striking distance of China. We heard about an Air Niugini flight from Cairns that connected with Hong Kong via Port Moresby. We booked the first available seats, and thus had a departure date— mid-January 1993.

Travelling by public transport might be a little haphazard (you count yourself lucky if you can find anything pointed in the right direction) but preparations for this sort of trip are simple: make sure your passport's in order, pack a minimum of clothes, take a first aid kit and as much money as you can lay your hands on.

Each of us found a small rucksack. The girls carried their own clothes, notebooks and toys. Dorcas carried her clothing, plus a toilet bag for the family, the medical kit and a 'hussif', her all-important travelling repair kit for lost buttons, split seams and broken straps. I carried my own gear, plus the family documents, maps, timetables and books. The most useful of these were Thomas Cook's *International Railway Timetable*, and Lonely Planet's excellent guidebook *China—a travel survival kit*. These two books were constant references, and the amount of research that had gone into them only became apparent when we needed them most.

We'd be travelling through China and Russia in the middle of winter, and warm clothing would be essential, but here we faced a problem. In the far northern tropics of Australia, there's not a lot of call for winter overcoats and thermal underwear. Our local shops were well supplied with board shorts, t-shirts and suncream, but their range of sub-zero mountaineering gear was limited. A few friends discovered long-disused overcoats in the backs of their closets, and happily loaned them for the duration. The rest we resolved to buy in Hong Kong.

The first step would be easy—Hong Kong is a well-equipped and snappily efficient city, where Chinese visas can easily be obtained in a few days. Our air tickets came with seven nights' stay in a tourist hotel (the package was actually cheaper than the normal economy air fares alone), so we would have a soft start to the journey. Braced with a week's final preparations, we'd be ready to leap into the maelstrom of China.

The last week before departure was frenetic. Dorcas had arrangements to make with the children's schools, so that they wouldn't fall too far behind in their study—particularly important for 13-year-old Clare, who was in her third year of high school. Her teachers were sympathetic, and the school principal remarkably encouraging. The girls were bright enough to catch up, she said, and the chance of a trip like this was not one to be missed. The house had to be packed up, then scrubbed from top to bottom to be made ready for tenants, who had obligingly agreed to take it for the five months we would be away. I had a business to secure, a task made easier by an accommodating partner, who would take over the reins for the time I'd be away. The pressure on all of us, to tie up all these disparate threads in time to catch the plane, saw tempers fray and occasionally snap. 'Let's just get out of here,' we thought, 'the travelling part will be easy.'

In a last-day flurry of tea-chests, written instructions, caged pets and checklists, it was done. On the night before we left, our old house was strangely quiet and bare, the bedrooms empty, the kitchen dark. We sat on the floor, the five of us, to eat a late-night supper of takeaway pizza and Coke. We laid out the clothes we'd need in the morning, and put the girls down to sleep on the bare mattresses. We were ready to go.

The short flight from Cairns to Port Moresby was over the Coral Sea, a blue-grey carpet of water studded with small islands. On the ground in Moresby the light was intense, the air billowing across the tarmac in hot gusts scented with aviation fuel. The airport was tatty and run-down, the waiting room grotty and plastic, but mercifully air-conditioned. Waiting while the larger jet that would take us to Hong Kong was re-fuelled, we looked ridiculously over-dressed, dragging the borrowed overcoats around in the 40° heat.

Seven-year-old Aislinn was already having a good time. Aeroplanes, she had decided, were just great. Nice people brought you games and things to eat. You could watch movies. Going up and down was almost as good as a roller-coaster, and you didn't have to queue up to get on. Kerry, our middle daughter, was not so easily placated. Moody and a worrier by nature, Kerry was the only member of the family who would really rather have stayed home. She was intelligent and interested in the world, but preferred things to stay the same around her, with familiar possessions and friends and foods—she would need lots of reassurance throughout the trip, we thought. We reminded her that the family would always be together, even if the scenery and people changed around us, and it was, after all, not the first time she'd travelled. In her 11 years, she'd already been around the world once, and had visited a dozen countries. She just liked staying put once she'd arrived. Clare, our teenager, was serene. Travelling was one of the things she liked doing best, and she was well used to it, having bounced along in the back of lorries, buses, trishaws and tuk-tuks since she was a baby.

The five-hour flight from Port Moresby to Hong Kong was comfortable. We reset our watches to local time as we drifted in towards Kai Tak airport for a late afternoon arrival. The girls were pinned to the windows for the dramatic landing between the towering buildings crowding the sides of Hong Kong's single runway. A few minutes later, we were down, and took our first steps into China.

Two

On the ground in Hong Kong, we were taken for an involuntary tour of Kowloon. The airport bus wound its way through the densely packed side streets of Tsim Sha Tsui, before taking us across the harbour to our hotel on Hong Kong Island.

It was a cold, grey evening, but Chinese New Year fever was in the air. The holiday started that night, and our bus driver and minder looked like they couldn't wait to get away. All the shops were ablaze with light, and signs in red and gold promised 50 per cent off everything. It's good luck to make big sales on the last day of the year, and also good luck to buy yourself new clothes and things for the New Year. Business was brisk.

The kids exploded into the two small rooms in the hotel, switching on televisions, activating air-conditioning, pressing any available button to see what happened. They were delighted with the panel of switches on the bedside table, which allowed them to dim the lights, set a wake-up alarm and ring room service all at once. They watched Cantonese soap operas and Hong Kong MTV while we unpacked. There's a big industry in what's called 'Canto-Pop', slushy romantic songs with accompanying video clips in nasal Cantonese. The story line is simple: boy meets girl, girl spurns boy, boy goes off and damages himself on a motorcycle, girl ends up at the hospital bedside with boy sporting a head bandage, they croon undying love to each other while she checks his pulse. The MTV presenters were terrific, dressed like Michael Jackson and slipping in and out of Mandarin, Cantonese and English with amazing facility.

We bundled up in gloves and scarves and set off to find dinner.

Aislinn had never worn an overcoat before, and had to be given instructions. It was raining, and colder than anything we'd been used to in the Australian tropics. Taxis hissed along the wet streets, while crowds of late-night shoppers prowled up and down Hennessy Road. The clanking trams ran in both directions, looking like overloaded bookcases on rails. We found a cheery, bright Cantonese restaurant full of steam and noise, and settled in for our first meal in Hong Kong.

It had all the right essentials. Plates of glossy, copper-coloured roast duck, bowls of lovely prawn dumplings and clay pots of braised mushrooms and fried bean curd appeared on the table, and we all hoed in. Because we so often cooked Chinese food at home, the three girls were already nimble with chopsticks, and adept at shovelling rice into themselves from a small bowl. The dishes were just the standards of Cantonese cooking, but the quality was superb. The sauces were no more than strengthened stocks with a touch of soya or oyster flavour, the green vegetables finished with a sheen of oil and salt. Like the French, the Cantonese rely on the quality of the ingredients and the skills of specialist cooks to make the meal. It was a lovely introduction, and we had a week to explore what else Hong Kong's restaurants could provide.

After dinner, the rain had stopped, so we walked down Hennessy Road to Victoria Park, which had been transformed into a huge flower market for Chinese New Year. Floodlit and thronged with people, the park was packed with stalls selling branches of pale blossoms and potted tangerine trees, symbols of re-birth and good luck in the new year. We put in some practice at crowd-following. There was no way the five of us could walk, and stay together in Chinese crowds, so we needed a method of finding each other if we became separated. I'd found a big wide-brimmed Akubra hat for the journey. It was easy to spot in a crowd, as I'm taller than most Chinese, and the girls could home in on the familiar hat if I stopped every 15 minutes or so. Aislinn was the hardest to keep track of: she could disappear into a crowd in moments. We bought her a bright red bobble-hat to make her easier to find.

Hong Kong never closes for business, but the New Year holiday seemed to slow it down a bit. All the offices and most of the big department stores were closed for the weekend but sensibly, the museums and parks were open. We joined local families out for a stroll with their children in Kowloon Park, then went to a *yum cha* restaurant recommended by a girl at the Hong Kong Tourist Association.

Yum cha, or 'drink tea', is the generic term for a lovely Cantonese habit of stopping for a bite to eat and a pot of tea, any time from early morning to late afternoon. Dozens of Hong Kong restaurants offer yum cha, often with seating for hundreds of customers at a time. Good ones will be packed around lunchtime, with a noisy, pleasant atmosphere and lots of good food. In fact, the queue to get in, and the noise level inside, are the best indications of a good restaurant, not just for obvious reasons. Great yum cha requires a fast turnover, so that the assortment of small steamed and fried snacks, collectively known as dim sum, keep coming fresh and hot from the kitchens. The restaurant we'd been recommended was in the Ocean Centre, the massive, interlinked shopping complex on the west side of Kowloon. Shaped like a theatre club, with a large central stage and hundreds of tables, the Ocean Centre Restaurant was already in full swing by 11.00 am, but the harried maitre d' managed to find us a table for five.

Cantonese dim sum chefs are specialists, and the first mark of their skill is the quality of the pastries they make to enclose the traditional fillings. There are five of them: bao dough for the light steamed buns often filled with sweet roast pork, egg noodle dough commonly used for siu mai (meat dumplings), rice noodle dough, glutinous rice dough and the semi-transparent wheat starch dough, used for the lightest of prawn dumplings, har gow. However good the quality of the fillings, dim sum will be spoilt if the basic doughs are too thick, poorly shaped or badly mixed. Working with the five doughs, skilled dim sum cooks can prepare at least 50 or 60 different varieties of sweet and savoury pastries to be served at a yum cha lunch. Hong Kong is a city that lives to eat, and has it the most demanding audience in the world for the dim sum chef.

We joined the crowd with enthusiasm, slurping tea and picking bamboo steamer baskets from the tea ladies who pushed their carts around the restaurant, calling out in Cantonese the names of the delicacies they had to offer. Pai gwat was a favourite, steamed pork ribs with black beans and a trace of fresh chilli, or crisp fried spring rolls, green pepper slices with fish cake or the delicious (and expensive) yee chi gow, shark's fin dumplings. The girls went at this assortment like starving sailors, while Chinese grandmothers at adjacent tables nudged each other to have a look at the little *gwailos* eating with chopsticks.

All of us had to get used to the notion that, with our pale skin and round eyes, we would stick out in crowds for the next few months of travelling. The Cantonese term for foreigners, *gwailo*, can be translated as 'ghost man' or more commonly, 'foreign devil'. The Chinese are still a xenophobic race, and regard the rest of the world with curiosity, if not suspicion. Hong Kong was a soft introduction. Thousands of Europeans and North Americans live there, and *gwailo* has become almost an affectionate term, commonly used by the *gwailos* themselves. Later, in the more remote parts of China, we would get the sort of reaction you might expect in Melbourne if you were to appear at the Lord Mayor's Ball in a chicken suit. It's rare enough to see a western foreigner in China, rarer still to see a matched set of three fair-haired girls and their parents, trudging through some backstreet fish market in Wuhan. We could expect to pull a crowd.

Hong Kong's imminent union with the People's Republic was a subject that we'd be discussing over and over again, but at that moment we were keen just to learn more about the place. With a population of nearly six million, it is one of the most densely packed cities on earth. Its political system is antique—there aren't many fully fledged colonies left in the world, and its dedication to capitalist freebootery is legendary. It's also a Chinese city. Take off a thin top-dressing of British judges, policemen and politicians, and the city is 99 per cent ethnic Cantonese, with a sprinkling of Filipinos and Indians. Visitors to Hong Kong, we were told, seldom get out of the Kowloon and Causeway Bay shopping ghettos, so we resolved to see more than the camera shops. We'd go to restaurants, too.

Our first expedition was a short one, over to Aberdeen on the south coast of Hong Kong Island, one of the colony's best natural harbours and home to a colourful fleet of fishing boats. The town is small and rag-tag, but the harbour is the attraction. Several thousand people live permanently aboard the fleet of ocean-going junks moored there. These are large, serious-looking working boats festooned with fishing nets and flapping laundry while in port. Dozens of small sampans buzz around like taxis, all of them with the high, bouncy look of the traditional junk hull.

On a holiday weekend, Aberdeen was packed with Chinese families on their way to Sunday lunch at one of the big floating restaurants in the harbour. These giant foodie emporiums are monuments to Chinese kitsch—every wall is red flock and gold trim, every chandelier is tasselled, electric-eyed dragons breathe fire from every doorway—a sort of Cantonese Disneyland afloat. The Jumbo Restaurant could provide seating for more than 2000 people at a time, and the blaze of decorative lighting it displayed at night was the subject of a hundred postcards. There was even a fish-viewing deck out the back, where thoughtful diners could inspect the tanks of live fish, crabs, crayfish, eels and prawns, before selecting what they'd have for lunch. A painted sign hung on the wall: 'Please Do Not Disturb The Seafood'.

The food was good, standard Cantonese *dim sum* and fried noodle dishes, delivered quickly. The din was extraordinary, several hundred people shouting at once, toasting each other with Tsingtao beer, arguing over the bill (it's good form to pick up the tab, even if you come to blows over it), waiters clattering plates and bowls—just the way the Chinese like a restaurant to be.

The following day, Dorcas took the girls off to visit museums, while I went on a quest for Chinese visas. Walking around the city streets, Hong Kong reminded me very much of New York, where I'd spent most of my childhood. The buildings were steel-grey and soaring, the streets packed with well-dressed businessmen and taxis. In both cities, the local colour erupts at street corners, where the newspaper stands, sandwich shops and snack bars do their business. In New York, it had been Italian-ice men in the summer and chestnut-roasters in the winter, in Hong Kong the assortment was much wider. Peddlers with tiny charcoal braziers on wheels supplied the passing trade with grilled dried squid, skewered fish balls, or light, sweet waffles cooked on a griddle. Fresh-juice carts dispensed carrot juice and sugar-cane drinks. Like New Yorkers, the Chinese hate to be far away from something to eat, and they're amply catered for in the street.

The Consulate of the People's Republic of China (Visa Division) in Wanchai was not hard to find, a plain office on the fifth floor of an unremarkable building. I took a form from a stack at the door, and read the details. We had to provide all the usual passport information, photographs and an estimate of how long we'd be in China. This was 1993, and the PRC had opened the doors wide to tourism, mindful of the hard currency it brought in and paving the way for overseas Chinese investment on the mainland. Only ten years previously, when individual travel inside China was still a novelty, many areas of the country remained off-limits to foreigners. Now the formalities were minimal.

Queuing up to lodge the forms, I was treated to my first taste of the Chinese civil service. I'd arrived just before opening time, anticipating crowds later. There were already 40 people in the line. The counter clerks, however, did not seem quite ready to meet the day. One woman appeared behind the glass, shrugged on a cardigan, and went off to lie down on a camp-bed. An older man walked in, sat on a stool with his newspaper and began a patient and thorough exploration of his left nostril. A grandmotherly sort made her entrance stage right, hoisted herself up on to a cashier's perch and proceeded to stare into space.

Twenty minutes past opening time, out in the queue, we conferred. Perhaps they didn't open until half past nine? Could this be some sort of workers' holiday? Would we all have to go away and come back tomorrow? A Chinese-American gent in a lime-green safari suit, gold Rolex and a Florida tan was getting impatient. His handler, a natty young Hong Konger with a portable phone tried to calm him down.

'What's the matter with these goddamn people, they work here or what?' said the senior citizen in a ripe Brooklyn accent.

'No problem, they will open soon,' said the handler.

'Hey, I'm supposed to be in Canton tonight, I haven't got time for this crap.'

'Relax, it's OK, I will make sure you catch your flight.'

'Geez, they think I got all day here or something?'

The old man looked like he was working himself up to something serious, like buying the building and firing everybody, when the glass window snapped open, and the line began to move. Grandma and her two companions, with world-weary expressions, were now processing forms and accepting cash. I presented our bundle of passports and said 'Good morning' in Mandarin, exhausting roughly half my vocabulary in one hit. Grandma looked at me as if I'd asked her for a loan to buy drugs. She tossed our precious passports into a bin and flicked a form back at me across the counter. We had 90 days, more than enough, I hoped, to see us through to the Russian border. We could pick up our passports in 48 hours.

Our second excursion took us into the New Territories north of Kowloon, which extend up to the PRC border of Shenzen province.

Everywhere in Hong Kong, the public transport was fast, inexpensive and brilliantly laid out. A combination of hovercraft, train, tram and bus got us quickly from Central out to the satellite town of Tuen Mun, on our way to the tiny village of Laufaushan, on Deep Bay. Most of Hong Kong's oysters come from here, raw material for one of the most essential condiments in the Cantonese repertoire, oyster sauce.

If we had pictures in mind of a bucolic countryside, with bamboo-hatted peasants planting rice in flooded paddies, they were quickly dispelled by Hong Kong's urban sprawl. Huge housing projects, reminiscent of Singapore, stood like pastel ice-cream blocks along the shoreline near Tuen Mun, and the town had a new, raw edge about it. The pavements were still unfinished, the trams gleamingly clean. We took a light rail out to Yuen Long, a town centre with crowds just as thick as Kowloon's. Hong Kong's six million people were being encouraged to spread out into the New Territories to relieve the terrible overcrowding near the city centre. Offered government-subsidised housing, and provided with excellent public transport, they were taking up the offer in their hundreds of thousands. The colony already imports most of its food, so the loss of another few hundred hectares of farming land matters little if the satellite towns ease the tremendous pressure of population.

We found our bus, an old blue double-decker going to Laufaushan and the oyster farms. The girls piled upstairs to secure the front seats and the best view. They needn't have bothered. The landscape was not picturesque. Outside the town centre, we entered a wasteland of grisly industrial slums, wreckers' yards, container dumps and seedy housing. There's nothing sentimental about Hong Kong's single-minded pursuit of industrial growth. If you need a desalinisation plant or a container dock, you just go ahead and build the damn thing wherever it's convenient. Environmental considerations come a long way down the list. The bus trundled its way out slowly towards the coast, through a bleak panorama of broken concrete and rusted iron.

The village of Laufaushan was, at first, no more promising. A couple of tired-looking restaurants guarded a scruffy village square, little more than a turning place for the bus. We wandered a bit, finding no sign of the sea, but eventually discovered a narrow village lane that led down to the harbour from the bus stop. This was packed cheek-by-jowl with seafood restaurants, fishmongers, oyster shuckers and old women selling fried octopus and squid on skewers. Down at the bottom of the lane we found the sea, and a remarkable shoreline. Over the space of a hundred years or more, the oyster farmers of Laufaushan have gathered their catch, shucked their oysters and dumped the shells back in the sea. As a result, a vast midden of broken shells extended from what had once been the shoreline out about 400 metres into the bay. From the edge of this crunchy white rubbish tip, we saw the bamboo poles that marked the oyster beds, and a few shallow sampans tending them.

The day was bright but overcast, and we could plainly see the Chinese mainland a few kilometres away. We'd be going this way soon, for Deep Bay is a part of the great Pearl River estuary, which leads up to China's largest southern city, Guangzhou. This was the way the Portuguese had sailed in 1516, to the city they called Canton, to tap the wealth of Imperial China.

We took lunch in one of the little restaurants, served by a giggling girl of about 15, who thought our attempts at Cantonese were hilarious. While Kowloon businessmen poked and discussed lunch at the glass tanks full of wrasse, coral trout and razor clams, we had a wonderful meal of fried squid and casseroled noodles, crisp fresh greens and soft bean curd. Mother and Grandma were called out to have a look at the girls, and without six words in common, we were made welcome. As a treat, they brought us a sort of dessert soup, made of sweetened beans and taro, which all of us politely supped, after a few swift kicks under the table.

I wanted to try some of the less familiar styles of Chinese cooking, and Hong Kong is well furnished with them. Cantonese predominates, but there are many Chiu Chow, Sichuan, Shanghai and Beijing-style restaurants, too. A style rarely seen in the West is Chinese Buddhist cooking, a strictly vegetarian regimen that has evolved over centuries in the Buddhist monasteries. The story goes that the monks were required to accommodate the local warlords when they came to call, but their religion prohibited the preparation of animals for food. Eager to placate their prickly visitors, they presented remarkable dishes made from vegetable ingredients, fashioned to resemble meat in texture and flavour. 'Mock duck' and 'mock pork', made from various forms of bean curd and wheat gluten, became mainstays of the style, and remain so to this day. We went to a famous Buddhist place in Causeway Bay, the Bodhi Restaurant.

'No Meat or Alcohol Permitted on the Premises' said the sign in the window, just in case we'd forgotten. The restaurant was large and busy, and we were shuffled up to the second floor to find a table. The menu listed dozens of variations on gluten (a chewy, savoury product of wheat dough with the starch washed away that it has a texture like chicken skin when braised) and bean curd, combined with a variety of dry and fresh mushrooms. We ordered boldly. The results were wonderful. A claypot of mushrooms included delicacies like wood-ear, white fungus, black mushroom and lily buds. Crisp-fried bean curd rolls and snap fresh green beans made a meal that we devoured with enthusiasm. That night, we wandered down to the harbour to see the New Year fireworks. The crowds were out to celebrate the Year of the Rooster. The girls craned their necks to watch the soaring chrysanthemums and the exploding stars. The Chinese do not applaud or shout at spectacles like this. They sigh. 'Waaaah', from all around us, like some collective breath, as the huge displays burst and fell in the sky.

Walking back to the hotel, we looked into the small restaurants that seemed to crowd every block in this city devoted to business and food. Even late at night, they were still crowded with locals stopping to take on a plate of roast pork rice. A cook came out the door of one small place with a flapping carp, fresh from the tank. He slapped it on a chopping block that stood near the gutter and delivered an almighty whack with the side of a cleaver. It was gutted and scaled in a moment, the entrails flipped casually into the street. He trotted back into the steamy warmth of the restaurant with the fish still twisting in his hand.

We shopped for winter clothes and railway maps, trying to judge carefully what we would need against what we wanted to carry. We'd not been able to learn any more about the Xinjiang railway, nor could we get any information from the Russian side of the border, since the CIS did not have a consulate in Hong Kong. There were two in China, we learnt, at Shanghai and Beijing. With a large-scale map unfolded on the hotel bed, Dorcas and I discussed the possible routes we could take. Ferries from Hong Kong regularly sailed up the east coast, stopping at Xiamen and Shanghai, but these would make us arrive too early in the north, where it was still bitterly cold. We elected to take it slowly, north from Macau to Canton, then up by rail through south central China. There was no way to book tickets in advance, so we'd just have to start in Canton and take it from there.

The week in Hong Kong ended happily, but the time had come to hoist the packs and leave the cosy luxury of posh hotels. The first stop would be Macau, that odd relic of Portuguese empire-building, 65 kilometres west of Hong Kong Island at the mouth of the Pearl River. Transport there was easy. Thousands of Hong Kongers made the journey every day, attracted by the one vice dear to the Chinese heart they could not legally indulge in Hong Kong—casino-style gambling.

Given directions by a friendly woman at the Macau Tourist Board, we hunted for a cheap hotel somewhere near the docks from which the Canton ferry would leave. Macau is a Chinese city (95 per cent of the population are Cantonese), with a very different look from the slick steel-and-glass canyons of Hong Kong. The creaking godowns, or warehouses, along the waterfront looked as if they had not changed much in a century. The older houses had iron balconies and shuttered windows that reminded us of southern Europe, and the streets were narrow, twisting and paved with cobblestones. Although the lanes were crowded with taxis, bicycles and carts, the pace seemed somehow slower. Outdoor cafes were commonplace, and after dark, couples and families strolled an evening *paseo* along the Rua Praia Grande, as if in Lisbon or Madrid. It's a place with a wonderful atmosphere and a strange history.

Macau was first settled by the Portuguese in the early years of the 16th century, and quickly established itself as a trading port for the lucrative India–China–Japan monopoly which the Portuguese controlled. The Catholic Church used it as a Christian foothold in Asia, sending Jesuit missionaries under the control of Francis Xavier, who died in China and was later canonised. Macau was the principal European outpost in the East long before the upstart British seized the island of Hong Kong in 1841. It has an extraordinarily long history of wars, truces, invasions and political skulduggery which somehow has allowed the Portuguese to keep hold of it continuously for more than 400 years. The Japanese, who took Hong Kong in World War II, never crossed the water to invade Macau. Even the lunatic fringe of the Red Guards failed to capture Macau during the Cultural Revolution. When a Marxist government in Lisbon attempted to hand the place back in 1974, the Chinese government wouldn't have it, and told the Portuguese to leave things as they were. Following the agreement to hand back Hong Kong, the PRC agreed to take Macau back in 1999. In the meantime, it remains the oddest European settlement in the East.

As always, food reflects history, and tends to last longer than the latest written version of events. In Macau, the Portuguese colonial influence and the melting pot of Malay, Indian, Eurasian, Japanese, African and Chinese people who, at one time or other, ended up here, account for one of the strangest mixes of culinary styles on earth. Macanese restaurants prepare dishes from local *bacalao*, or salted dry fish, which is a Portuguese inheritance. The Cantonese have picked up the taste for it, and slabs of dried salt fish are now top of the list for take-home gifts for visiting Hong Kongers. The same restaurant will serve Cantonese fried noodles alongside something called 'African chicken', a Macanese speciality derived from Mozambique. (The Portuguese administrators who served in Africa often brought their cooks with them when posted to Macau.) Spanish *chorizo* is as likely to turn up in a dish as Chinese black beans, and it will probably be served by a Thai or Filipina waitress. This is the only Chinese city which serves good, crusty bread rolls with your dinner as a matter of course, and you can actually get a glass of nice white wine with which to wash it down. If a dedicated foodie died and went to heaven, it might not be unlike Macau.

Tearing ourselves away from the restaurants, we wandered up to the ruins of the Basilica of Sao Paulo, a sort of Hollywood-style frontage (there's nothing behind the splendid front wall) which is nevertheless almost 400 years old. Local kids were using the massive plaza in front of the church to set off New Year's fireworks, which echoed satisfyingly against the saint-encrusted wall. The Fortaleza do Monte above it commanded a great view of the Pearl River mouth, and had been useful to the Portuguese for blowing up Dutch, English or Spanish ships arriving without an invitation. The ancient cannon emplacements started me off on an extended lecture on the principles of ballistics for the girls, who yawned politely and enquired if we would be leaving soon. We caught a taxi down to the southern tip of the island, to the temple of A-Ma-Gao, from which the colony gets its name. Thunderous strings of explosives (Macau manufactures most of the fireworks that supply Hong Kong) were being detonated in the courtyard of this 17th century shrine to the goddess who protects the local fishermen and sailors. Retreating from the din, we went into Macau's brilliant Maritime Museum, where I learned a lot about Chinese nautical exploration. Some 70 years before Columbus, the Ming emperor Chu Ti sent out a great war fleet which conquered and extracted tribute from places as far away as Ceylon, Mecca and the east coast of Africa. This threw a rather different light on the notion of a closed, inward-looking Middle Kingdom, and an aggressive, expansionist Europe in the Age of Exploration.

We had one more restaurant pilgrimage to do, before boarding the ferry that would take us up-river to Canton. On the southern island of Taipa, connected to Macau by causeway, there is a Buddhist monastery which does lunch, so to speak. We took a local bus, and hopped off where we thought the temple should be. A little park near the bus stop was almost knee-deep in the red-paper debris of fireworks, and children supervised by their parents and a benevolent policeman were setting off whizzers, bangers and rockets. A short row of stalls offered every sort of explosive novelty I'd ever wished for as a kid, and I turned our girls loose with a few dollars to buy what they liked. When they proved a little shy of lighting the fuses, I got down on hands and knees and became a 10-year-old boy again for a few short minutes.

The monastery was almost full by the time we arrived. It was a pleasant, rambling compound with handsome shrines and temple buildings, and large gardens which provided fresh vegetables. A spacious kitchen served an even larger restaurant, where two or three hundred people were already seated, tucking in to lunch. The women serving food were pleasant and friendly, and took us to a spare table. A menu written in Cantonese was produced, and I was struggling to identify some of the characters when our hostess appeared with a little girl about Kerry's age, who shyly translated some of the dishes for us. The food arrived quickly. Cleverly textured bean curd imitated squid in a light savoury sauce, gluten had been transformed into a close approximation of roast pork, and the mushroom and green vegetable dishes were delicious. The centrepiece of the meal was a surprise—plump, juicy oysters fried in a crisp batter. I later found an explanation for this unusual exception: of all the living creatures in the world, it seems the humble oyster is the only one that lacks a brain, making it fair game for the Buddhist epicure.

THREE

We had a last dinner of excellent Macanese food, watched the fireworks over the water for a while, and strolled down the Rua Praia Grande to a busy supermarket, still open at nine o'clock. We were due to board the ferry for Canton at 10.30, and thought we'd take the opportunity to stock up on a few essentials. The girls argued for chocolate biscuits, Dorcas filled her basket with soap and toothpaste, while I weighed up the cost/benefit ratio of expensive French brandy versus cheap Portuguese *grappa*. This was a very classy supermarket, patronised by what looked like the embassy set, and the shelves were full of English and American comfort foods, like Bird's Custard Powder and Campbell's Mushroom Soup. We presented at the check-out with a basket of goodies. The girls got their chocolate digestives, Dorcas got her Colgate and I settled for the *grappa.*, figuring two bottles in the rucksack were worth one on the shelf.

The Macau–Canton ferry is operated by the Chinese government, and the terminal had the right sort of air about it. It was painted in institutional green and furnished with hard class wooden benches. Everyone seemed to be asleep. It reminded me of an English dole office. A half-hearted duty free counter offered mouldy pistachio nuts, strange Chinese medicines and cheap Taiwanese watches.

The MV *Xiangshanhu* was a bit of a rust-bucket, but not too bad. A second class cabin for five came with a shower and toilet, and the restaurant looked likely to stay open late. The girls were very tired, so we wrapped them up into bed, and went out on deck to watch the lights of Macau. We rounded the southern end of the peninsula and passed under the hump-back causeway that connects Taipa Island to the city. The hotels and casinos were a blaze of light, and the occasional rocket still whizzed up into the heavy night clouds. The ship's engines made a low, growling vibration, while the propellers churned up the viscous brown water astern. It did not look like the sort of stuff you'd want to fall into. We turned up into the Pearl River, and the lights fell away behind us. Dorcas and I shared a beer in the restaurant, then went off to join the girls and sleep.

The wake-up call showed no mercy. Someone switched on the wall-mounted loudspeakers in our cabin and blasted us with shrill Chinese marching songs, interspersed with even more shrill announcements in rapid Chinese. We didn't have to speak the language. The gist of it was 'get off the boat'. This racket was going on all over the ship, while the predatory cabin staff banged on doors and demanded bedding from passengers still mostly asleep. The engine noise had stopped. I peered out the grubby porthole window at a grey, misty dawn and a ramshackle customs shed. We had arrived in China. It was six o'clock in the morning, and cold with it.

Clare, Kerry and Aislinn shouldered their packs like sleepwalkers, and we followed them down the gangplank into the customs hall. We were expecting the third degree, but the dishevelled officials in crumpled green uniforms were half-asleep as well. We passed through without a fuss.

I went to the Bank of China counter to change some money. The Chinese government, when it opened the Big Red Gates in the 1980s, devised a whole new currency for the use of foreigners. The Chinese yuan was in the same basket with Polish zlotys and Romanian levs, which is to say worthless outside the country. The new currency, FEC (Foreign Exchange Certificates) was supposed to keep us rampant capitalists from cornering the market on dog-eared bits of grubby paper, and prevent the citizenry from getting their hands on hard currency. It was a spectacular failure from either angle. Tourists couldn't wait to trade in FEC on ordinary money (it went much further), and the Chinese were very keen to accumulate FEC (with which to buy washing machines and Sony Walkmans, smuggled in from Hong Kong). The result was a thriving black market. A rascally bunch of touts and taxi drivers were already on hand but, wary of thievery, we evaded them and set off for the city on foot.

This was our first glimpse of the real China. Trudging up the street at 7.00 in the morning was as good a way as any to see it, and the city was already awake. The buildings were old and run-down, coated with the same grey, gritty rime you see in the industrial slums of London or New York. The air was more polluted than in Hong Kong, although there were fewer cars on the road. Hundreds of bicycles were carrying everything from fresh sides of pork to little girls dressed in frilly white frocks on their way to school. The people were generally well-dressed in casual clothing, and we saw few of the blue Mao suits. Only the old men sitting fishing along the river bank wore them. I couldn't help wondering what they might catch, for the river was grievously filthy, with unidentifiable rafts of brown gunge floating down it.

We were headed for Shamian Island. This low-lying sandy island in the Pearl River had an interesting history. The xenophobic Qing emperors had grudgingly allowed European traders to set up shop here back in the 1750s. British, French and Portuguese companies were quick to take advantage of the opportunity to trade for Chinese silks, porcelain and tea. They built their warehouses and offices on the island, although they were only allowed to stay there during the winter trading season, and were booted out each spring. In 1773, the English sailed up the Pearl River with 150 000 pounds of good Bengali opium, intending to set right the imbalance of trade caused by the Chinese demanding cash on the barrelhead for everything they sold. Canton became the drug capital of China overnight. When the Qing emperor tried to outlaw the trade, the British replied with the Opium Wars. The Chinese lost, and ceded Hong Kong as part of their war debt. Shamian became a prosperous British–French concession, and the other European powers opened embassies and missions on the island.

All this had faded by the time we arrived, washed away by the various wars and revolutions of the 20th century (Chinese political history has never been dull), but the old colonial architecture was still there, and the district had become a hunting ground for cheap hotels and restaurants. It had a quiet, residential air, separated from the crowded streets of central Canton by a narrow canal. The landmark was the White Swan Hotel, a massive joint-venture palace built to accommodate the Taiwanese businessmen and American Express tourists who flooded in with the opening of the doors in the early 1980s.

Like a huge spacecraft, the White Swan had been settled on reclaimed land at the western end of Shamian Island, and once through the doors, you were in Five-Star International Hotel territory.

The shopping arcade was paved in cool marble, the reception desk was the length of a small playing field, and there was a two-storey waterfall in the lobby. Groups of locals dressed in Sunday best were gaping at the sheer wealth of it all, and posing for group photographs in front of the waterfall. Our European features got us past the stern look of the restaurant manager, and we slumped down in the lap of luxury to have breakfast.

It was wonderful. Fresh croissants and Swiss jams, curls of sweet butter and endless cups of good coffee arrived, followed by perfectly scrambled eggs and grilled sausages. The girls were in heaven. After just ten days away from their regular diet of fresh milk and cereals, they were becoming rebellious. Rice gruel with pickled egg was not their idea of breakfast, and they approved very much of the White Swan Hotel. While they laid into a fourth serving of buttered toast, I went looking for somewhere less breath-takingly expensive to stay. Just across the street, I found a clean and cheerful youth hostel which offered rooms at a reasonable price. We moved in after breakfast.

The rooms were surprisingly large and airy, although the hostel had strict rules about how many they'd let stay in one room, so I was banished to a men's dormitory across the hall. The limits of Chinese service were made clear when Dorcas asked for more towels. One towel, one bed, she was told, also one slip of soap and one slim toilet roll per room per day. The sky might fall before any more were issued, but you could have all the hot water for tea you wanted. This is delivered in all Chinese hotels twice daily, the Chinese being even fonder of tea-drinking than the English. The tea was also provided, either the mild fermented red tea or the thinner, sharper green tea, both of them drunk neat, without milk or sugar. Downstairs, the people at the front desk spoke good English, rented out bicycles, and were not averse to a little currency exchange themselves. We were well content with the place, and planned to stay a few days, while we sorted out tickets for the journey north.

Just across the narrow canal, the maelstrom started. Canton (we were gently reminded by Chinese students to use the correct name for the city, Guangzhou) is a city of just over three million. At least it was, before the economic changes of the last few years started a great migration from the countryside into the city. Now, no one was sure how many people there were, but the authorities reported as many as 10 000 people a day were pouring into Guangzhou, and they regarded it as a problem. The attraction for the peasant farmers was money. As the great collective farms were dismantled, and private businesses allowed to flourish, so the word spread that anyone could have a shot at getting rich. Even the English-language newspaper, China Daily, carried stories of rags-to-riches peasants, making their fortunes by selling postcards or repairing bicycles in the streets of Guangzhou. So the population swelled, faster than the city could cope with the change.

The avenues were packed with people from early in the morning to long after dark. Just walking down a street was an exercise in pushing, squeezing past, losing track of each other and coping with the awful traffic fumes generated by a fleet of badly maintained buses and trucks. It proved exhausting, even for short distances. We kept retreating back to Shamian Island, defeated by the weight of numbers and the 'staring squads'—groups of urban peasants so astonished at seeing a family of non-Chinese foreigners that they would stand, gaping open-mouthed, in a circle around us every time we stopped moving.

On a pedestrian bridge near the city centre, a man had set himself up as a shoe repairman and boot polisher. Kerry's leather boots badly needed attention, so we stopped and negotiated a price to have them cleaned and polished. For the meagre sum of Y2, his expressive sign language assured us, Kerry's boots would be transformed into a model of well-maintained footwear. Kerry sat down on the stool, and the shoe-shine man went to work. An audience began to gather at once.

The shoe-shine man had a good idea of the promotional opportunities provided by a family of gwailos using his services. He kept up a running sales pitch, aimed at the crowd, as he worked. His cloth stretched and snapped, twirled in the air. He was hamming it up something rotten. The crowd grew bigger, as more people stopped to see what was going on. The shoe-shine man started on the second boot. By now, we were causing a serious obstruction on the bridge. I was wondering when the police would arrive. As he finished the second boot with a flourish, popcorn-sellers were beginning to work the edges of the crowd. I gave the man five yuan, and he tipped me a wink as he pocketed the note. We resisted the urge to bow, and without waiting for change, exited stage left.

The combination of the traffic, the smog, the attention and the overwhelming crush of people began to take a toll on us. Everything was so hard to accomplish, especially as we had been rendered illiterate at one stroke. Road signs written in Chinese characters meant nothing to us. We would pass shops, entirely ignorant of whether they sold groceries or armature windings, unless they happened to have a pile of them outside the door. Because spoken Chinese is a tonal language, even our best attempts to say 'Where is the post office?' were met with uncomprehending looks. We were beginning to slip into culture shock, and found it easier to retreat to our hotel room than to deal with the streets of Guangzhou. But there was one major hurdle I couldn't avoid—somehow, we had to get tickets out. And that meant going to the train station.

The Canton Railway Station is located north of the city, and although it was only about six kilometres from Shamian Island, it took more than an hour of gruelling traffic to get there. I set off alone on our third morning, my mission to get five tickets for anywhere out of Canton. I first tried the CITS office, which, in theory, sold tickets to foreigners travelling in China. They lived up to their reputation, in turn denying that anyone spoke English there, that they sold any sort of tickets at all, or that the ticket-selling person would be back from lunch before Thursday. They chivvied me out of the office like a bothersome Jehovah's Witness, presumably so they could get back to their cots.

The main railway station was just across the way, and the first sight of it did nothing for my spirits. In a great concrete square, a crowd was gathered which would have done justice to a biblical epic. I estimated some 40 000 people milling about, camping, making tea over charcoal burners, selling sugar-cane and standing in formidable queues which showed no signs of having moved in living memory. The People's Army had erected defensive barriers in front of the building to prevent any more people from moving in permanently. Even to get near those barriers meant a full-on assault on the crowd, something like trying to reach the front row at a rock concert. As for which queue to join, or where the right counter might be, I hadn't a clue. I squatted on my heels and lit a cigarette, wondering how I was going to get around this one. A modest audience gathered to watch me think about it.

'Hello, you want to buy tickets?'

A young, tall Chinese guy in a blue suit was speaking, in passable English.

'Yeah, you have tickets?'

'No problem. Plenty of tickets, where you want to go?'

'Changsha.'

'OK, Changsha, train leaves 4:30 today. How many tickets?'

'Wait, not today. Tomorrow or the next day. I need five tickets.'

'OK, no problem, you come with me to my hotel, get tickets.'

'Where's your hotel?'

'Not far. Please, you follow me.'

I was getting nowhere with the crowds, so I followed across the avenue, up and down a few pedestrian bridges, and into the lobby of a large, busy hotel. We took a table in the coffee shop.

'You pay for tickets now, I go get them for you,' he said.

'No chance. You get the tickets, then I pay you for them.'

'OK, you stay here. Five tickets for Changsha tomorrow, yes?'

'How much are they?'

'Chinese price, very good price, no problem.'

He was referring to the government rule that all foreigners must pay double, or sometimes more, for tickets on any Chinese train. You also had to pay in FEC, which made them more expensive still. If you could obtain Chinese-price tickets, we'd been told, no one asked how you'd got them. Chinese train conductors were usually too busy sleeping to bother with such details. We agreed on a price somewhere between the counter price and the foreigners' price. This gave me the tickets I wanted without battling the crowds, and my friend would pocket the difference in profit. It was a reasonable arrangement. He was back in fifteen minutes.

'OK, Changsha, five tickets hard sleeper tomorrow, 4.30.'

He produced five little cardboard stubs, richly decorated with Chinese characters, numbers and stamps. The trouble was, I couldn't read them. They might have been laundry stubs for all I could decipher. I took them to the hotel counter, where a bored-looking desk clerk confirmed they were, indeed, train tickets for Changsha. Back in the coffee shop, money discreetly changed hands. In 1968, both of us would have been dragged out to the nearest courtyard and shot by the Red Guards, for taking the capitalist road. Now we were cutting a deal over lunch. Times had changed.

'Your English is very good,' I said.

'I am a student six years, studying English.'

'What job will you do?'

'I want to make business. Better for me, make a business, than to be a student. Everyone wants to make business now. Good money.'

'But what were you studying for?'

'Engineering. Civil engineering.'

'Thanks for the tickets.'

'No problem, you tell everyone in your hotel, they want tickets, look for me.'

'I'll do that.'

Back on Shamian Island, I announced we were going to Changsha the following day. We went out for dinner, taking advantage of the superb cooking in the local restaurants. The exchange rate was such that we could wander into quite classy restaurants and order freely, without spending much more than $25 on the five of us. Cantonese chefs are regarded as the best in China, and we were never disappointed. Some of the European backpackers we'd met at the hotel bragged of having found noodle stalls where you could fill up for 20 cents. This seemed to me like saying that you could visit the Louvre and save money by staying outside.

I got up early the next morning to visit the Qinping Market, one of Guangzhou's largest and busiest, not far from Shamian Island. At seven o'clock in the morning, the *dim sum* houses were already packed. The Cantonese say they will eat anything that walks, swims, crawls or flies, and Qinping is the proof of it. Hundreds of stalls lined Qinping Donglu and the side streets running off it, selling every sort of fish, animal and bird in the whole Cantonese repertoire. In the space of the next two hours, I saw chickens, ducks, pigeons and guinea fowl, sparrows, quail and geese, all sold live and despatched on the spot with the flick of a sharp little knife. There were fish, prawns, eels, snakes and salamanders, frogs, crabs, terrapins, turtles and even centipedes for sale. (I have yet to learn what you do with centipedes.) In the street of the butchers' stalls, you could choose freshly killed and perfectly trimmed cuts of pork, beef, lamb, dog (whole bow-wows, relieved of their skin, hung from steel hooks), cat or deer meat. If none of that caught your fancy, you could always pick up a nice bit of monkey or raccoon for dinner. This was more of a menagerie than a market, but you had to give them full marks for freshness—there was nothing being sold that hadn't been walking around a few minutes before. I was relieved that I'd come on this expedition alone.

Given that all this was going on in the open air, with not a refrigerated cabinet in sight, it was enough to make an Australian health inspector scribble a hole in his clipboard. By western standards, everybody should have been writhing around on the ground in the last agonies of food poisoning, but clearly, no one gave a hoot. In fact, food poisoning is rare in China, and in all the weeks we spent there, sampling the most unusual foods, we would never once suffer from a food-induced illness.

The explanation lies in the way Chinese cooks handle food. Their obsession with freshness means that nothing gets to lie around long enough to develop slow-acting toxins. Most cooking is done either by high temperature stir-frying or long steaming or casseroling until very well done. Chinese cooks never re-use cooked foods, and there's almost nothing in the way of the pâtés, terrines and cream dishes that cause so much trouble in European kitchens. Dairy products are almost unknown. What preserved meats they use are dried, smoked or pickled. The Chinese regard our habit of holding meat chilled or frozen for weeks at a time as peculiar and unhealthy.

Shamian Island had been a gentle introduction, but the overwhelming sensory shock of Guangzhou's noise, pollution and crowds had affected us all. This was going to be hard going, but we had to make some sort of a start before we lost our nerve. We packed our bags again and set out for the railway station. With a couple of hours to spare, we didn't want to face the crush inside the railway station just yet, so we found a public garden a few hundred metres away, and paid Y10 to get in. Inside it was remarkably well-kept, with fountains, green lawns and shady benches under ornamental trees. Dorcas and I settled in for a rest while the girls ran off to play. We were talking to a student when the girls returned with a young, fashionably dressed woman who wanted to ask a question.

'Excuse me, do you mind if I take your daughters?'

'Ah, where would you like to take them to?'

'We are making photographs . . . making movie,' she mimed.

Aislinn and Kerry had already been adopted, it seemed, by a local film crew who had arrived to make a television commercial in the park. Seated in a neat circle on the grass, nine or ten impeccably lacquered Chinese children were posing for the camera. Our girls, in travel-stained t-shirts and crumpled trousers, stood out like sore thumbs. On cue, the group sang an incomprehensible song, danced about a bit, then sat down again.

'What do you think they're advertising?' I asked Dorcas.

'Whose Mum doesn't use Persil?'

'I see what you mean.'

Battling our way through the crowd, we gained the barrier at Guangzhou Railway Station and waved our tickets at a policeman, who let us through. Inside, several thousand people had set up semi-permanent camp in the station, sleeping, eating and milling about. Whole families were living in stairwells. Gangs of children were riding the escalators up and down again for fun. One kid of about ten was crouched inside a dustbin, reading a comic book. He looked pretty comfortable in there. Each of the six waiting rooms was packed like a Kurdish refugee camp. All the signs were in Chinese, and we hadn't the slightest idea where the Changsha train might be. This wasn't going to be easy.

I found a railway official who spoke a few words of English. He was a coin collector, and asked if we had any Australian coins with us. Dorcas had to do an emergency rummage through her rucksack to find a few lonely 5 cent pieces. I was amazed at the things Dorcas could produce from her rucksack on demand. We handed them over, and the railwayman herded us into one of the waiting rooms. There was no room at all to sit down, so we crouched on our bags, while our guide gave instructions to the guards to point us at the Changsha train when it arrived. All around us, Chinese grandmothers poked each other in the ribs and gestured at our family. They asked questions in expressive sign language. Are they all yours, the three of them? Yes, we nodded, all three. Eeeehh, to have three children! Very good! The thumbs up sign is universal.

A ripple of panic spread through the crowd. The train was approaching. There is nothing on earth like a Chinese crowd boarding a train. They would work themselves up into a near riot, then rush the barricades, carrying staggering loads of baggage and children. Once free on the platform, they would storm the carriages all at once, climbing into windows, flinging parcels aboard, fighting at the doors and almost weeping with desperation to get aboard. In the cheapest hard class carriages, people were piled six deep, sitting on each other's laps, hanging out windows and shouting at relatives still on the platform. In the second class carriages, sleeping berths were booked in advance, and never over-sold, so the mad rush to get aboard was unnecessary, but the passengers went at it anyway. We hung back for the worst of it to pass, then climbed aboard.

Chinese long-distance trains come in three classes: hard seat, hard sleeper and soft sleeper. Hard seat is the cheapest, and since there are no booked seats, carriages are massively over-crowded. It's all passably congenial, but foreign travellers agreed that it was really a last resort. Sixteen hours in hard seat was an exercise in cramped, seedy misery. Hard sleeper was twice the price, but offered quite good sleeping berths, stacked three high in open bays of six. The highest bunk took some acrobatic manoeuvres to reach, but was correspond-ingly removed from the sociable sprawl at ground level. The Chinese loosen up on trains, changing into slippers and track suits, folding away their street clothes, and breaking out the magazines, knitting and decks of cards. Along in soft class, the top government cadres were reclining in four-berth compartments, equipped with frilly pillow covers and plastic flowers.

We found our berths, staked out a bit of territory with bags and coats, then settled down to a window seat. The view was obscured by a thick layer of oily grime on the outside of the train which rendered the windows almost opaque. You could open them, though, and as long as the winter sunshine kept the temperature mild, that's what we did. The lowest sleeping bunks, facing each other over small window tables, were effectively park benches during the day. Passen-gers would stroll up and down the carriage, visiting each other, chatting, playing cards and eating. When the children hung out the window and waved at the passing local trains, the effect was comi-cal—first blank looks, then alarm, then a wave of excitement as relatives were dragged to the windows to see.

Hot water was drawn from a coal-stoked boiler at the end of the carriage, and kept at each table in heavy steel thermos flasks which slipped into a cage-like holder bolted to the floor. The custom was to half-fill your jam jar with tea leaves, pour on hot water, then slurp the contents throughout the day, topping up from the flask as required. Screwing the lid on the jar between slurps neatly avoided spills. If you emptied the flask, it was good manners to go and fill it again from the boiler.

The toilet cubicles were horrible. A hole in the floor opened directly on to the track, and the difficulty of maintaining a balanced squat while the train swayed wildly along lumpy, bumpy Chinese railway tracks meant that the aim was not always good. Nor had they been cleaned within living memory, so they were best avoided except in case of dire need. The whole train, in fact, sorely needed the attention of a dozen German housewives with lots of buckets and soap. Our sleepwalking conductors would make an effort every few hours, but they did little more than shovel the worst of the debris down toward the end of the carriage, run a black, greasy mop over the floor, then retire back to their compartment for a nap.

The train left neatly on time, pulling out of Guangzhou Railway Station in the late afternoon, leaving undiminished crowds on the platform. We passed through miles of urban sprawl—not the squalid shanty-towns of South America, but almost as crowded. Every building looked overloaded with people, every road packed, every bus full to overflowing. Chinese cities are not so much poor as hammered, pounded into shabbiness by the weight of 1000 million people.

FOUR

We nodded and smiled at Mrs Woolly Boots, who occupied the second-tier bunk opposite. She did not attempt a conversation, but rather left her hairy footwear at ground level, removed her stockings and climbed upstairs to read a novel. The bottom berth was occupied by a dapper young man in an officer's uniform of the Red Army. He carefully set out his tea-jar, his magazines and his food supplies on the table, then adjusted his uniform, removed his shoes and buried himself in a newspaper. The Captain was clearly too sophisticated to gape at a bunch of foreigners, and having no English, he politely ignored us. He wasn't counting on Aislinn, who had been assigned the top berth on his side.

Like an agile tree kangaroo, Aislinn clambered up and down the berths every ten minutes, to fetch a book, put her pencils away or change her clothes. At least half a dozen times, she managed to step on some part of the poor Captain as she descended. He was stoic. He did not flinch. He did not complain, but rather sank further behind his newspaper, like a huffy English vicar on a suburban train. Dorcas made apologetic noises in his direction, and whispered urgently to Aislinn, telling her to be careful where she put her feet. Aislinn decided that if people were going to be huffy about being stepped on, then she'd go and explore the rest of the train.

Mrs Woolly Boots produced a packet of the salty black melon seeds that were so popular at the station buffet, and offered them encouragingly to Kerry, who was being shy.

'It's all right, Kerry, take some,' I said, smiling politely at Mrs Woolly Boots.

'I don't want any,' said Kerry.

'I know that, but this lady is being very nice. Take some.'

'I hate them.'

'Go on, they're not that bad.' Mrs Boots was shaking her packet more insistently, taking Kerry's reluctance for good manners. 'Just have a few.'

'They taste like poison.'

'No they don't. Just eat a few to be polite.'

'If I eat them, I'll be sick.'

'If you don't eat them, I'll kill you myself,' I said between clenched teeth, grinning at Mrs Boots like a demented chimp.

Kerry reluctantly helped herself to a fingerful and managed to secrete them somewhere about her person without actually going near her mouth. The basic decencies observed, Mrs Boots went back to her novel. Kerry glared daggers at me then ascended to her own bunk in a huff. I thought it must be time for a drink.

Now, there are countries where it is permissible to fetch a bottle of whisky out of your bag and have a long snort at 4.30 in the afternoon, and countries where this sort of thing is frowned upon. In Poland, for instance, there would be no problem. If you do the same thing on a Melbourne tram, people are inclined to change seats, and if you try it in Saudi Arabia, they take you away at gun point. I was not yet sure where the Chinese stood on the matter, so I thought I'd try the idea on the Captain.

I produced a bottle of Portuguese brandy and placed it on the table. I waited for his eyes to lift, then invited him, with a gesture, to join me in a drink. He looked alarmed, and refused the offer with a wave of his hand. Good manners, Chinese style, require that you refuse anything offered at least twice, so I persisted. Please have one, I said, pouring him out a glass. Perhaps he thought I was trying to recruit him as a spy. He wouldn't have it, and retreated further behind his paper. This was a bit of a worry. Maybe he was just a teetotaller. Then again, maybe afternoon boozing was highly illegal. I thought about this one while I polished off my brandy. After fifteen minutes, he hadn't arrested me, so I drank his, too. Things were looking up.

Before long, it was quite dark outside and everyone on the train was getting to know each other. The Chinese are very sociable people, and after overcoming a little initial shyness, they were calling around to see us, the only foreigners on the train. Students stopped by to exercise their English, with fairly straight questions—'Where are you from, where are you going and how do you like China?'. Aislinn had already adopted several surrogate aunties who would walk her along the corridor by the hand, stuffing her full of odd sweets and melon seeds. Clare was being withdrawn, and retreated to an upper bunk to read her book. Within an hour or two, we had the feeling that everyone in the carriage had the gist of our story, and basic curiosity had been satisfied.

We still weren't getting far with the Captain, who suffered in silence while a stream of visitors perched on the edge of his bunk, flicked cigarette ash on the floor and generally kept him awake. When the queue died down around 11.00 pm, he composed himself for sleep. He went away for a wash, returned and laid out his bunk with military precision. He arranged his clothing, set out his things on the table and retired to sleep. It was beginning to get quite cold, so Dorcas decided to turn in, too, wrapping herself in the heavy woollen blanket provided by China Railways and climbing into her upstairs berth for the night. I sat up a bit longer, reading a guidebook, then finally clicked off the light and went to sleep.

The sound of passengers pulling down their luggage woke me while it was still dark. It was very cold now. We'd come about 500 kilometres north, and away from the sea. The children were still sleeping soundly, as was Dorcas. I went for a piss in the swaying, smelly toilet, and joined the early risers in the corridor for a cigarette. I'd given up smoking back in Australia, but in China, just about every adult male smokes, and it was part of the ritual to exchange cigarettes and lights. Refusing the offer of a cigarette was almost impossible, so I'd caved in for the duration, and loaded up with a few packets of English and American cigarettes to offer around when language failed.

The conductors had roused themselves, and started preparations for arrival in Changsha. They swept a considerable pile of rubbish down the length of the carriage, arranging it in a neat heap near the door. We'd been very good about keeping ours in a plastic bag, unlike the rest of the passengers, who were inclined to fling it out the windows of the train. I deposited our bag of orange peelings and biscuit wrappings on top of the heap, had a brisk face-wash in cold water, and went back for another half-hour's sleep before we arrived.

Dorcas was up first, and began to pack bags in the dark. We whispered to avoid waking the Captain, who was still snoring soundly under his sheet.

'How did you sleep?' I asked.

'Cold, but it was all right. What about you?'

'Great. I woke up thirsty. Sorry, I finished off that bottle of water. We'll get some more in Changsha.'

'What bottle of water?'

'The one you left on the table.'

'I didn't leave any water on the table.'

'Oh, Christ, wasn't that ours?'

'You mean you finished off the Captain's water?'

'I didn't know it was his.'

'He'll probably shoot you.'

'Wake up the girls and let's get off this bloody train.'

As we stepped down from the train, it still felt like the middle of the night. A chill fog haloed the lights on the station platform, and all the passengers were huddling into their coats for warmth. The place felt lost and empty, but that was probably just the awful hour. We gathered up our bags and hefted them on to our shoulders. The girls had that bruised and confused look of children woken up when they should be sleeping. Further down the platform, the conductors were cleaning the train by opening the windows and throwing all the rubbish out of them, including our neatly packed little plastic bag full of scraps.

Changsha was dark, cold and bleak at five o'clock in the morning. The fog was thicker, and it had an irritating, stinging feel about it. We ducked in to a small, garishly lit café and sat down. Near the door, a bamboo steamer was simmering over a charcoal stove and a few people gathered around it to warm their hands. We sat, cold and awkward, at a skinny steel table at the back of the shop. Nothing much happened. I went up to the woman at the stove and asked, as well as I could manage, for a pot of tea. No tea, the woman said, '*mei you*', the endemic phrase in China that means 'not have'. I couldn't work this one out—everywhere in China has tea, even if they have little else, and if we needed anything on a dank, foggy morning in Changsha, it was a cup of tea.

'No tea,' she repeated firmly, 'dumplings', pointing to the steamer. I caved in quickly and ordered a plateful of dumplings. These steamed bread lumps are more common than rice in central and northern China, where wheat takes over as the staple grain. Imagine a loaf of white bread which has been boiled rather than baked to get a good idea of the consistency. They are the size of bread rolls, but have a chewy, elastic texture and an utterly bland taste. The Cantonese call them *bao*, and have a very light touch with them, adding fillings of delicious roast pork or sweet bean paste. Here in Hunan, they were solid fodder, good for filling the belly but little more. The girls looked at them without enthusiasm. Clare was hungry enough to reach the centre of one of them.

'Oh, ecck, it's seaweed in the middle,' she said.

It was, too. Some sort of fibrous, salty filling that tasted of ship's bilges lurked in the middle of the buns, enough to put anyone off their breakfast.

'Let's find a hotel,' Dorcas said.

'I'll see if I can get a cab.'

I went off to haggle with the taxi drivers hanging around a small, battered fleet of ancient Soviet Fiats. I practised my finger counting, a useful Chinese invention which substitutes finger signs for each number up to several hundred. I negotiated a price in rapid sign language, ended up with a willing driver, but was a little unsure whether I'd agreed to $3 or half a week's wages. We piled into the car anyway.

The driver, a wizened man with bad teeth and a flat cap, refused to turn his lights on, even though it was still pitch dark. He seemed to think he was saving electricity. He'd flick them on occasionally, when we were bearing down on the rear end of a lumbering bus, but snap them off again when we pulled out to overtake. All of this happened in a sort of slow motion, because Chinese vehicles do not go very fast. It's the secret of Chinese traffic safety. You can drive any way you like, because nothing goes more than 30 kilometres an hour, so there's always time to get out of the way.

We had picked the first hotel mentioned in the guide book, and managed to get the message across. A few minutes later, we were deposited in front of a big, dark building which seemed to be closed for business. The driver found an open door, so we paid him (it was $3 after all) and moved our bags inside. A cavernous lobby was illuminated by two dim table lamps, and an old man in some sort of uniform snored soundly in a comfortable armchair. There was no other sign of life, but it was still only 6.00 am, so we curled up on the 1950s vintage sofas and did a bit of dozing ourselves.

Just on 7.00 am, the hotel woke up. From behind the reception desk, two desk clerks rose from their camp beds, yawning and scratching, fully dressed in their hotel uniforms. A few taxis arrived. A cook or two appeared and headed off in the direction of the restaurant. The bad news was that rooms were an astronomical price, at least for foreigners appearing uninvited in the lobby so early in the morning. I couldn't shift them from their insistence that we pay more than $100 each for dim, gloomy rooms in their hotel. As this was more than two month's wages for the average Chinese, I thought we ought to be able to find something better.

We took another taxi. The driver looked mildly terrified to have five large, live 'ghost people' in his cab; worse, they kept shouting incomprehensible Chinese and waving directions. He couldn't wait to get rid of us somewhere, anywhere. We stopped at two more hotels, where I got the stony-faced '*mei you*' which means 'you are far too much trouble to deal with, so go away'. At last we found a smart, cosmopolitan hotel which offered (with a little persuasion) to put us all in one room at a reasonable rate, the equivalent of $A50.

We all had a sleep and woke up hungry. Dorcas set off with the three girls to a place they'd seen near the hotel, the Happy Children Restaurant. This looked like a sort of fifth-rate McDonald's clone, decked out in garish plastic and grinning clown faces. It promised a Chinese version of western fast food, something which was becoming very chic among the post-Tiananmen Chinese youth. I stayed at home, nursing the first of several bouts of the endemic winter 'flu all of us were to suffer at times. I took the opportunity to read a handful of the 'China Facts and Figures' booklets thoughtfully provided in a rack in the lobby.

These booklets, published by the government-run Beijing Foreign Languages Press, quoted the current Communist Party line on a variety of topics, from agricultural reform to medical care, textile production to economics. They were written in a breezy, *Newsweek* style which made them less grindingly dull than they sounded.

The gist of it was that China had taken a dim view of private enterprise since the Communist victory in 1949, and during the Cultural Revolution, the self-employed 'were regarded as capitalistic bourgeoisie and therefore criticised'. I gathered that criticism by the Red Guards sometimes involved dropping people off tall buildings, so I felt some sympathy for all those bourgeois bicycle-menders and toffee-apple men. The interesting bit was that the policy had changed in 1979, and now small businesses were allowed to flourish. Since it's difficult to keep the Chinese out of business, there had been a predictable surge towards a free market. The booklet wound up with a few Hero-of-the-Revolution stories about individual businesses solving production bottlenecks, getting the goods to the market and paying huge amounts of taxes. One Zeng Fa-Zhen, a ceramics peddler in Guangzhou with 5 square metres of floor space, had paid Y140 000 in taxes in 1985. This is in a country where the average yearly wage was about Y2000 at the time.

Dorcas returned to say that the Happy Children Restaurant was abysmal. They'd eaten dreadful Hunanese attempts at hamburgers and milkshakes, prepared by cooks who seemed to be unsure which one got the pickles. I had a fleeting premonition that Ronald McDonald was going to be the next Hero of the Socialist Revolution.

Hunan has its own cuisine, one of the Eight Great Schools of Chinese cooking (the Chinese passion for assigning numbers to everything doesn't miss out cooking). It is in turn part of what's usually called South-western style. Sichuan, the next-door neighbour, has had more exposure in the West, and although the styles are not the same, they do have a few things in common. Hunan is a long way from the sea, so the fresh seafood and vegetable dishes common in Guangzhou are difficult to make. The food relies more on pickles, salted ingredients, hot chillies and dried mushrooms. Meats are often prepared in 'twice-cooked' style, cooked once in a spicy and fragrant marinade, then deep-fried or steamed with vegetables. Sauces are much oilier than their southern cousins, and meats are simmered or casseroled, rather than stir-fried. We set out on our second day in Changsha to find some real Hunanese food.

Down the road from the hotel, the bright red signs over a small restaurant caught my eye. A number of well-fed cadres were piling in the door for lunch. Tanks of fresh crabs and lake fish bubbled, live chickens and pigeons were displayed in cages. We went in. We couldn't have made a bigger impression if we'd gone naked and painted ourselves blue. The cute young girl in the air-hostess uniform gaped at us with alarm, then fetched her boss, a very smooth business type in a silk jacket. His expression said 'Foreigners? Sure, we get 'em in here all the time, no problem,' but he was looking a little nervous, too.

The clientele was exclusively male, and well-dressed. The hostesses were wearing short blue suits with dinky little stewardess caps. Two televisions, mounted high on the walls, played Cantonese-pop video clips. The *mao tai* bottles were already on the table. I wondered if we had inadvertently walked into a brothel. There was no telling, but we were getting a lot of strange looks. The kids didn't give a damn. They peeled off their hats, scarves, gloves and jumpers and hung the lot on the backs of their chairs. They were watching TV; they were happy.

One of the waitresses must have drawn the short straw, because she was firmly sent over to our table to take an order. There was no menu, but there was some very nice-looking food coming out of the kitchen.

'Tea?' I asked. The girl nodded her head with relief. Tea, yes, they had tea.

'Do-fu?' I tried, and named a simple tofu dish. Great, yes, she agreed, writing quickly on her pad, do-fu, yes!

'Soup?' I was on a roll here. She understood me, and wrote more characters on her docket. We were getting along fine.

'Rice?' Brilliant, she nodded, rice! No problem there, they could do rice, yes, not a worry, rice would be fine. She scribbled. We smiled at each other. Yes, that would do it, thank you. She went away.

The tea arrived promptly. We all had a cup while four or five of the hostesses huddled close by, pointing out our three girls, giggling and smiling, waving at Aislinn. The businessmen were not exactly giggling, but they were having a few surreptitious looks, too. We drank more tea. Silk Jacket came over to break up the waitresses, who went back to serving tables. Food started to flow out of the kitchen, wonderful platters of whole, crisp-fried fish, braised chicken, green vegetables with crabmeat. The businessmen tucked in with gusto. We had more tea. It was very nice tea, but we were all hungry by now.

Our waitress came back to top us up. We smiled at each other again. I didn't have the words to ask her where the food might be. She wasn't offering any clues. The televisions were crooning slushy love songs to each other.

On our fourth pot of tea, I was getting the feeling I'd missed something important. Our waitress did seem to have understood me, and she had written something down on her little pad. Maybe it said 'five pots of tea'. The businessmen were finishing their lunches and getting into the *mao tai*. Still no food for us. When they appeared with the fifth pot of tea, we had to give up. It was all very amiable, but we rose from our seats, put our coats back on and headed for the door. At the desk, Silk Jacket wouldn't accept any money for the tea.

Without three words in common, it just wasn't possible to find out why we missed out on lunch. On the way out, I got a closer look at those cages, spotted a few puppies on display, and shooed the girls past them before they could ask any questions. Perhaps missing lunch hadn't been such a bad idea.

Changsha, we learnt, had been Mao Zedong's home town, the place where he began his career as a school-teacher, and later got into local politics. During the height of his personality cult in the 1960s, special trains had run from Guangzhou and Shanghai, bringing the faithful to see his birthplace, not far from the city. These days, the Great Helmsman had been downgraded a little, and Changsha was promoting other tourist attractions. One of these was the remarkably well-preserved tomb of a Han Chinese woman, discovered by archaeologists under a mound of earth within the city limits. Like an Egyptian pharaoh, she had been buried with a large number of funerary objects, which gave an interesting glimpse of Chinese life 2000 years ago. Ancient corpses, as they were described in the tourist brochures, were a growth industry in China. Most of the provincial museums we visited were proud to display at least two or three of these desiccated relics, complete with remnants of clothing, jewellery and often, a full head of hair.

Walking around Changsha was not like our struggle with the crowded streets of Guangzhou. Here, the streets were broad, the pavements wide and the sun shone. We were able to take long walks, and although we attracted some attention, there was none of the claustrophobic feel of the larger city. We stopped to have a shoe mended, buy a few more bits of warm clothing, and watch another New Year's lion dance. These dances were performed by local sports clubs, and they made a spectacular job of it. An orchestra of drums, cymbals and pipes kept up a lively rhythm while the lion pranced and the red banners waved. Strings of industrial-strength firecrackers were detonated, deafening everyone within 30 metres. This traditional ceremony, in which the good-luck lion dances into business premises to frighten away evil spirits and ensure prosperity in the coming year, was frowned upon during the hysterical purges of the Cultural Revolution, but was making a strong comeback.

We found another restaurant, and had a second attempt at Hunanese food, this time successful. We tried the local dumplings and cold pickles, salted fish and radishes with chilli. The rice was much coarser than in the south, and steamed bread was served as a matter of course. Foods were often deceptive: we had a savoury-looking soup made with mushrooms, abalone and corn, only to discover that it was a sweet dessert. The sauces were heavy with oil, and the brilliant roast duck and pork of Cantonese cooking had disappeared altogether. The tastes were strange, pungent and unexpected.

In the streets, dozens of food stalls offered snacks: boiled chicken wings with sesame, fish balls braised in broth, crisp-fried sardines and peeled water chestnuts. All of these were served with crushed red chillies. Even slices of fresh pineapple got the chilli treatment. One peddler had a clever foot-powered machine for making candy floss. The sugar syrup was melted over a charcoal fire, then spun out of a whirling gizmo and caught up on a splint of bamboo.

Buying railway tickets for Shanghai was easy, compared to the mob scenes in Guangzhou. A desk at the hotel looked after travel bookings, so we had only to specify how many tickets we wanted, what class, and when we wished to go. They even accepted payment in Renminbi, much the easiest booking arrangements we were to find anywhere in China. We reserved seats on the overnight sleeper for the following day.

In the morning, we lolled about in the hotel room as long as we could decently stretch it, then packed up for the 27-hour trip to Shanghai. Changsha station looked a bit better in the light of day, and we joined a considerable crowd waiting for the train. Railway stations were always interesting, if crowded, places. Every class and type of person seemed to be on the move. Snappy-looking officers and baggy-trousered soldiers, business types with briefcases and peasants with bamboo baskets were all mixed up in the waiting rooms. Only the very highest ranks of military and government elite were spared the public waiting rooms. These privileged cadres had their own soft class salon, well removed from the masses, where the tables were covered with lace doilies, tea was served by hostesses and the water ran hot from the taps in the wash room. We occasionally parleyed our 'foreign guest' status into admittance, but after two weeks of living out of rucksacks, we were beginning to look as if we belonged with the peasants.

The Shanghai Express arrived on time. We boarded promptly, claimed our berths and settled in for another night on the train. There were more students to meet, more grandmothers to take an interest in the girls, and for me, more cigarettes to be handed round in the smoking compartment between the carriages. The train was not long out of Changsha when the dining car opened, and we joined the rush to secure a table for our first proper dinner aboard a Chinese train.

The dining car staff were a race apart from the ticket counter dragons—affable, noisy and good-natured, they trotted plates of food out of the kitchen speedily, and made no great fuss over our difficulty with the language. I pointed, they wrote chits, and a few minutes later we were eating. The food was not brilliant, but it was very good, easily a match for many of the restaurants we'd been in. Six or seven dishes were offered for each meal, different each time, served with soup and rice. Prices were, by local standards, moderate, and beer was cheap. Half an hour into dinner service, the dining car was a bedlam of clattering plates, half-shouted conversations, crowded tables and noisy disputes over who would pick up the bill—everything the Chinese like in a restaurant. We'd come to like it, too. It was the healthy, cheerful racket of people who enjoy eating together, and look forward to it all day.

After dinner, we drifted back to our berths and began to get the girls ready for bed. The train was too full to get really cold, but it was chilly enough to be more comfortable in bed than out of it. When they were all wrapped up, Dorcas and I sat in conversation with a doctor from Changsha, who had introduced himself earlier. His name was Dr Peng, and he was a surgeon on his way to Shanghai to take up a new posting there. His English was very good, if a bit rusty, for he had served as a government interpreter some years before, working with a Chinese engineering project in Iraq. Dr Peng was to become a good friend, and explained a great deal about modern Chinese history and the changing social conditions in his country. We sat up late, talking about the differences between Australian and Chinese medical care. He was a literate and intelligent man, full of curiosity about the outside world. He was also a life-long member of the Communist Party, and from what I could gather, he had been a member in good standing straight through the Cultural Revolution. I had a lot of questions I wanted to ask Dr Peng, but I held most of them back, out of politeness. I felt that Dr Peng was doing the same with me.

We made a breakfast of instant coffee, oranges, biscuits and hard-boiled eggs. At every station, there were licensed carts, wheeled along the platform by young women in white coats. From these you could buy buns, peanuts, soya eggs, chicken feet, pressed tofu, apples, sausages, beer, mineral water and small bottles of *bai jiu*, the lethal Chinese vodka made from millet. The carts did a busy trade, because Chinese people on trains seem to be worried about starving to death between one station and the next. They stocked up with extraordinary quantities of snack foods, then worked their way through them all day long. A slim, smartly dressed young woman joined the train just after breakfast and took the berth opposite us. In the space of the next few hours, she consumed a stack of boiled chicken feet, three sticks of raw sugar-cane, a bag of pickled radishes, some sesame dough sticks, a bag of sliced tofu, three boiled eggs and a packet of biscuits. I was fascinated with the performance, as her sharp little teeth champed and gnashed their way through bone, flesh, gristle and biscuit like a chaff-cutting machine. I was reluctant to leave my fingers lying around on the table.

As we drew closer to Shanghai, the stations grew more frequent, and there were many people getting on and off at each stop. Dr Peng came by for a chat. He told us that we really should visit Hangzhou, through which we were passing, and the famous West Lake. He said it was one of the most beautiful parts of the country. We explained that we were eager to get to Shanghai, to find out more about the Russian visas we needed, and about the railway line beyond Ürümqi. We had no idea how much bureaucratic red tape we might have to deal with, and wanted to allow plenty of time for it. Dr Peng was going to visit his family in Shanghai, but insisted that we call him when we had found a hotel, so that he could see us again.

From the window of the train, we watched the countryside wane and the urban sprawl of China's largest city grow. Just after noon, the train pulled into Shanghai Station, and we gathered ourselves up for another battle with the crowds.

FIVE

Shanghai is China's Big Apple, the financial capital, the largest city, the centre of manufacturing and trade. Beijing has the military parades, the demonstrations and the Great Hall of the People, but Shanghai is the centre of fashion, of new ideas, new money. Shanghai has embraced every major political upheaval in China from the Taiping Rebellion to the Cultural Revolution, and has started more than a few of them itself.

We walked out of the railway station, open-eyed. The air was cool and clear, the streets busy, and banners everywhere proclaimed Shanghai's participation in the East Asian Games. The city was buzzing with traffic and people, all of it moving with a purpose, and quickly. I was impressed. Even the taxi system worked. We jumped into one and set off for the Pujiang Hotel.

'I would like a room for five people.'

'Sorry. All full up. No rooms.'

These were only the opening feints in the game, I'd come to understand, like the first few pawn moves in a game of chess. The desk clerk and I were just limbering up. If we had warm-up jackets, we'd still be wearing them.

'OK, I'll take two double rooms,' I said.

'No more double rooms, all full up.'

'You will have some rooms later, yes?'

'Maybe later. You come later.'

An opening. The possibility of rooms available for rent was now on the table. We were making progress.

'It's eleven o'clock now. What time will you have rooms?'

'Maybe two o'clock. You come two o'clock.'

'How about dormitory beds? Do you have dormitory beds?'

'No more dormitory beds. Only rooms.'

The desk clerk was looking uncomfortable. I wasn't going away. When you've got to the desk in China, you never, ever give it up. You have to hang in there for the distance, or twenty other people will take your place. The desk clerk fiddled with his tie. I fiddled with a colour brochure on the Pujiang Hotel. One of the pictures was of a spacious, five-bed room.

'What about this room? Can I have this room?' I said, pointing to the picture.

'This room only for five people.'

'How much is this room?'

'This room is Y200 for one night,' he said, naming a sum that was meant to frighten anyone off. Three weeks' wages, perhaps $A40.

'Can I pay in Renminbi?'

'No Renminbi. You must pay in FEC.'

'OK, I'll take it.'

Game, set and match. He'd walked into that one. If we'd settled on a price, then he'd have to give us the room. He passed the key grudgingly across the counter. A young German couple came up behind me.

'*Bitte*, do you haff room for two people?'

'No rooms. Sorry, all full up.'

The Pujiang Hotel started life as the Astor Hotel, a gentlemen's club built in the 1860s, when Shanghai was just beginning its career as the European capital of China. The great Hong Kong traders like Jardine Matheson and Victor Sassoon, growing immensely wealthy on the opium trade, occupied European 'concessions' on the Huangpu River from 1842. The British, French, Americans and Japanese each maintained and policed their own districts, packed with sweatshop factories, brothels and opium dens. Robber barons competed with each other to erect impressive buildings along the river frontage which came to be known as 'the Bund'. The city's heyday in the 1920s and 1930s saw the construction of superb Art Deco and neo-classical buildings, including the Hong Kong & Shanghai Bank, the Customs House and the enormous Cathay Hotel, all of which are still standing. The Astor Hotel had seen better days, but the atmosphere lingered on.

Our room was enormous. A polished wooden floor proved perfect for games of marbles, and the girls each had a bed of their own (a luxury they were not often to enjoy on this trip). The ancient enamel bath was big enough to float in. Dorcas declared a laundry day, and everyone had to shed clothing and scrub it clean on the tile floor of the bathroom. Two hours later, the room was decorated with dripping socks and t-shirts, the girls were bundled up in their beds with comic books and packets of biscuits, and I set out to see where a man might buy a drink.

The hotel corridors were panelled in dark oak, the floors were creaky and ancient, and the Pujiang still had a lot of style. A wide marble staircase descended the five floors to the lobby, uniformed bellhops operated the lifts, and the intricate plaster ceilings and chandeliers looked original. In the lobby, a shop sold everything from razor blades to calligraphy supplies. The place hummed with new arrivals, businessmen off to meetings (the new Shanghai Stock Exchange was next-door) and a small army of desk clerks and cashiers.

Outside, the sky was clear and the temperature bracing. The moan of ship's horns echoed off the buildings. Motorised sampans were churning up the noxious waters of Suzhou Creek as I walked across the bridge and along the riverfront for my first good look at Shanghai. It reminded me of Manhattan, as it was when I was a kid, before all the brown-brick skyscrapers had given way to steel-and-mirrored-glass corporate headquarters in the 1970s. There was a hint of the Chrysler Building about the Peace Hotel (formerly Sassoon's Cathay), and the Hong Kong & Shanghai Bank would not have looked out of place on Wall Street. These buildings were contemporaries, of course, but here in Shanghai, they'd slipped into a sort of time-warp, escaping the redevelopment that had destroyed their sisters in Hong Kong and New York.

A sleek-looking fellow in an expensive leather jacket approached me. He was about 45, I guessed, greying at the temples and wearing a pair of amber Ray-Bans.

'Hello, where are you from?' he asked.

'From Australia.'

'Your first time in Shanghai?'

'Yes. I think it's a beautiful city.'

'You are travelling with friends?'

It seemed an odd question. This kind of conversation usually got straight into what you did for a living and how much you earned.

'No, with my family.'

'Where are you staying?'

'Near here. In a hotel.' A little buzzer went off in my head.

'Would you like to change some money? I can give you a very good rate. Since I speak English, we can understand each other.'

'No, thank you.' Something familiar about the style, the way he behaved.

'It's better to have Renminbi. You can use it in restaurants. I can give you 130 Renminbi for 100 FEC. I can change as much as you like.'

'No, thank you. Excuse me, I must go.' I had it now. He was a cop, I was sure of it. The smooth routine, the slight hint of arrogance, the expensive clothes.

'You should consider changing at least some. If you don't change with me, you may be cheated by bad men.'

'Thanks, no. See you later.'

I pushed off back to the hotel. Outside the Stock Exchange, I saw the local money-changer on duty. He was a small, round guy with the blunt-saw haircut of the Chinese peasant. He did not look like a cop. His trousers were hanging halfway down his arse, and he kept hoisting them up again. He sniffed with the cold.

'Changsh marney?' he asked, hopefully, as I opened the door of the hotel.

'Sure,' I said, smiling, 'step into my office.'

The restaurant at the Pujiang was closed for renovations, and we were all feeling a bit fluey, so we opted for the nearest place, the restaurant at the Seagull Hotel across the road. It was an elegant little hotel, more modern than the Pujiang, and devoted mostly to tour groups. The restaurant on the first floor had a great view of the Bund and the Huangpu River. The menu was standard Cantonese, but a few local dishes were included, and they served Shanghai's own Seagull beer, a change from the premium Tsingtao brand found all over China.

The history of beer-making in China goes back to the same colonial era that left its mark on the Shanghai waterfront. German brewers set up shop in Shanghai to take advantage of cheap supplies of grain and a rapidly expanding market. Although the Germans are long gone, the Chinese developed a considerable thirst for beer, and breweries all over the country are kept very busy. All the brands I tried were in the same Czech–German style—a pleasantly flowery scent, light body, and remarkably good quality. A handful of British and Australian enthusiasts, I learnt, had already devoted themselves to beer-tasting tours of China.

Our first priority was to obtain the essential Russian visas which, we hoped, would see us across the border in Xinjiang. I found the Russian Embassy, just across the street from the Pujiang Hotel. It was a massive, blue-grey building, handsome and imposing, bristling with high-tech antennae and microwave dishes on the roof. The new CIS tricolour hung from the flagpole. A notice in Chinese and English announced that the visa section was open on Tuesdays and Thursdays. I presented myself to the Chinese guards at the gate-house, produced a passport and was let in. A crowd of people hung around the gate, to what purpose I couldn't guess, but then crowds of people hang around any sort of official bureau in China, just on principle.

Inside, a notice on the wall gave the various fees charged for visas. There was a basic visa fee, a fee for processing within three days, and an even higher bounty for same-day work. In addition, all foreigners had a 'consular fee' to pay, which varied wildly according to which country you were from. The English, Australians and Americans got away reasonably cheaply. The French were stung an extra US$20 for their visas, and the Cayman Islands must have really done something to upset them, because they were up for an extra $75. Accordingly, the waiting room was not over-crowded with Cayman Islanders carrying backpacks.

Behind a glassed-in counter, two young men were dealing with the queue. Both of them looked like British Foreign Service juniors, well-bred young chaps doing their hard time until they could be appointed Ambassador to Zimbabwe or Bahrain. They were snowed under by a crowd of excitable Chinese who were shouting, weeping and pushing documents at them. The young Russians were coping well with the language, but looked harried. I made it to the counter at length, and we exchanged weary looks.

'Can you give me visas to cross the border from Ürümqi to Alma-Ata?' I asked in English.

'Yes,' he said, neatly demonstrating that he was at least trilingual, 'Did you want them today? It's an extra 200 yuan each.'

'No, thanks, we're staying in Shanghai for about a week. Can we pick them up next Thursday?'

'Sure. I'll need photographs and your passports.'

I produced the documents.

'Do you know if the border is open? Is there a train running?'

'Sorry, I don't know. We haven't been asked before.'

'But you've no objection to us going in to Alma-Ata, and then by train up to Moscow?'

'Your transit visas will be good for ten days. You can go wherever you like in that time, but you must leave the CIS by the last day marked on your visa, and you cannot extend them. Where do you plan to go?'

I named a few cities, the most likely stops along the way from the southern province of Kazakhstan to Moscow in the north. We planned to leave the CIS by taking the train south to Kiev and Budapest. The young man noted all this on his form.

'OK, they'll be ready next Thursday. You can pay for them when you collect them.'

'That's great. Thank you very much.'

'*Pazhalsta.*'

I couldn't believe our luck. This was the major hurdle I'd been dreading. If it wasn't confirmation of the train connection, at least there was nothing to stop us using it if it was there. Negotiating something like that at a Chinese government office in Shanghai would have been a nightmare. I was elated, and raced back to the hotel to tell Dorcas the good news. We decided to celebrate with a good dinner that night, and see about tickets for the Yangtze ferry the next day.

Having studied the map again, we thought we'd have a look at Central China from its most ancient thoroughfare, the Yangtze River. From Shanghai, regular ferries steamed up-river to Nanjing and Wuhan. From Wuhan, we could take the train further west, or continue by ferry to Chongqing. The trip to Wuhan would take about four days. The Russian visas specified particular dates in and out of the country. If we missed these, it would mean an 8000-kilometre return trip to Shanghai to get new visas, for there was no Russian consulate in Ürümqi. We'd left ourselves four weeks, but we'd have to keep an eye on the calendar.

That evening, we strolled over the Suzhou Creek bridge together. Along the Bund, the traffic was thick. There was a lot of construction going on. Huangpu Park, at the confluence of Suzhou Creek and the Huangpu River, was being rebuilt. This was the park made infamous in pre-revolutionary days (when it was known as the British Public Gardens) by its signs prohibiting 'Chinese and dogs' from admission. Now a great concrete monument of some sort was being erected, and the grounds refurbished with fountains and flower beds. Across the river, a gigantic tower was rising into the sky, festooned with cranes and bamboo scaffolding. The streets were in chaos, because Shanghai had decided, belatedly, to install an Underground, and if that meant digging up every major avenue in the city, then that's what they would do. Something had to be done about the grid-lock traffic jams that seized the city every day. Walking was much faster than taking a bus, and a taxi could take an hour to go 5 kilometres across town. We walked up Nanjing Donglu, the busiest avenue, and gaped at the crowds.

The avenue was packed with thousands of people, all of them intent on shopping 'til they dropped. Department stores, jewellers and gold merchants, electronics shops, restaurants and market stalls were all doing a roaring trade. The crowds were well-heeled, well dressed and very busy. United Colours of Benetton vied with Daimaru and Kentucky Fried Chicken for the biggest attendance. Shanghai had taken to capitalism with the same ferocious enthusiasm with which it had previously embraced European colonialism, the infant Chinese Communist Party, Maoism and the Gang of Four. Whatever the Shanghainese decide to do, they do a whole lot of it, very hard, at a high rate of knots.

The city is a foodie's dream—the Shanghainese are renowned gourmands, and look down on Beijingers as crude, country fellows who are content to stuff themselves with steamed bread and boiled meat. The Shanghainese are a more rarefied bunch, and they take their eating seriously. Even in the dire days of the Cultural Revolution, when the fanatics were attempting to stamp out traditional cooking along with everything else, the workers' dining halls of Shanghai were thought to be a cut above the rest. Within 100 kilometres of the city, several famous areas have contributed classical dishes to the Eastern School of cooking.

The city of Nanjing, just up the river, was the capital of China during the Ming Dynasty. The whole coastal plain from there to the sea became a sort of aristocratic Disneyland, where poets and princes disported themselves, and imperial chefs vied to outdo each other in composing dishes of refined elegance. The noble ancestor of the now humble spring roll came from Yangzhou, a town on the Grand Canal just north of Shanghai. It was, in those days, a lacy-thin crepe filled with finely shredded threads of the very first, tender vegetables to be picked in the spring, thus the name. Hangzhou, south-west of the city, is known for the real *haute cuisine* of the East. It was here that the Ming emperors built their summer palaces, complete with artificial mountains, dwarf trees and mirror lakes. The palace cooks, no doubt grumbling about having to make do with makeshift summer kitchens, invented such novelties as sizzling rice cakes (a dish in which hot, deep-fried rice crusts are combined with sauced meat in a noisy, showy finale) to amuse the bored exquisites reclining on embroidered silk in the pavilions. From West Lake came the classical steamed carp with vinegar sauce that carries its name today, and the prized Dragon Well tea, which found its way into the cooking, often in the form of tea-smoking. Shanghai itself has its own urban style, and the street-food scene is lively and interesting.

We'd read about a Yangzhou restaurant in Nanjing Donglu, and set out to find it. Getting a table in a Shanghai restaurant was no joke. By six o'clock, every place in town would be jammed, and by 8.30 or so, it was all over. Chinese people eat early, so that they have plenty of evening left for playing mah-jong, gambling and drinking wine. Sensible, really. You couldn't go out later, because the kitchens packed up early, except in the flashier night-clubs and the international hotels.

Shanghai is a cosmopolitan city, but we still carried a certain shock value when we sailed into a restaurant with three girls in tow. We learnt to keep on going, and lay claim to the nearest empty table, before the waiters had the chance to shove us out the door, claiming they had no room. Once we'd shed hats, coats and scarves and taken up residence, they were more or less forced to come up with a menu, clear the table and bring us some food. At the Yangzhou restaurant, the effort was worth it. We tried the speciality, air-dried chicken, which was mild and moist, and a wonderful dish of braised mushrooms, cooked very soft with anise and spices and served cold. A Yangzhou-style pork shred dish was cooked with slivers of green pepper and a rich, sweet sauce flavoured with wine lees. Braised noodles came with an assortment of seafoods and meats, in a style softer and less salty than the Cantonese equivalent. These Eastern dishes make much use of flavoured oils and wine, and slow-braising rather than stir-frying. The results were delicious.

As we walked back to the hotel, the wind off the river was turning cold. Even in the bitter breeze, peddlers camped on the street corners sold hot snacks from tiny charcoal braziers. Hard-boiled eggs and slices of tofu, boiled in soya, were offered for a few fen. One old man selling street maps and postcards had a nifty pair of ear-protectors, little fur-lined pockets the size of a coin purse, perched on the ends of his ears. They made him look like Mr Spock, down on his luck.

The weather was taking its toll. We were now battling recurrent 'flu symptoms that would hit one of us after the other. Achy, feverish and miserable, Dorcas was confined to bed the next day with a bottle of lemonade and a packet of aspirin. Our spacious room, with the five beds in a row, began to look like a hospital ward. As soon as one of us recovered, another would come down with it. The hotel room was comfortable, if a little chilly, so we bundled the girls up under their quilts. We wanted everybody healthy before we set off up-river, where it was likely to be colder still. The maids, who came in on their own schedule to sweep the floor and replenish the hot water (in Chinese hotels, there is no such thing as privacy), were bemused by the sight us all limping about in our long-johns, spending most of the day in bed. We were confirming all they'd heard about the strange habits of foreigners.

It was my turn to feel well, so I made twice-daily expeditions to bring back more food, aspirin and drinks. I also had to get tickets for the Yangtze ferry, and I wasn't looking forward to it. The Shanghai CITS office, while more helpful and better organised than most, could not issue tickets for this particular trip. I would have to go to the shipping office, they explained, and gave me directions. I found the building eventually (it had 'Yangtze Ferry Ticket Office' plastered all over it in 4-metre high letters, but I couldn't read them). My heart sank. Outside, there was a long queue of utterly hopeless-looking people. They looked as if they'd been camped there for weeks. The doors were almost invisible under the press of the crowd. I couldn't speak Chinese, so I couldn't ask directions. Which was the right queue? Where was the foreigners' office? Could you beam me up please, Scotty? I took a deep breath and plunged in.

I am not a little bloke. Sometimes I regret this. In department stores, I'm the guy down at the end of the shirt rack looking for the XXXOS with the wide fit. These always seem to come in a limited assortment of noxious plaids and pale-blue polyesters. Not for me the fashionable pleated trousers, the louche linen jackets with the sleeves pushed up. Twenty years of cooking, eating and drinking have left their mark on my already large frame. The only place in the world where I have ever felt petite was in Tonga, where adult males grow to the size of farm machinery. Here in China, I learnt to be grateful for every excess kilo. I could plough through crowds like a tugboat in a harbour full of dinghies. I tried to be polite, excusing myself frequently, but the essential thing was to keep moving, at least until I got inside the building. On the ground floor, a cavernous ticket hall was occupied by several thousand people climbing over each other to get at a row of tiny ticket windows. On the walls, huge charts gave destinations, times, distances and prices. I couldn't read a word of it. A smaller flow of people climbed the stairs to the first floor. I decided to have a look up there, where it might be less crowded.

Forty years of socialist rule has left China with some odd class distinctions. There is, for instance, no such thing as first class on trains, boats or aeroplanes. Prices start with second class, and go on down to third, fourth and fifth classes. If there is a particularly cushy berth, it will be described by a euphemism, such as 'soft' class or 'special' class. Very comfortable arrangements are available to high-level government officials, known as 'cadres'. These powerful bureaucrats are provided with separate ticket offices, waiting rooms and cabins. There are also special arrangements for officers in the People's Army, and for Overseas Chinese (visitors from Hong Kong and Taiwan). When China opened its borders to non-Chinese, similar arrangements were made for 'foreign guests'. There are foreigners' ticket offices at most train stations and shipping offices, if you can but find them. At these, you will be spared the masses, and may even find clerks who (at least in theory) speak some English. In return for this boon, you will be charged double for every ticket you buy, and be required to pay for it in inflated FEC currency. It is worth every penny.

At the foreigners' window, there were only a few people in line. When my turn came, I tried to explain that I wanted second class berths for two adults and three children to Wuhan. An older woman in a pearly cardigan was summoned to exercise her English, and after some discussion, the tickets were written out. This exchange was pleasant and friendly (if expensive) and I was delighted. I thanked her profusely. She smiled and nodded at me.

'Christ, that was easy,' I said to a young Australian woman who had been just before me in line, 'I thought that was going to take hours.'

'How long have you been in China?' she asked.

'Oh, just ten days or so.'

'Wait until you get out of Shanghai. It gets worse.'

She was right.

Dr Peng, the surgeon we'd met on the Changsha train, had been insistent that we contact him once we had settled in a hotel. We'd been feeling rotten, but resolved to ring him out of politeness before we left Shanghai. He was pleased to hear from us, and I asked if he would come and have dinner one night. He agreed, and said he would bring his wife and daughter along. We arranged to meet at our hotel the following night.

Peng was in his middle forties, and had moved to Shanghai to take up a new appointment as director of surgery at one of the city's largest hospitals. He arrived with his family, and we went up to our room to have a chat before going out to dinner. His daughter had brought presents for the girls, and we were a little embarrassed that we had nothing to offer in return. This business of gift-giving is a subtle and important custom in China, and we had yet to master the intricacies. Still, I thought, dinner would be on us, and we would be coming back to Shanghai on the return journey, a few months from now.

Peng had been concerned when I explained on the telephone that Dorcas and Kerry had been very ill with 'flu. He took a moment to examine Kerry, and then produced some medicines from his pocket. These were mild Chinese medicines, he explained, to be taken as tonics to restore health. The principal ingredients were herbs and snake bile extract, considered to be very good for the lungs and the chest. If she became any worse on the trip, he advised, we should give her antibiotics. He wrote out a prescription in Chinese, which he said we'd be able to fill at one of the city pharmacies before we left.

This mix of Chinese and western medicine was normal, he said. Although Chinese doctors were usually trained in one or the other, they borrowed freely from each system. Traditional medicine was generally aimed at prevention and long-term restoring of health and vitality through the choice of foods, herbs and teas that a person consumed. Western medicine, he said, was accepted to be essential for trauma, acute disease and life-threatening illness.

At the Seagull Hotel, Peng was kept busy all evening, translating for all of us, since his wife (a civil engineer working in the Pudong New City across the river) and his daughter did not speak any English, or were at least as shy about using it as we were of our primitive Chinese. The conversation was lively, though, as we fired questions back and forth about how things worked in our respective countries, what plans our children had, how we lived at home. It was a special occasion, and everyone was being polite, but we had a lot to ask each other. Peng was delighted at the idea of the trip we were making, and that we should be taking the girls along with us.

'This will open their minds,' he said, 'to see other countries and meet so many people. But won't they miss out on their schooling, and fall behind?'

I explained the arrangements we'd made. Peng said that his daughter was still undecided about a career, but that one of her dearest wishes was to be able to study overseas. This was hugely expensive, he said, since the government would provide little assistance. The student's family were expected to come up with the money, and even then, permission was hard to obtain.

While we were talking, an American 'adventure tour' group of about 30 people wheeled in for their evening meal. They all looked to be in their sixties, and were making jokes about eating snake and dog. A trio of musicians set up in the corner. They had traditional instruments—the one-string Chinese violin, the hammer dulcimer and a sort of drum.

At the table, we were into finance. Peng asked how I could afford to take four months off my job, as well as pay for such a long trip. I explained that I owned a small business with a partner, and that my partner was running things while I was away. She'd just returned from a four-month trip herself. As for the expense, we spend almost all our disposable income on travel. At home, we live simply, don't own a car, save for the next trip . . .

'And how much rent must you pay for your house?' Peng asked.

'We're buying it with a bank loan. About $200 a week.'

'Shhh!' The Chinese intake of breath, amazement, as Peng calculated the exchange in yuan.

'How much rent do you pay, then?'

'No rent. Our apartment is supplied with my job, by the hospital.'

'That's good, isn't it?'

'Yes, but it's impossible for us to buy a house. Now in Shanghai, there are many houses being built in the new development zones, but they're very expensive.'

'How much?'

'As much as one million yuan.'

About $A200 000, a staggering amount of money in China. Peng told me earlier that he earned about Y300 a month as a senior surgeon.

'But how can anyone afford them?'

'Only overseas Chinese from Taiwan or Hong Kong. High-up people in the government. Foreigners.'

The food arrived. It was a Cantonese restaurant, and the cooking was excellent. Peng had helped me choose the dishes. Mrs Peng ate like a bird, a tiny bowl of rice, a few vegetables. Peng and I were drinking local beer, everyone else was sipping tea. The girls were ploughing through the food like factory ships through a school of herring. I glared at them to be polite, offer the dishes to our guests. Dorcas kicked Clare under the table for wolfing down the last of the roast duck.

The adventure tour group got their dinner, whisked out of the kitchen all at once. More jokes, this time about using chopsticks. Most of them settled for spoons, like aged infants. The band launched into a tune that sounded familiar.

'The shops in Nanjing Donglu are very busy. Everyone seems to be buying things, especially clothes and electronics. Where is all the money coming from?'

'Business. Now, everyone wants to be in business. Some businessmen are making a lot of money, very rich.'

'What kind of business?'

'Importing things, export. Investing money in stocks.'

The new stock exchanges were recent additions to the Chinese financial system. In Shenzen, the special economic zone near Hong Kong, there were riots when the first share offers were made in public companies, and the army was called out to control the mob. The latest exchange to be opened was in Shanghai, in the Pujiang Hotel building. I'd caught a glimpse of the big electronic board through a phalanx of security guards, and the place was constantly busy. Shares had soared since they were first offered, and fast fortunes were being made, at a cost of disastrous inflation. Government employees like Peng were left behind on fixed salaries, while anyone with a few thousand yuan and a lot of nerve could have a go at becoming a millionaire. Cellular phones were the badge of the 'new businessmen' and there were plenty of Mercedes and BMWs in the streets.

'In Australia, a doctor is quite well paid. In America, they become millionaires,' I said.

'Yes, I have heard. Here, doctors are trained by the government, so we are expected to work where we are needed. There's no private medical business.'

'Is medical care free for everyone, then?'

'If you work for a government company, it is free. If you are a farmer, you must pay for it yourself. A kidney operation, for instance, would cost about Y1000.'

I tried to imagine what sort of kidney operation you would get in the US for two hundred bucks. Something with an electric tin opener, perhaps, and a set of instructions. The tour group had already finished their dinner, and were being shown out to a waiting bus, presumably for 1.5 cocktails at the Peace Hotel's Jazz Bar. The Chinese band saw them out with a perky rendition of 'The Yellow Rose of Texas'.

SIX

For the next few days, we lived in the Pujiang Hotel, making sorties into the city as our collective health and the weather allowed. We went to the Mandarin Gardens, the Peace Hotel, the Museum of Unusual Collections (pieces of grotesquely shaped rock, landscapes carved on the heads of ivory pins, jade, lacquer and 19th century cigarette tins). We went shopping, again, in the warren of tiny narrow streets near the Mandarin Gardens, where the remnants of the old Chinese city had survived the Boxer Rebellion, World War II and the Cultural Revolution. Tiny shops and noodle-stalls were packed tightly up against each other, and the bicycle traffic was dense. We stopped to buy Aislinn a new pair of shoes. The little shop was crammed with cloned Nikes and bootleg Hi-Tops, in diminutive children's sizes. The two rosy-cheeked women behind the counter were delighted with Aislinn, but held their hands in front of their mouths when they saw the size of her feet. They had the decency to avoid kangaroo jokes.

Next door, an even tinier shop contained one ancient man, working at a bench with a grinding wheel. In the dusty window, a set of exquisitely made scissors was laid out. From kitchen shears down to delicate embroidery scissors, each pair had been fashioned by hand from a single piece of steel—heated, bent, nipped, ground and sharpened to a keen edge. They were simple, strong and beautifully functional, like so many Chinese tools.

We stopped for dumplings, the 'pot-stickers' the locals call *jiao-tse*. These were everywhere on the streets; wherever a charcoal burner and a small table could be set up. A heavy, round, iron griddle plate, well-oiled, is put on to heat. Small lumps of elastic dough are filled with a seasoned pork mince, then deftly twisted and sealed to leave the filling enclosed. The finished dumplings, about the size of golf balls, are set on the plate close together, then fried to brown the bottoms. Finally, a domed lid is put over them, and they're left to steam-cook for a few minutes. When the lid comes off, people crowd to buy greasy bags full of the delicious hot dumplings. If you take your *jiao-tse* in a café, they're served with a teapot of dark vinegar so that you can season them yourself. The atmosphere and smell reminded me of fish and chip shops in the north of England.

On the streets just off the Bund, in the business district, instant restaurants appeared each day around lunchtime. A couple of women would appear in a doorway, set up a small stove and a table, then dish out takeaway lunches for the crowds of office clerks and shop assistants pouring out of the surrounding buildings. This really was home cooking; most of the food was spooned out of small saucepans and containers obviously brought from their own kitchens. A portion of steamed rice provided the base, and customers chose two or three dishes to go with it. I queued up one day to collect four lunchboxes (Dorcas and the girls were back in the hotel room, shivering under their blankets). The jolly, broad-faced woman in a white smock and hat was loudly amused by the presence of a foreigner in her lunch queue, and kept up a cackling repartee that involved repeatedly poking me in the belly and slapping my arm from time to time. Her daughter, a pretty girl of twenty or so, was mortified with embarrassment, and concentrated on filling the lunchboxes. As she finished, and passed me my change, she pushed a wisp of hair out of her face and said, intently, in English, 'Welcome to China!'

We packed our bags with some regret. The Pujiang was a comfortable old barn of a place, the Shanghainese were good-humoured and friendly, and the city was endlessly interesting, but we had many thousands of miles to go, and thought we'd better get on with it. As we checked out, I had a half-hearted attempt at booking a room for the return journey. 'Sorry, all full up. No more rooms,' was the reply. Well, I could have told you that.

At the Shanghai ferry terminal, we were back amongst the masses. Thousands of people thronged the waiting rooms, sat on the stairs, mobbed the snack-shops and staked out space with enormous piles of luggage. Kerry asked me what river this was. I told her that we were going up the Yangtze River, but that the river here in Shanghai was called the Huangpu. Kerry and Aislinn thought this was hilarious. 'Huang-poo, Huang-poo' they chanted, delighted with a fitting name for such a smelly river. An ancient grandmother on the next bench looked on indulgently. She leaned over to talk to Dorcas. 'Were they all her children?' the grandmother mimed.

'Yes, all three,' Dorcas said.

'Ahh,' said the old woman, 'very good, to have many children. And their ages?' Dorcas used the finger signs to indicate 13, 11 and seven.

'Very pretty girls,' the woman smiled, pointing to Clare and Kerry, . . . and so lucky to have had a boy at last!

Dorcas realised that Aislinn, with her hair tucked up under a woolly cap, was easily mistaken for a 7-year-old boy. 'No,' said Dorcas, reaching across to lift Aislinn's hat off, allowing a mane of blond hair to tumble down—'she's a girl, too.'

'EEAAAGH!,' cried Grandma, 'you poor woman! Another girl? Three girls? THREE GIRLS? Never mind,' she consoled, patting Dorcas' hand and glaring darkly at me—'it's probably him.'

People at the front of the hall were getting excited, indicating that the boat was ready for boarding. Peasants hoisted giant sacks on bamboo yokes, students gathered up shiny boxes of cassette players and videos, and we hefted our packs. The line moved slowly forward. We emerged, at last, on to the dockside, to join the queue climbing the long gangway that scaled the side of the ship. Suddenly, there was a burst of intense light, skewering us against the side of the ship while a great commotion erupted on either side of us. Scenes from the film Midnight Express flashed briefly in my head, encouraged by the presence of several soldiers with green uniforms and machine-guns on the other side of the blinding light. Then I made out the camera, and the fellow with the sound boom. It was a television crew. 'Whayayoufom?' called the interviewer. 'Australia,' we shouted back, giving the universal thumbs-up as the camera panned the five of us, lingering on little Aislinn, with her bobble hat and school-bag. A busy steward struggled down the gangway, welcomed us lavishly on board his ferry, and escorted us up to our second class cabin. We waved at the camera all the way up, like the Rolling Stones on tour.

The cabins were plain, but comfortable enough. A long room contained six double bunks. A sink and hot water were provided at either end. One door led on to the promenade deck, the other opened into the corridor which led to the showers, toilets and the rest of the ship. Forward of our cabin was 'special class' country, where four-berth cabins were daintily appointed with plastic flowers, lace doylies and carpets. We stowed our gear and went exploring. There was a restaurant on the same deck, already full of people. A shop dispensed comic books, playing cards, snack foods, cigarettes, soap and bottles of *bai jiu*. There were four decks altogether, the lowest taken up with a kitchen, another dining hall, and the more spartan sleeping arrangement for third and fourth class passengers. These were basically large dormitories, segregated by sex. I guessed that the ship carried about five or six hundred passengers. We would be on it for three days, as it steamed up-river to Wuhan.

Morning on the Yangtze River was cold, foggy and other-worldly. I stood at the rail, watching a wan yellow sunlight begin to lift the veil on a wide thoroughfare of water. Out of the mist ahead, a procession of river-craft materialised. Coal scows, smaller ferries, tiny sampans and great straining lines of heavy barges were on the move. There were no pretty pleasure yachts with colourful sails; these were all working boats, dun-coloured, grimy and heavy-laden. Diesel engines chugged. Coal smoke drifted across the flat expanse of the water. I could not see the shore in either direction.

The river is older than Chinese history. It's always been there, like a great highway running through central China. In Mandarin, it's called the Chang Jiang, and it rises in the chaotically glaciated folds of the Tanggula Shan mountains in remote Qinghai province. It then flows down through Tibet, almost to the border of Burma (where, at one point, the Irrawaddy, the Mekong and the Yangtze thunder within 100 kilometres of each other) before hooking north and east, seeking the flat central Chinese plain. At 6300 kilometres long, it is the world's third longest river, emptying into the East China Sea near Shanghai. The Chinese government regards it as the frontier between the north and the south. Public buildings south of the river are not permitted to burn coal for heating in the winter; those north of the river may. Further up the river, near Chongqing, the famous river gorges form a serious hazard to navigation and have been the inspiration for many classical scroll paintings. The government had already announced plans to drown the gorges in a great hydroelectric scheme, similar to the one that had changed the ancient cycle of the Nile at Aswan. What effect this would have on the Yangtze was beyond my scientific ken, but the unique freshwater dolphins that survive (barely) in some stretches of the river were unlikely to benefit from the new arrangements.

Chinese people get up early. By 7.00 am, there were already a score of people on the deck, twisting and shaking themselves, exercising with the sinuous movements of *tai chi chuan* or simple calisthenics. All this was accompanied by the dawn chorus of hawking, honking, coughing and spitting that greets every new day in China. There's no getting around it, the Chinese like to spit. Anywhere, everywhere. No piece of floor is safe, whether it's packed dirt, parquet or carpet. As long as it's floor, it's fair game, inside or out. The presence of China's largest river just over the rail did not prevent the passengers from anointing the deck frequently. Entire political campaigns have been mounted by the government to stamp out the habit, but so far without success. The cost to public health is obvious—if anyone's got the 'flu, everyone's got it. In the grip of moist, foggy winter cold, the whole country wheezes and coughs for four months of the year.

Breakfast consisted of tea, packets of sweet biscuits, and a few oranges. The restaurant was open, serving bowls of hot rice porridge and soup, but we were not keen to face the brawl for a table just yet. Several fellow passengers called over to try their few words of English on us. This intense curiosity about foreigners was endemic. If we were walking down a city street, people might just stare, but if we stopped somewhere, in a restaurant, a waiting room or a hotel lobby, we learnt to expect that someone would inevitably come over and ask questions. Some travellers find this a wearying experience in China, the constant attention and questioning, but we felt obliged to respond. They really didn't see very many foreigners; we were lucky enough to be able to travel distances which were absolutely out of the question for most Chinese nationals, and we were, after all, their guests. We met dozens of people—teachers, factory workers, students and civil servants—most of whom asked the same questions. What country were we from? How many were in our family? What jobs did we do? Why were we in China? Did we like it? Where were we going next? Since we couldn't speak Chinese, these interviews with English-speakers provided our only chance to ask questions in return. The answers gave us a very different picture of China from the one we'd gleaned from books. Most of what we'd read was political history or geography. Jung Chang's brilliant *Wild Swans* had come closest to explaining how ordinary life in China survived the cataclysms of recent history, but even that book swept along on a pretty grand scale. We just wanted to know why Chinese kids so seldom cry, how much a bicycle cost, why no one ever used a rubbish bin.

The ferry stopped several times a day, at major and minor ports along the river. Passengers would disembark or come aboard, freight was unloaded on to stout wooden carts, and then they'd take on more food, essential for maintaining supply for 600 people who seldom stopped eating. The docks were busy. At each stop, a blackboard was hung near the gangway, advising how many minutes the boat would be there. Crowds of passengers scrambled off to queue up at the food stalls and souvenir shops which opened specially for the boat's arrival. The selection of goodies changed as we steamed further up-river. Instant noodle soups, sticky buns and boiled eggs were regular favourites, but each town had its own specialities. At one place, blue and white ceramic jars were filled with candied ginger. Another stop offered roast ducks, hung by the neck at butcher's stalls. An odd pudding, not unlike a Scotsman's haggis, put in an appearance later. Boiled chicken feet, pink manufactured sausages, dried melon seeds and chillied peanuts, even bananas, were on offer.

Dorcas and I left the boat at Nanjing, where we had an hour to look around. The girls were perfectly well looked after by a network of surrogate aunties they'd gathered on board in the previous 24 hours. We were hoping to get a glimpse of the 14th century city walls, but in China ancient monuments are more likely to be buried behind a tractor factory, hung with lines of drying laundry or put to use as a bus station. The city walls had survived British bombardment from the river during the Taiping Rebellion, but we couldn't find the damn things. With time running short, we settled for a stroll along the waterfront, then joined the throng re-boarding the ferry.

Around noon, general movement in the corridors indicated that lunch was being served, so we made our way aft. The second class restaurant was a utilitarian dining hall with steel chairs and tables bolted to the floor. There were already 200 people in there, making the usual amiable racket. Near the door, a caged-in counter dispensed bottled beer and grimy glasses. Lunch orders were placed at another counter. Blackboard menus listed eight or ten choices, with prices. These were all in Chinese characters, and no one at the counter spoke a word of anything we could understand. While Dorcas nobbled a table, I had to drag a scruffy waiter around, pointing at dishes on other people's tables and gesturing for him to write it down. The patrons thought this was hilarious, and took it in good form. If it wasn't elegant, it was certainly quick. We got bowls of doughy rice and several dishes of tofu, chicken and indeterminate meat with green vegetables. It was all reasonably good, and ridiculously cheap. Half the restaurant was waving in our direction, exchanging notes on the habits of foreigners or chuckling over the one about the *lao-wai* and the farmer's daughter. As we finished our lunch, one group of happy youths came up to the table and presented us with a small bottle of *bai jiu*. Dorcas declined, having sniffed the stuff from ten yards away, but they insisted that I drink a toast to international friendship then and there, so I had to swallow the bottle in one draught, as is the custom. This brought a great cheer, several slaps on the back and handshakes all round. We bolted before they could find another bottle.

One of the advantages of travelling with your children is that they, of course, find other children and bring them back. This provides an opening to introduce yourself to the parents, and so starts many a conversation. In most cases, we were limited to smiles, nods and sign language to settle exact ages and number of offspring. Occasionally, the parents might speak a few words of English, but usually they drifted off with our kids in tow for a session of card-playing, finger games and boiled-sweet consumption. Once the ice had been broken, the students would turn up. Perched on our berths, they would launch into intense discussions of politics, sociology and popular culture. Their enthusiasm and politeness were impressive. We exchanged addresses and learnt a great deal about what they were studying, the plans they had for the future, and how eager China was to 'open to the West'. There was no political coyness. Deng Xiao-Ping's latest initiatives, the Cultural Revolution and the role of foreign investment in the New China were all fair topics of discussion. There was a notable lack of the pseudo-cynicism and radical chic which were considered suitable attitudes for undergraduates when I was at university. These bright and well-scrubbed young technocrats reminded me a little of Mormon missionaries, but smarter.

After dinner that night, the ever attentive students returned. I had had almost enough political and economic discussion for the day, and I was not keen on another few hours of it before bed. But they weren't there to chat, they had an invitation for Clare.

'Will you come with us to a dancing party?' one girl asked.

'A what?'

'A dancing party. We are having dancing party downstairs,' she beamed.

'Dad, is that OK? Can I go?'

'Sure, go ahead. Don't fall off the boat.'

'Thanks, Dad, I'll try not to.'

As Clare brushed her hair and hastily found her earrings, the students had a whispered conference. Someone must have pointed out that the oldies might possibly know how to dance, too. A young male was elected to do the talking.

'Excuse me, sir, would you and your wife also come to the dancing party?'

'Ah, thank you, not for me, but my wife would love to go. She likes dancing very much.'

'Very good! You must have many dancing parties in Australia.'

I couldn't answer immediately, because the pinch-grip Dorcas had on the back of my hand brought tears of pain to my eyes.

'AAhhh,' I squealed, 'yes, very many.'

Dorcas brushed her hair, gave me a look that said there would be a reckoning for this later, and sailed off with Clare to the student disco. Kerry and Aislinn were already in bed, so I read for a while until they were asleep. After an hour, I was bored with the book. I checked on the girls, then decided to go and have a look at the 'dancing party' myself.

On the deck below us, in a forward cabin, the furniture had been cleared away, and a set of coloured lights draped from the ceiling. A tape cassette player fresh from Hong Kong had been plugged in and the BeeGees were turned up loud. There were at least 50 people crammed into the room, as I peered in the door. I couldn't see Clare, but Dorcas was very visible in the middle of the room, held in a fierce but chaste grip by a young man who was attempting to waltz to 'Stayin' Alive'. I bailed out quickly.

'Wei! Wei! Lao wai. Ni hao ma?'

The shout came from the porter's office, next to the stairs. I was wandering about aimlessly, stepping carefully over the informal passengers snoring underfoot. A broad-faced, unshaven fellow in a uniform jacket was leaning out the door. Lights were on inside, and he had a few mates in there with him.

'Ni hao ma?' he repeated.

'Hen hao, xie xie,' I said, exhausting the other half of my vocabulary in Mandarin. The porter waved me closer. The tiny cabin held five or six men, cramped up on three chairs and a counter-top. This was where the lads hung out, when all the passengers were asleep. The fug of cigarette smoke said they'd been in there a while. They made room for me, and insisted I sit down. Fresh cigarettes were distributed, and everyone lit up.

'Whayayufum?' said the one in the porter's jacket. One or two others had the same jacket, the rest wore white cotton t-shirts.

'Ao-da-li-ya.'

'Ah, Ao-da-li-ya. Seedeni. Mehbone?'

'No, Cairns. In the north. North Australia.'

This prompted a bit of quick question-and-answer around the room. What did he say? Did all Australians have black beards and big bellies? What about the women? I produced a pen and used the back of an old timetable. I sketched out a map of Australia, indicating the relative locations of Seedeni, Mehbone and Cairns. This was passed around with a lot of sage clucking and nodding. Time for more cigarettes all around. A bottle of *bai jiu* came down off the shelf.

'Ao-da-li-ya,' my friend asked as he pointed at the bottle, '*bai jiu*?'

'No, no *bai jiu*. We have Bundaberg. It's worse.'

'Ahh, Bun-da-buq.'

All of us agreed that this was enough conversational foreplay. It was time to start drinking. There were lots of toasts. Australia! *Zhongguo* (China)! *Bai jiu*! Bundaberg! The liquor was appalling. It had a repulsive diesel-oil smell and a terrifying alcoholic content. The bottle was almost empty, so I produced another one from my coat pocket. Hurrah! Australia! *Zhongguo*!

Half an hour later, we were all drunk. We'd given up struggling with language, and resorted to slapping each other's backs, digging each other in the ribs and laughing uproariously. The noise was starting to carry, and a few of the fifth class passengers called out complaints. Would we please shut up in there, decent people were trying to get some sleep. Get knotted, my comrades called back, can't you see we're entertaining a foreign guest?

It wasn't easy to disengage from my new-found buddies, but I thought I'd better get back and see how the girls were getting on. We all shook hands, and I weaved off down the corridor. Now to find my cabin. Just look for the number. Christ, what was the number? The corridor lights were turned down, and sonorous snoring noises drifted out from every cabin. It had to be along here somewhere, 320-something . . . or was that the berth number? It was on this deck, wasn't it? I peered into the second class cabins through the windows, but they all looked the same in the gloom. Bloody inconsiderate, really, turning all the lights off when a fellow's trying to find his cabin. I turned a corner into yet another long corridor, full of bundled sleeping people on the floor. I stepped carefully through them, getting the occasional muffled curse when the ship gave a lurch to one side.

At the end of the corridor, a figure appeared, gnarled and bent. It was one of the women who swept the corridors. She cackled at me in rapid Chinese. Her tone was demanding, interrogatory. I couldn't understand a word. She beetled down the corridor towards me, uttering scolding noises. I stood firm, gently belching diesel fumes. 'Tcch!' she said. Grasping my sleeve in her horny brown fingers, she pulled me halfway down the corridor, opened a cabin door, and thrust me in. In the dim light, I could just make out Dorcas and the three girls, peacefully asleep. I rolled in to my empty bunk and shut down for the night.

I risked opening one eye the next day around ten o'clock. A couple of fresh-faced students were already camped out on Dorcas's bed, chatting pleasantly. I felt like I had bubonic plague, or possibly something worse. I groaned. Dorcas looked over, without sympathy.

'Serves you right,' she whispered.

'Have pity.'

'Try dancing lessons.'

'Does you good to get out.'

'You can start by getting out of that bed.'

I did, but regretted it. A splash of cold water on my face and a visit to the loo did little to improve my condition. Just as I settled back on my bunk, yet another student descended, and launched into an interrogation in strangled English. He'd obviously been cutting classes, because every phrase was an enormous effort. Listening to him was even harder. I had to go outside; he was making me ill.

The river had narrowed as we approached Anqing, a river port in Anhui province. This was the industrial heartland of modern China, and the river traffic grew busier still. Along the banks of the river, I could see peasants harvesting great sheafs of reeds from flat coastal fields, bundling them and loading them on to barges for transport.

Oil tankers specially constructed for shallow draught, and long strings of coal barges, plied up and down. Factories on either bank belched out smoke. The air was grey and misty, as much from pollution as the winter weather. If they can ever overcome their terrible population problem, China faces another monumental job: cleaning up the industrial mess made by Mao's Great Leap Forward in the late 1950s and the early 1960s. In a frenzy of heavy construction, power stations and steel mills were built near the river for easy fuelling, while agricultural land was spoilt and wasted. Serious pollution of the river with heavy metals and chemical wastes created more problems, and the traditional fishing resource of the Yangtze was all but destroyed. Coal is still China's principal fuel, and its grimy, eye-stinging residue is ever-present. The awareness of pollution so familiar in the West just hasn't sunk into the Chinese mind. The average man in the street sees nothing wrong with disposing of rubbish, however noxious, by throwing it out the nearest window or into the nearest waterway. The arrival of western packaging has made the problem much worse. Where once bamboo or paper containers eventually decomposed, now foam clam-shell packs, plastic bottles and wrappers litter every road and waterway.

After lunch, and a restorative bottle of beer, I was feeling much more chipper, and decided to have a better look around the boat. I passed a few of my new buddies, who tipped me the wink as they went by. They didn't seem to be suffering any ill effects. On the deck nearest the water, I poked my head into the kitchen, as any cook will do in a strange place. The lads in there were working in white trousers, t-shirts and aprons, with natty little hats and white gumboots. It all looked pretty ship-shape, except for the frozen chickens that were skidding around the floor like so many footballs. I was impressed with their cutting boards, which were entire sections of tree trunk, sawn off flat at top and bottom, standing 4 feet high. A row of big steamers stood for the rice against one wall. A series of benches did for vegetable preparation, and against another wall, six giant woks were built in. It was a big kitchen, but quiet now, in the after-lunch lull. A couple of prep cooks were peeling onions, another was washing rice. Over near the coldroom, a butcher was dismantling a whole pig. A second dining hall, behind the kitchen, served as a takeaway counter. For Y3, you got a box of rice, some fried cabbage and a bit of braised pork or whole fried fish. Each day, on the ferry, hundreds of these cheap meals were served up in foam containers. The used containers went over the side. They formed a sorry trail in the water after each meal, as they drifted away behind us.

The following morning dawned raw and cold. It was raining fitfully. We packed up our things and shared a cold breakfast. Quite a few of the students were getting off here, and stopped by to draw us maps and offer advice. The ship's siren moaned across the grey water, as we approached the dock. We'd arrived in Wuhan.

SEVEN

We were beginning to understand a comment we'd read, not long before we set out, in another traveller's account of a trip through China. He said that Chinese people, in particular the students, were sometimes *too* helpful. Now that we had gained our close-knit group of student chaperones, it was very hard to get away from them. Granted, the weather was dismal, Wuhan looked grey and threatening, and we hadn't a clue where to go. When the students insisted that we accept a ride in their school bus to the other side of the river, we accepted. We waited for some time. It was raining. The students fidgeted, assuring us every few minutes that the bus would be here soon. It got colder, and began to rain harder. We would have been happier to stagger off to the nearest café and wait for some improvement, but the honour of Wuhan University was at stake, so we crouched, miserable, under a tin roof and waited for the damn bus. Finally, it arrived and we all piled on board, getting drenched in the process.

The bus was packed with wet clothing and luggage, but the students found seats for Dorcas and the girls. I was being noble, refused a seat, and chose to stand in the stairwell, as we lumbered across the Wuhan Bridge. This noteworthy feat of engineering, completed in 1957, was the first bridge to span the Yangtze, and Mao Zedong was particularly proud of it, as a symbol of the industrial might of the revolution and the leadership of the Communist Party. By the time we had crossed it, we had heard just about every statistic one can quote about a bridge, from the metric tonnes of concrete that went into it, to the number of lampposts along its length (one for every something or other that must have been important at the time). I was feeling ill, feverish and claustrophobic. Dorcas leaned over and talked to me.

'You look unhealthy.'

'I feel awful.'

'Something you drank, was it?'

'No, really, I think I've got the 'flu again.'

'Let's see if we can find a hotel and some breakfast.'

'If we ever get off this bus.'

'Do you want to sit down?'

'No, it's OK, I'll stay here.'

'Come on, I'll stand for a while.'

'No, really, I can't.'

'Why not?'

'Because my trousers are falling down.'

'What?'

'I must be losing weight. My trousers are halfway down to my knees, and I'm too wedged in here to hoist them back up. So I'd better not move just at the moment, if it's all the same to you.'

'Honestly, I can't take you anywhere.'

'It's a worry, isn't it?'

Twenty minutes later, I had managed to hoist my trousers discreetly back into place, just in time to climb off the bus. We'd stopped outside a Chinese hotel, and two of the students insisted on escorting us into the hotel. They talked the desk clerk into letting us in to the place, and left after refusing an invitation to stay to lunch. The rain was getting heavy and the light gloomy. From our window, Wuhan looked an unlovely place with dense traffic and pressing crowds, but the hotel was just around the corner from the railway station, where I hoped we'd get tickets for the next train to Xi'an.

Food was the next step. We'd missed breakfast in the confusion of disembarkation, and had to wait for the hotel restaurant to open for lunch. It was the sort of Chinese medium-expensive hotel where we'd expect to find party cadres and businessmen impressing each other over long lunches with plenty of *mao-tai*. A raggle-tag family of foreigners with children was slightly out of the ordinary, but the restaurant staff put a brave face on it and found us a table. There the communication hurdles began. No one on the staff spoke English, nor was there a translated menu. My Chinese was still at a primitive level. The best I could do was bark the words for 'pork', 'vegetable', 'chicken' and 'rice' at the embarrassed waiter, dipping into my phrasebook for a triumphant 'and squid!'. The waiter smiled, nodding. They brought us tea.

'What have you ordered?' Dorcas asked.

'I hope I've ordered some chicken and pork and squid, with vegetables.'

'Will you go to the railway station after lunch and see about tickets?'

'Yes. Shall we take the first train we can get?'

'I suppose so. I'd like to have a bit of a look around, but the weather's so miserable. No point in sitting in the hotel for three days.'

The first course arrived, to the girls' approval. Steamed rice there was, and a plate of green vegetables, rather plainly boiled. The pork was cold, slices of grey meat on a platter, but it was a start. At least they had served us food. We had an audience of local patrons, too sophisticated to gape at us openly, but discreetly staring at our every move with chopstick and bowl.

I watched a series of platters emerge from the kitchen, variously flaming, sizzling or wreathed in steam. 'Ooohs' and 'aaahs' rose from the diners, impressed with the artistry of the chefs. Brass-funnelled 'steamboats' were brought to many of the tables. This is a northern specialty in China, called Mongolian hot-pot. A round trough of savoury broth is kept on the simmer by a charcoal fire inside, the fumes riding through the chimney. Platters of thinly sliced meats and fish are presented, along with assorted vegetables, mushrooms and dipping sauces. The diners use their chopsticks to dip morsels of food into the boiling broth to cook, then add their own combination of soy, chilli or vinegar to their bowl and wolf it all down. When the platters are exhausted, the rich broth is ladled out into bowls and drunk to finish the meal. It's a very popular style, and the steamboat sign was to become a familiar sight in restaurant windows as we got further north and west.

Our waiter was back with the second course. There were two platters. On one, a pair of pale, rubbery cuttlefish reclined like half-deflated footballs, entirely unadorned by sauce or garnish. On the other, a large, naked white chicken, plainly boiled, was similarly unsullied by any form of condiment or decoration. I had asked for a chicken, and they'd brought me a chicken. I hadn't said anything about how I wanted it cooked, so they had played safe and boiled it, whole. Likewise the squid. Bizarre tastes in food, these foreigners, but then what could you expect from barbarians?

Back in the room, the girls were much cheered up by our spartan lunch, and declared themselves fit for a little shopping if the rain abated. I was feeling worse; feverish and clammy. It was all getting a little much for me. The bloody weather, the bloody railway stations and the constant battle to make ourselves understood was taking its toll. I was fed up with China. I wanted to get out to somewhere where I could order a coffee in Italian, French or English and have a reasonable chance of getting it. I wanted to get away from the grotty rubbish in the streets, the unrelenting crowds everywhere, the unreconstructed diesel fumes that passed for an atmosphere in China. It was all too bloody difficult, and on top of that I was getting the 'flu again. Dorcas force-fed me three aspirin, gave me a large glass of brandy, and rolled me up under a pile of woollen blankets.

'Stop moaning,' she said, 'I'm taking the girls out for a walk. Go to sleep.' The door closed behind them, and I followed instructions.

They returned a couple of hours later, having browsed the local market for the supplies we replenished whenever we could—toilet roll, bottled water, instant coffee (this was something of a luxury, and expensive—it came in neat little Nestlé's packets complete with milk and sugar). Dorcas said that the rain had slowed a bit, and that the area around the station was full of stalls and tiny restaurants. I felt better for the sleep, and set off to try the railway station for tickets.

The ticket hall was the normal confused and crowded scrum, with lines of people everywhere attempting to get at the ticket windows. I had a crumpled scrap of paper, which the students had written out for me, asking for five tickets on the next train to Xi'an, hard sleeper. Getting near the window was a matter of queuing up for an hour or so. As I got closer, the knot of people around me became more and more panic-stricken, climbing and pushing and shouting at each other. It was mainly by force that I got to the window. This was a tiny aperture, less than a hand's breadth high, through which one could glimpse the dragon woman behind the counter. In order to speak to her, it was necessary to assume a sort of supplicant's crouch, dangerously close to a kow-tow. This seemed to suit her just fine. Hard-faced and grim, she snatched the bit of paper from my hand and read it as if it were a bit of particularly unpleasant news. She shook her head with an imperious '*Mei you!*' and tossed it back at me. This was a disaster. My sorry scrap of paper was the only chance I had of obtaining tickets, and it had been found wanting by the Dragon Lady. I had no idea why, and I could neither question her nor argue with her in Chinese.

Chinese ticket clerks hate to give anything away. If you ask for an afternoon train to Beijing, they'll say '*mei you*' and send you off with a flea in your ear, without letting on that there is an 11.50 am train, and that it's the last one for the day. Ask for an upper berth on the express to Xi'an and you'll be banished to the outer darkness, unaware that there are plenty of lower berths available, but you didn't ask for a lower berth, did you? I was on the point of despair, when an English-speaking woman in the next queue offered to help. Grateful beyond expression, I let her ask questions for me, and learnt that I'd simply come at the wrong time. Tickets for the Xi'an train were only sold in the morning, and I'd have to present myself at 7.30 am to have any chance of getting them. I thanked her at length, then left.

The area around the station was busy, as evening grew darker, and the crowds seemed to be getting thicker. The streets glistened, illuminated by garish neon tubes above the market stalls. With rain pouring off my hat, I picked my way through foul pools of brown water and rotting vegetables. Faces loomed up out of the rain, blank, staring, hostile. Terrible, distorted pop music shrieked out of a dozen tinny speakers at 1000 decibels, and the whole scene took on a nightmarish, hallucinatory quality. I wasn't feeling well.

Back at the hotel, I confessed that I'd been unable to get tickets, and would try again in the morning. Dorcas offered to take the girls out to one of the restaurant stalls for dinner, while I crept back into bed for more sleep. I didn't wake when they returned, and slept straight through until morning.

Just before 7.30 am, I was present and accounted for on the Foreigners' and Overseas Chinese Visitors' ticket line at Wuhan Railway Station, clasping my bit of paper and full of hope. Even at this hour, there were several hundred people in the place, but happily, only a dozen or so on my line. My fellow (intending) passengers were a mixture of well-dressed Taiwanese businessmen and young Hong Kong tourists in Reeboks. The only other non-Chinese in the line was a young American who bore an uncanny resemblance to the comedian Eddie

Murphy. He was immaculately kitted out in an expensive track suit, gold chains, Rolex watch and an earring. We weren't close enough to hold a conversation, but we nodded to each other over a few heads. 'Where you going?' I called.

'Beijing. How about you?'

'Xi'an, if I can get tickets.'

'Good luck, man. Woman on this counter a little hard to get along with.'

I was thinking about all the 'staring squad' treatment we'd had in the last couple of weeks. However innocently curious, it got a little overpowering at times. What must it be like then, to be a single black American touring around China? If European faces are rare in China, black faces are about as common as lunar landings. Still, Eddie Murphy seemed to be holding his own. When the ticket window finally snapped open, he'd repelled a couple of late runs from the sidelines, and successfully staked his claim at the counter. He'd just begun to speak to the Dragon Lady when he was pushed aside by an aggressive Chinese man waving a handful of passports and money. Eddie rounded on the Chinese with a loud, fluent and expressive stream of perfect Mandarin, cursing the astonished man's breeding, manners, personal hygiene and political correctness. The intruder staggered back, stunned. Eddie turned on the Dragon Lady and made it clear that he wanted one ticket to Beijing, first class, right now, and none of your bullshit about no room, either. Even the Dragon Lady was cowed by this incredible performance, and meekly pushed the ticket across the counter. I felt like cheering as Eddie Murphy shook his shoulders, readjusted the fall of his jacket, and bopped out of the station with a spring in his stride. When my turn came at the counter, I tried to convey with a look that if there was any trouble, my main man Eddie would be back to sort her out. It worked, and I left the station with five stubby tickets for the Xi'an Express that evening.

We checked out of the hotel later that afternoon, parked our bags with the desk clerk, and set out to find dinner at one of the ramshackle restaurants that sprang up at dinner time in the station forecourt. There were dozens. We chose one that consisted of a couple of rickety tables, a few stools, and a little cook's bench with a large wok on a gas ring and a pot of boiling broth. On the bench, various vegetables and slices of fish and meat were displayed. You pointed to the variety of noodles you wanted, indicated a few ingredients to go with them, and the cook obligingly stir-fried them while you found yourself a seat. We hadn't a word in common, but I mimed cooking methods and pointed to combinations of ingredients while the chef smiled and nodded comprehension. Steaming bowls of soup arrived first, then tasty plates of broad rice noodles with beef and a spicy sauté of cuttlefish, green beans and fresh chillies. The chef was beaming proudly as we devoured his cooking, and his wife exchanged smiles and giggles with the girls. Aislinn did her party piece, lifting her woollen hat to reveal a tumble of long blonde hair, and the woman shrieked with good-natured laughter. The contrast with the stuffy hotel restaurant couldn't have been greater, and the whole bill came to less than $5. We left in good humour, ready for the overnight trip.

This leg would take us north, more than 1000 kilometres, and we could expect the weather to become much colder. It would also be the start of the seriously long trip out to the far west of China, into the Xinjiang Autonomous Region. We'd be on the train for nearly 24 hours. We joined the crowds at the station shops, stocking up on everything from melon seeds to sticky cakes. The girls had their pocket money in local currency (they were becoming quite expert at exchange rates) and did their own provisioning, which leaned heavily in the direction of Mars Bars and odd Chinese sweets.

The locals were gathered around the steamed bun carts, stoking their bellies with the large, puffy grey dough-balls, seasoned with a little crushed chilli or chilli oil. In Mildred Cable's book *The Gobi Desert*, she recounts her extraordinary travels in western China in the 1920s and 1930s. She describes how the carters who worked on the caravans were fond of carrying twists of dried chilli and salt tucked in the folds of their garments, to season their plain boiled noodles at the end of a day's march. A little oil was considered a luxury, and they were not averse to stealing some from the drum of linseed oil carried along to grease the axles of the carts. This habit of pouring a strongly flavoured oil over a dish as a garnish is rare in Cantonese cooking, but common in central China and the north.

When the train arrived, we got on and secured our berths. Every place was taken, and our neighbours made their own preparations for the night, rugging up in double socks and woolly cardigans. We followed suit, piling on clothes against the cold. The girls climbed up to their bunks with their books, so that they could read themselves to sleep. The fug of cigarette smoke and the click of melon seeds hitting the floor started before we even left the station, but there was a sort of crowded, noisy bonhomie about the whole thing. It was pitch dark when the train pulled out (for all their shortcomings, Chinese trains are remarkably good at running on time) and the cold began to seep into the carriage. Everyone curled up in their blankets, and the conversations lulled. I don't normally suffer much from the cold, but that night I wore an overcoat to bed, and checked the girls before I went to sleep.

EIGHT

During the night, the train passed through Henan province, making for the rail junction at Zhengzhou, where it turned west along the valley of the Huang He, the Yellow River. The Yangtze, China's longest river, is a broad and busy industrial highway through the heartland of China, but the Yellow River has a better claim to be the ancient home of the Han people, the original inhabitants of the Middle Kingdom. Like the Nile, the Yellow River carried a massive burden of rich silt, and its annual floods deposited this fertile topsoil on the valley lands. These floods were often disastrous, but they left behind them muddy fields suitable for the cultivation of barley, millet and wheat. (Rice came much later to China, probably from Thailand or India.) As a pale and dusty sun rose the next morning, I sipped black tea from a tin cup and looked out the window of the train at a landscape that might not have changed very much in thousands of years. Far in the southern distance, I could see a range of mountains, rising steadily as we travelled west, dusted with the first winter snows we'd seen. Between the mountains and the railway, the land was a vast, yellow-brown plain of the stuff they call 'loess', softer and more crumbly than sandstone, deeply cut by wandering, gravelly rivers and the work of man. Everywhere the land was terraced for agriculture, and villagers were already up and working in their fields. A few ancient tractors chugged along the dirt roads, but buffalo are more common as beasts of burden, and most of the work is still done by hand. In the chill morning, a woman stood alone in a large field of young maize plants, patiently tending them with a long-handled hoe.

The land looked ancient; biblical, somehow. Hundreds of caves were hollowed in the low, crumbling cliffs. Some seemed to be storehouses, but others were occupied by families, and chickens ran in and out of the doors like startled children. I saw few surfaced roads, mostly village tracks potted with holes. The buildings and pens were made of flat, dun bricks, often built on top of older mud-brick walls, so that it was difficult to tell where the ancient ruins ended and the newer work began. The terracotta armies of the emperor Qin lay buried near here for 2000 years, and I wondered how many other reliquaries and manuscripts there are still sealed up in ancient caves, in the tombs of long dead emperors. I saw rice, maize, onions and straw being harvested with the most primitive tools and almost no machinery. The earliest excavated sites on this plain are neolithic, and I realised that what I was looking at was not biblical at all—those villages were already twenty centuries old when Jesus preached in Palestine. People have practiced agriculture here for more than 6000 years, and yet in my own country, we're suffering from soil degradation, erosion and rising salt after less than 200 years of farming. Clearly, we're not as clever as we think.

The girls were up and breakfasted early, and we had a visit from a young woman from Wuhan, a teacher whose English was faultless. She was escorting a group of French high school students on a three-week tour of China. There were 40 of them, all girls, travelling in soft class with their own teacher. We met this woman later. She spoke fluent Chinese, but no English, so we had an odd, but interesting, four-way conversation in three languages. Clare disappeared into soft class, where she spent the day with the students, exchanging horror stories about Chinese toilets and eating habits, and pining for soft cheeses, chocolate and crispy baguettes. Wherever people go, it seems, it's their own food they miss first.

I was recovering quickly from my bout of the 'flu, but Aislinn showed every sign of coming down with it next. She was running a slight fever, so we kept her well rugged up and gave her a mild dose of aspirin. This constant round of illness hadn't stopped us travelling yet, but it was definitely a nuisance, and it all seemed so preventable, if the locals would just improve their sanitary habits a little.

Dorcas and I took turns paging through Mildred Cable's book, now that we were close to the eccentric Englishwoman's old haunts. Cable had been a missionary, but an unusually tolerant and observant one, who had lived with the nomads she sought to convert, travelling back and forth along the ancient camel routes of the Gobi wilderness, from oasis to oasis. This extraordinary woman spoke and wrote fluent Chinese, and taught herself the principal languages of the Turki, Mongol, Uzbek and Kazakh tribespeople. *The Gobi Desert* was written after she retired to an English seaside town, and was first published in 1942. It was the most vivid account of life in Central Asia that we had come across, and in Xi'an we would pick up her trail.

Xi'an is ancient by any standard, and at one time boasted a population of two million souls. This was in the 7th century AD, which made it then the largest city in the world, larger than Rome or Byzantium. Chang'an, as it was called in those days, was the imperial capital of the Sui Dynasty, and later of the Tang emperors. They had built a great city near the ruins of an even older one, established by the emperor Qin Shihuang in the 3rd century BC. It was Qin Shihuang who had tried to guarantee his immortality by burying a great army of clay soldiers, horses and officers to guard his grave. Interred at the time of his death in 210 BC, they would not see the light of day again until 1974.

Seventh century Chang'an was a purpose-built capital, laid out in formal style, a stately capital designed to accommodate the Imperial Court, the bureaucracy, the civil service schools and traders from India, Turkestan and distant Byzantium. There were markets, stables, caravanserai, and formidable city walls to protect those inside from the wild northern tribesmen who occasionally swooped down from Mongolia. As the capital of China, it would last more than 300 years, and when successive dynasties took their capitals elsewhere, Chang'an would remain a powerful city.

It was to the mountains north of Xi'an that Mao Zedong led the Long March, and there the tide turned for the Communist Revolution. Xi'an has grown steadily since, so that it once again has a population of more than two million. It still marks a sort of boundary, between the Han majority homeland, and the autonomous regions to the north and west, where the Han Chinese are outnumbered by the ethnic 'minorities' over which they maintain political control. All sorts of things change beyond Xi'an: culture, language, appearance, religion . . . and of course, the food.

The train rolled in to Xi'an Station in the late afternoon, and there was a great rush to be off it. We jumped into the maelstrom of people on the platform, and were carried by the tide out on to the great open square in front of the station. This was the first railway station I'd seen in China that could claim any architectural merit. It was a huge, imposing building with an ornate traditional roof, just outside the city walls on the north-east corner of the city.

We chose the closest hotel, a place called the Jiefang, across the plaza from the station. After a brief negotiation about room rates, number of beds and length of stay, we were given a comfortable suite with two rooms and four beds for the equivalent of $A55 a night. It was the most luxurious accommodation we'd had since leaving Shanghai. I was eager to see the city, especially the 15th century Ming Dynasty walls surrounding it. I liked my first impression. The place was busy and lively without being oppressively overcrowded. There were lots of food stalls (always a good sign), and the hotel rented bicycles by the day, which seemed a good way to get around. Once we had settled into the room, Dorcas announced another laundry day and I went for a preliminary explore in the neighbourhood.

There were a few 'change money' touts near the hotel door, but they were a sorry, cold-looking group who were loathe to get too far away from the charcoal stove at which they were warming their hands. The temperature was dropping fast, but I felt brisk and full of energy, and I enjoyed the novelty of seeing my breath puff out in front of me as I walked along. The shopkeepers and the cooks at the little food stands looked cheerful enough. Their faces were broad, apple-cheeked and friendly, wreathed in great clouds of steam rising from the dumpling trays and soup pots. At a few street corners, I saw old women set up what looked like a local specialty, a low table with tiny benches, on which was spread an assortment of bowls. There were bowls of shredded vegetables, of peanuts, chillies and pickles. At the end of the table, a boiling pot of maize or millet gruel was kept stirring, and a stack of flat pancakes to hand. When a customer took a seat, he'd be given a deep bowl of porridge, to which he added the various garnishes. The stall-keeper dipped one of the flat pancakes into the boiling gruel with a pair of long chopsticks, then rolled it up deftly and served it on a side plate. This was eaten with the fingers, while the porridge was ladled up with a spoon.

I noticed that I was not getting quite the same number of incredulous stares I'd become used to in Guangzhou and Changsha. Perhaps the presence of minority peoples in Xi'an made the inhabitants more cosmopolitan, but whatever the reason, I was glad for a little relief from the gob-smacked looks on the faces of Chinese peasants who had just seen a six-foot, bearded *lao wai* (barbarian) for the first time. Then I turned the corner and did the same thing myself.

Standing in a group outside a noodle shop were four men who looked like no one I'd ever seen before. Their heavy green ponchos were made of some sort of felt or wool, edged with brightly coloured embroidery. They wore loose trousers, tucked into high leather boots, and on their heads, black hats something like bowlers. Their faces were aquiline, copper-coloured, the features Asiatic, but definitely not Chinese. I was reminded of American Indians, the impression strengthened by their long black hair, caught up in a simple pony tail at the back. One of them carried what looked like a leather whip in the crook of his arm. We all stood still and stared at each other. Finally, the one nearest me gave an amused grin, and lifted his hat. I tipped my Akubra in their direction, and carried on down the street.

People in the shops were busy buying up foodstuffs, watches, radios, televisions, clothing, bicycle parts, kitchen tools and even refrigerators in designer colours. (Kitchen appliances are seldom white in China; it's the colour associated with mourning and death, and by association, it's unlucky.) There was no apparent shortage of consumer goods, nor of willing customers ready to snap them up. Department stores lined the principal avenues, and in the back streets, tiny factories and shops turned out everything from footwear to electric motors. It was hard to imagine it any other way. The Chinese passion for business and trading is familiar to anyone who's ever been to a large-city Chinatown in the West, and here in China it seemed entirely normal. We had to keep reminding ourselves that this had been out of the question only fifteen years ago, when the Communist Party strictly controlled what was made and who was allowed to buy it. Not for the first time, I had to think of Mao's revolution as one more blip in the long saga of Chinese history. However violent the change or radical the revolution, it had all happened before in the Middle Kingdom.

The real horror of the Cultural Revolution, which lasted at its worst for only five years, was the amount of destruction done in that short time. From 1966 to 1970, Mao's Red Guards went into a frenzy of book-burning, temple-smashing, looting, terrorism and vandalism. Their actions were not insane, though—they actually had a purpose. The idea was that a new age had dawned, and it was only by purifying China in a blaze of destruction that it could be released from the bad, old influences of history. It's possible to understand that if you want to start the Brave New World, you might not want 5000 years of history breathing over your shoulder.

This idea had occurred to the man who founded his city close to the site of present-day Xi'an. Qin Shihuang had also wanted to blot out the past, and he used much the same methods. When he defeated all his rivals at the end of the Warring States period (476 to 221 BC), he took upon himself the title Yellow Emperor (*shi-huang*), a name which he borrowed from a half-legendary emperor who had lived 2000 years before him. He was the first to marshal all the various tribes and petty lords into a single state, and forge a central government. If he'd had trains, they would have run on time. As it was, he codified the laws, organised a standing army, started a civil service and built a lot of roads. He also burnt every book in China. To keep, or even quote from, the ancient texts became punishable by death. Hundreds of scholars and intellectuals who just couldn't get the hang of the new idea were put to death. History officially began with Qin Shihuang, and all record of what had gone before was destroyed.

Qin Shihuang was eventually overthrown by a peasant bandit named Liu Pang, who went on to found the very successful Han Dynasty, which gave its name to modern Chinese culture. The Red Guards were eventually overthrown by Mao Zedong himself, who used the People's Army to quell all those excitable teenagers with automatic weapons. Then Mao died, the Gang of Four were denounced, Deng Xiao-ping was wheeled out again, Richard Nixon was invited to dinner and the Opening to the Capitalist West was announced. Chinese history just goes on and on.

We did hire a couple of bicycles the next day, although we couldn't go out together, since Aislinn's fever was worse and she needed nursing. We started her on a course of antibiotics which Dr Peng had given us in Shanghai, and kept feeding her liquids at regular intervals. I had learnt my lesson, and decided that the first order of business would be to secure tickets for the next leg of the journey, out to Lanzhou. The hotel, conveniently, had a CITS office on the second floor, so I thought I'd try there first. The woman behind the desk spoke good English, and said that although she could not get us tickets straight away, she would reserve some on the first available train. I was surprised; could it really be this easy? She still couldn't tell me whether the train continued beyond Ürümqi to the Russian border. As far as CITS was concerned, Chinese trains ran to the end of

Chinese railway lines (Ürümqi, as far as they knew) and what they did after that was no business of theirs. This was a bit of a worry, since Ürümqi was 2500 kilometres away, and if there was no connection there, we'd have to come back 4000 kilometres to Shanghai for new Russian visas. We'd have to take the chance. I decided not to argue with good fortune, and left her some money as a down payment on five tickets.

Collecting my bicycle from the hotel counter was a little more difficult. The hire of the bicycle was about a dollar for the day, but they insisted on a large deposit against its safe return. This wasn't so bad, but they also wanted to hold my passport, and would almost certainly have taken one of the children hostage if I'd been unwise enough to mention them. The lady behind the desk, I thought, must have been a Chinese Railways ticket clerk earlier in her career, but had been retired for being too surly even for that hallowed calling. Since she kept her valuables in an open cigar box on the counter, I was not keen on the idea of leaving anyone's passport with her. She was adamant. No passport, no bicycle. I offered more deposit money. No go. I produced our room key, and explained we were guests in the hotel. Not a chance. Playing my trump card, I produced a wedge of passports, credit cards, visas and identity cards from an inside pocket and spilt them on the counter.

Chinese people have an absolute fascination with official bits of paper, probably because they play such an important part in their lives. The more stamps, seals, photographs and signatures, the better. Mrs Bicycle was entranced with all those important-looking plastic cards on the counter. I held each one up in turn. Passport, I indicated, not negotiable . . . need it to change money at the bank. Can I interest you in a nice credit card? No way, she said. How about a Russian visa; very official, lots of seals and a fine photograph? No, not that either, but she was wavering. She liked the ones with the photographs. Look at this little hummer, I said, a genuine International Youth Hostel Membership Card, very low mileage, colour photo . . . ? She was still not entirely happy. She teased one more card out of the pile with the end of her pencil. Snappy colour scheme, good photograph, very impressive stamp in red ink. Would that do? Mrs Bicycle harrumphed and supposed that it would do. The card disappeared into her cigar box, and I was out the door with my rattletrap bicycle. Whatever I got up to for the rest of the day, I would not be doing any open-water scuba diving in north-central China.

The streets were full of bicycles and I blended right in. At least as well as you can blend in when you look like a circus bear with a very large hat. The day was impressively cold, but sunny and clear. The bicycle traffic behaved much like the automobile traffic in Hong Kong. That is to say, there was plenty of it, and it was reasonably well-behaved. Bicycle roundabouts, bicycle parking lots and bicycle repair stations dotted the city streets, and several thousand people were on the move. Only the occasional bus or lorry came along, and since these moved at about the same speed as the bicycles, everyone got along just fine.

I pedalled along Heping Lu until I came to the city walls, which run 14 kilometres around the old city, enclosing it neatly in a rectangle of huge fortification. The walls were built in the 14th century, on the foundations of the much older walls of the Tang Dynasty (618 to 907 AD). They are 12 metres high, and a massive 18 metres thick at the base. Faced in blackened stone, they form a barbaric structure which conjures up great violence and ancient power. On a cold day, with the leafless trees set against a watery sun, they made me wonder what sort of enemy deserved such formidable defence-works.

The city fortresses and towers seemed to be built on the same giant's scale. I cycled around the Bell Tower, from which a great iron bell once tolled the hour, and continued to the Drum Tower, in the Muslim quarter. The white hats of the hajjis, and the smell of roasting kebabs confirmed that Muslim life was alive and well in Xi'an. During the Cultural Revolution, mosques had been desecrated, and devout Muslims persecuted, but it has always been a dangerous game in China's north and west, where Islam has often been the fuse for popular risings against the Han. The government in Beijing was now taking a conciliatory tone, and had decided to allow the open practice of religion in the autonomous regions. Even Buddhism was once again permitted. Mosques, which the Red Guards had used for pig-sties, and Buddhist temples, used for public lavatories, had been rebuilt and re-consecrated by the devout.

I completed my partial tour of the city by cycling down a few quiet lanes at random. In the back streets, puff-ball babies in winter clothing were entertained on their grandparents' knees and old men sat on stools, smoking. Tiny bakeries and shops offered flatbreads and bottles of local beer, and women washed vegetables under taps on the pavement. I stopped at a cobbler's stand for running repairs to my boots. He did the work quickly and well, took a few yuan for it, and waved me on my way. I felt almost normal. I decided I liked Xi'an.

The next morning, I was up early and pulled back the curtains for a peek at the weather. I crept over and woke each of the girls in turn, whispering for them to come and see, without waking Dorcas. They pressed their noses against the glass to watch the dusty white flakes falling on the street below. Australian kids all, growing up in the tropical north, they had never seen snow before.

NINE

Hanging out the back window of our room at the Jiefang, I had a box seat on the restaurant alley that runs behind the hotel. Directly across the way, on a level with my first-floor window, was the glass-walled kitchen of a busy Cantonese restaurant. Down below there were boiled noodle and dumpling shops, *halal* (Muslim) butchers, Chinese pork butchers and a few barrows selling shiny brown pig's trotters cooked in soya sauce. It was a busy little alley, and a good illustration of the cross-over between Muslim and Han Chinese cooking that we'd notice more as we travelled west. Aislinn was confined to bed, so I had hours to kill. I wrote my journal, did some damage to a bottle of Chinese brandy and watched the day's progress in the restaurant kitchen across the street.

Work started around 9.00 am, when half a dozen cooks turned up to prepare for lunch. There was a lot of chopping and mincing on the round wooden blocks, some bored-looking kitchen hands stuffing *wan tuns*, and a gaggle of scruffy hangers-on sitting on the rubbish bins, smoking, spitting and telling each other stories. This Greek chorus of unemployed extras is a familiar sight all over China—in railway offices, bicycle shops, bus stations and hotels. There's no certain age; there'll be a few old men in greasy Mao jackets, and younger ones in the familiar running suits, camped out in the same place all day, hawking and slurping at jam jars full of tea for hours on end. I never managed to work out whether they were on the payroll, members of the family, or just content with a warm spot, but they could be relied upon to offer a range of opinions on any subject from international geo-politics to the best place to get your boots mended. This particular bunch stayed in place right through the lunchtime rush, while busy waiters stepped over them. Some of them were so galvanised by the excitement that they lay back and snored.

The noodle shop on the ground floor did a busy trade from early in the morning, at six rickety tables outside the shop and another few inside. From the boiling pot on the pavement, billows of steam rose into the cold air. The noodle-maker set up his bench beside it, the better to survey the passing trade as he worked. He was a big, amiable-looking fellow wearing an apron that had once been white, before the local laundry had had a few goes at it.

From a tin bowl covered with a damp, grey cloth, he pulled a lump of dough of about 2 kilos. Working on his floured board, he rolled the dough out into a long sausage, folded it over itself three times, then rolled it out again. Now he took it by the ends and whipped it around in the air like a child's jump-rope, stretching the dough until it almost brushed his shoes. With a neat flick, he spun the dough into a long twist, and dropped it back on to the board. This he repeated seven times. The long dough was now rolled into a sausage, and cut into portions. Each portion got the stretching treatment again, whipped in the air to draw out the skeins, doubled and stretched, until, with a final casual toss, the bunch of string-like noodles left his hands to describe an arc into the boiling water. A waitress would fetch it out a few moments later with long chopsticks, drop the noodles into a bowl, add a ladle of boiling soup from a second pot, and finish the dish with chopped fresh chillies and green onions. This steaming bowl of nourishment for Y2 served as breakfast, lunch or evening meal for a steady stream of customers late into the night.

The kids were fascinated by the onion-cake man, and they worked out an efficient system to get the delicious, crispy cakes while they were still fresh and hot. One of the girls would watch from the window, as the man at the street-stall below deftly rolled out the stretchy, thin pastry, incorporating a spoonful of spicy ground pork and chopped onion. He flattened the cakes with a calloused palm, then set a few dozen to fry in a covered pan for fifteen minutes or so. When they were almost ready, another of the girls, bundled up in six pairs of long-johns and armed with a fistful of tatty 5-mao notes, would rush downstairs, just in time to arrive as the fresh cakes come out of the pan. Clutching her greasy paper bagful, she'd run back upstairs, and the savoury, oily scent of cooked meat and flaky pastry would fill the room.

The weather had turned really cold now, and the slight falls of snow had turned to grey slush on the pavements. The local touts had gotten used to us (we were there several days) and the 'change money' hisses were less insistent, partly because I'd acquired a firm of brokers who inhabited a ramshackle shed just outside the Bank of China. Uighur taxi drivers with a thriving sideline in currency exchange, these guys could have been lifted straight out of an old Humphrey Bogart movie, with black trilby hats squashed down over their eyes, and a way of speaking out of the side of their cigarettes that made their broken English even harder to understand.

Negotiations were fierce over the daily rate of exchange, with much slapping of the hand to the heart, protestations of impending bankruptcy and appeals to heaven, but eventually a huge roll of grubby Renminbi would be produced from an inside pocket. The swap would be made, my crisp new 100 FEC notes disappearing into yet another inside pocket with a little grunt of satisfaction from my broker. We'd nod at each other gravely, have a quick scan up and down the street for effect, and go our separate ways. They knew I'd be back in a few days—the black market rate was rising steadily, and we now relied upon the exchange of 100 FEC for 150 Renminbi to stretch our food and incidentals money to cover the regular over-charging we met everywhere.

The next day, Aislinn's fever was not much improved. She was a very sorry little red-eyed bundle under a swathe of blankets. Dorcas suggested that she'd skip the Qin tomb excavations, having been out to the neolithic village site at Banpo the day before. I said I'd take the older girls out to see the buried army, while Mum stayed home and fed antibiotics and lemonade to the patient.

There were a number of mini-buses that offered day tours to the Qin sites, but booking one was to take the risk of being torn limb from limb by an assortment of frenzied ticket women with wizened brown faces and long graspy fingers. In a perfect brawl of free-market enterprise, these dun-coloured harpies would latch onto an arm or a child, and drag you off towards their ancient Toyotas, while three or four competitors hauled in the opposite direction. I emerged from the hotel with Clare and Kerry in tow, ran a quick end-play through the screen and set out to find the public bus for Qin Shihuang Tomb.

Chinese buses operate on the when-we're-full-we'll-go system, and we were unlucky to find that business was slow, with a dozen empty buses standing by at the railway station. We were dragged on to one by an enthusiastic conductor, and had a brisk argument over the fare, which eventually settled down to roughly twice the local's price—about average. Money changed hands for tickets, and we sat shivering, waiting for the bus to fill up. Nothing much happened for an hour or so, and I decided to change buses. Another tortuous negotiation followed.

'Please give me my money back, we'll get another bus.'

'No problem, leave right away, you sit down!'

'Forget it. We've been here an hour. Money back.'

'No, no money. Not me got money.'

'Where is the money?'

'Driver have money, she gone away.'

'Exactly. Get the money, we want to go.'

This deteriorated into a slanging match, enthusiastically joined by half a dozen of the station forecourt extras. I caught sight of a skinny, rumpled policeman shambling towards us, so I started roaring and waving my arms at the little ticket man. Then he caught sight of the policeman, gave it up as a bad job, and handed the money over briskly before the military got involved.

'Dad, didn't you say we just had to be patient and insistent with the Chinese?' Clare asked.

'Yes, that's right.'

'And not lose your temper or anything?'

'Right, you lose face.'

'So why were you shouting and waving your arms at that guy?'

'Because we were about to lose money, that's worse.'

'Oh.'

The next bus leaving the station was already crammed to the gills, but pulled up when I stood in front of it and shouted my practised Chinese for 'We want to go to the Qin tombs'. This caused everyone in the bus to crane forward to see the crazy, giant foreigner in the funny hat barking gibberish. The overloaded bus popped its doors, and I handed up the two girls, to much amusement and grinning from the sardine-packed passengers, who made room on knees and baggage. Their grins quickly faded when it became apparent that I, too, was planning to get on the bus. This caused a lot of consternation, since I am roughly the size of three Chinese, but room was somehow made, and we settled in for the 40-kilometre run out to Qin Shihuang's tomb. Once the doors were closed, the windows firmly shut, and the various arms, legs and bums evenly distributed, everyone produced cigarettes and happily lit up. The inside of the little bus was like an oven, dense with smoke and steaming wool, just the way the Chinese like it. At least no one had started eating chicken feet yet. We rattled along a busy highway, out into the flat, hazy countryside. The fields were barren, covered in a thin layer of snow, and had a melancholic look in the thin sunlight. Everyone was half asleep, drugged by the acute lack of oxygen inside the bus. An hour's driving saw us arrive at a medium-sized market town, where we changed buses, and had another brief negotiation over fares. The conductor didn't seem to have his heart in it, though, and charged us something like the real price. Further out into the countryside, I was peering out the window to see some sign of the massive excavation, begun by a chance discovery in 1974 while some local farmers were digging a well.

What they found was a jumble of broken pottery figures, remarkable in that they were life-sized, and that there were a whole lot of them. Having called the local militia in, wise heads decided that this might be a major archaeological find, and that the farmers should go dig their well somewhere else. What eventually came to light has been amply described in colour magazines—the 'Silent Army', the 'Terracotta Warriors'—the strange legacy of a Chinese emperor who lived 2200 years ago, and made his imperial capital here. Emperor Qin had the notion that if he was going into the afterlife, he had better bring a few things with him, and his artisans were given the task of building an entire army in terracotta clay. Thousands of life-sized figures of soldiers, captains, generals and their horses were modelled in extraordinary detail. These were buried in pits, standing rank upon rank, staring into the distance, in anticipation of the emperor's enemies, who would come from the east.

The three of us were unceremoniously dumped at a bus stop, near a pair of stone gates, in the middle of nowhere. 'Qin tomb, Qin tomb' the bus conductor reassured us, pointing emphatically at a hill in the middle distance. The snow was crunchy underfoot, the wind brisk, as we trudged back a few hundred metres to the gates. There was a distinct lack of tour buses or crowds, but a few shivering souvenir-sellers were on hand to poke miniature figurines, embroidered table-cloths and rabbit pelts at us as we approached the entrance. An ancient woman wrapped in quilted jackets emerged from a hut and cackled at us, wagging a book of shrivelled tickets. She relieved me of Y10, and let us pass.

A long path led up to a stone staircase, which in turn climbed straight up the snow-covered hill, to what looked like an observation platform at the top. The girls lit off like a pair of jackrabbits, while I stumped purposefully up the endless stairs, wondering when we'd come upon all the terracotta soldiers. At the top, more ancient and toothless old people lay in wait. They gathered around us like insistent goats, pushing bits of lurid-coloured plastic junk under our noses, finally retreating, grumbling, when it became clear we were not going to buy their entire stock. The view was marvellous, a winter landscape straight out of a Breughel painting, the light pale, the peasant farmhouses crumbly and dark, the lines of the hedgerows visible under the snow. But soldiers there were none.

As Clare and Kerry started a loud, shrieking snowball fight, it dawned on me that we were indeed standing on the Qin tomb—in fact, his fabled necropolis was buried under this vast man-made hill. I retreated into my guide book. The tomb of the emperor Qin Shihuang, it was written, contained fabulous treasures, artificial lakes of mercury, the Imperial Throne Room and Treasury, and presumably, the crumbling remains of old man Qin himself, but this, in a remarkable fit of restraint, the Chinese government had decided not to excavate, until the larger work of unearthing Qin's army had been completed. His army, the book said, was arrayed some 1.5 kilometres to the east of the Emperor's burial chamber. Now, if I could just work out which way was east, and find a road that went in that direction, we might see the soldiers after all.

Back down the stone steps, we passed through the agitated crowd of souvenir-sellers, who were at a loss to understand why the foreign devils did not want to buy a hundredweight of clay statues and gaily-coloured cushion covers. They were also at a loss to explain which way was east, probably because I didn't know how to ask them.

We tramped through the half-frozen mud on the roadside through what little there was of a village, out into the open fields in a direction I hoped was approximately east. Walking along that deserted road, I had an odd sense of looking at ourselves as if from above. One middle-aged bearded fellow and two Australian schoolgirls, plodding along beside a ditch in the back-blocks of western China on a wintry Tuesday afternoon, at least 4000 kilometres from anyone we knew (I wasn't counting Dorcas and Aislinn back at the hotel). We were a long way from anywhere. Still, this is why you go travelling—to walk along some road, savouring the poignant feeling that nothing could have predicted that you would happen to be just here, just at this time, and that you're unlikely ever to be here again. It's very moving, even if you are lost.

The few bristle-headed peasants who cycled past put their lives in danger by pedalling in one direction while staring incredulously in the other. I tried to flag one down, waving the guidebook. He took off like China's next entrant in the Tour de France, pedalling for dear life. The road wasn't getting any shorter. There was no sign of what I thought must be a very large building, the aircraft-sized hangar the Chinese had built over the excavations. There were no buses, tour or otherwise. It was getting colder, and the light seemed to be failing, possibly my imagination. We trudged some more. At a crossroads, we stopped for a breather.

'It's nice here, Dad,' said Clare.

Sound child, I thought, that's the spirit.

'We've walked a long way,' Kerry said, 'do you think we're going in the right direction?'

'I hope so.'

'Are there horses, too, with the soldiers?'

'So the book says.'

'That's good. Can we go and see them now?'

'Certainly. Which one of these roads do you fancy?'

'This one,' she said, pointing right, 'I can see something down the end of it.'

She could, and so could I, soon—a definite bit of bus activity in the middle distance. Another ten minutes walking brought us to the bus station, and the same muddy Nissan mini-bus, now empty, which had deposited us at the Qin hill-tomb. A few small groups of tourists, all Chinese, wandered towards the impressive entrance gates of the Xi'aansi Regional Museum. Business was slow in the middle of winter, but there were a few stalls open, flogging cheap earthenware copies of the warriors, and the luridly coloured gee-gaws so dear to the Chinese heart.

When we approached the gate, a solemn-faced soldier in a greatcoat pointed us at a tiny ticket booth off to one side. There were no English signs, but I'd learnt enough ideograms to work out the admission price, a mere Y5 each. At that price, I didn't even bother negotiating children's rates, but bought three tickets and returned to the gate. We were waved through by the sombre soldier, and had made it halfway across the wide courtyard towards a huge modern building, before the shouting started.

Two very important-looking officers were hurrying towards us from an office door, hitching up their trousers and their gunbelts as they came, obviously disturbed from some well-deserved lolling about back at guard headquarters. They had a lot to say to me, but none of it in any language I could understand. The gist of it was that the three of us were to accompany them back to HQ at the double. Command central turned out to be a comfortably warm office complete with radio, a couple of desks, the Chinese equivalent of a girlie calendar, and an impeccably turned-out senior officer with one polished shoe on his desk.

'Whayufram?' he enquired, giving me the hard look that said I could quite possibly be a covert CIA agent smuggling schoolgirls into the People's Republic.

'Australia.'

'Ahh . . . Ao-da-li-ya ren,' he informed his staff officers.

'Ao-da-li-ya,' they concurred, slurping thoughtfully at their jam jars.

'You mus pay,' he announced, writing a figure on his desk blotter.

It was something over $A10 each, about what these guys earned in a month. All of them.

'That's too much. Small children,' I said, indicating Clare and Kerry, and encouraging them to slouch.

'Sssssssuh,' he said, making that peculiar noise the Chinese use to mean 'this is a big problem and we're going to have to struggle with it'.

Working out the tourist (child) price, giving due consideration to our nationality, the time of the year, the position of the planets and the projected wheat crop in Baluchistan, took ten minutes. The inevitable search for the correct form, a working ballpoint and carbon paper took another ten. At this rate, they would have unearthed the rest of the buried army by the time we got to see it.

Finally we were released, and fair sprang up the steps in anticipation. And there they were. Hundreds and hundreds of them in ranks, eerily staring at the blank wall of their pit, as if they might still receive the order to march out of it. Infantrymen in studded leather uniform, their empty upraised hands formed in a neat 'o' where their pikes had been. Each face was uncannily different: Mongol features and flat, unseeing eyes, but each distinct—the sly one, the pompous fellow, the brave one and the country bumpkin. Buried for 2000 years, they had been crushed and jumbled by the weight of clay, and the shudder of earthquakes, so that the archaeologists must piece each figure together like a puzzle, but the several hundreds already restored stood square and silent under a vaulting roof. I couldn't look at them enough.

After the crumbling museums we'd already visited in China, this one was remarkable for its smart layout and functional signposting. Explanatory panels were in Mandarin, English and Cantonese. A separate hall featured individual figures in full regalia, with good (if slightly florid) descriptions of what they signified. 'A General of the Qin Army gazes purposefully to the east,' said one, 'His face shows courage, determination and commitment to the successful overcoming of obstacles.' The copywriter had resisted the temptation to mention Marxism-Leninism and the heroic struggle of the workers' and peasants' collectives, but only just.

Back at the Jiefang Hotel, the five restaurants proudly listed in the directory seemed to exist only in the mind of the writer. We tracked down the only remaining choice, a cold, gloomy room on the first floor that looked as if it had once been a discotheque. A grubby mirrored ball hung over a battered dancefloor. The tablecloths showed the scars and stains of a chequered past. Service was provided by a crew of dishevelled waitresses in crumpled uniforms who lounged around the cash desk, spitting melon seeds and glaring malevolently at anyone who took a seat in the restaurant. A brief squabble in rapid Mandarin was lost, and one of them shuffled reluctantly over to our table to drop a greasy menu decorated with soup stains and cigarette burns. A request for a bottle of beer and some juice was greeted with a curled lip and silence.

The menu was notable mainly for the number of dishes crossed off in leaky ballpoint. All that remained was a handful of pork-with-something and chicken-with-something dishes that are the mainstay of tourist hotel restaurants all over China. A dusty bottle of local beer did arrive, but getting an opener and glasses to drink it out of required a special invocation at the cash desk. I took the opportunity to drag a waitress back with me so that we could place an order. We settled in for a long wait. At the next table, a couple of Scandinavian girls with mournful expressions poked at plates of fried rice and glutinous chicken. At another table, a group of local cadres stubbed out their cigarettes in the remains of a multi-course lunch and saluted each other with repeated cups of *mao-tai*.

This cult of lunchtime drinking seemed to be an essential part of Chinese culture. Eight or ten men (rarely did I see a woman included) would take their seats at twelve o'clock and tuck into an enormous meal of duck, pork, tofu, vegetables and whole fish; the number of dishes was more a matter of face than what they could actually consume. Beer would be served with the food, but once appetites were satisfied, the white bottle of *mao-tai* would appear, with small porcelain cups to sup it from. Elaborate toasts to each other would get louder as the bottle dwindled, cigarettes would be passed, and the rest of the afternoon written off. If there was any sign of slowing up, they'd launch into a noisy game of 'one-finger, two-finger', a guessing game in which the loser is required to polish off a cup of *mao-tai* in one go, only to have it refilled immediately.

Mao-tai is just one of the many types of distilled spirit sold in China. All have in common a ferocious alcohol content, often as high as 70 per cent, and that dreadful smell of turpentine. Most are made from millet, a grain with a particular pong that doesn't go away in the distilling process. The price of a bottle can vary from a few mao (less than $A1) to considerable heights ($100 plus, more than a month's wages for a senior civil servant). The older and rarer brands command the top prices, and if you need something for what ails you, there's a range of medicinal spirits, flavoured with such delicacies as snake bladder, ginseng or chicken. No one need be caught short of a snort, either, because small pop-top bottles of generic *bai jiu* are sold at every corner shop and station kiosk.

After serious attempts to acquire the taste, I had written the stuff off as undrinkable, and stuck to Chinese brandy when I could find it. This was not unpalatable, although it was nothing likely to worry the French distilling industry. Real French cognac was readily available in the larger cities, at real French prices—a bottle of Martell VSOP in Shanghai cost as much as three bicycles, in a country where a bicycle is a lifetime investment decision.

Our lunch arrived in the fullness of time, a sorry-looking collection of dishes swimming in oil, served with cold rice. Half of what we ordered never appeared at all. We ate what we could, then I packed the girls off to the room, anticipating another battle over the bill. The seed-spitting hag at the cash desk saw no reason why she shouldn't charge for everything on the bill, whether they'd actually brought it or not. Battle was joined, made the more bitter by my insistence that I would pay in Renminbi, the people's currency. This was really too much, the hag screamed, how dare we come in here and make nuisances of ourselves, then refuse to pay for things we hadn't eaten. Barbarian! Foreign Devil! A wad of cash notes waved under her nose caught her attention, and she snatched them from my hand, muttering and grumbling as I walked out the door. I'd recall the Jiefang Restaurant every time I saw another 'Beijing Awaits the 2000 Olympics' billboard. Keep waiting, I thought.

We got out of Xi'an with some difficulty, the trains often booked out by passengers travelling through from Beijing. The CITS office in the hotel was reassuring, so we left our fate to them, checking daily if they'd come up with any tickets. Finally they announced that China Railways had decided to put another coach on the afternoon express to Lanzhou, and if we were quick, we'd catch it. We hustled over to the railway station. The usual teeming horde occupied the ground level, and we battled our way through to reach the right platform. The train had not yet arrived, but there was a good crowd of people, mostly older cadres, waiting for it. When the Beijing express rolled in, we spotted our carriage, hastily bolted on to the back of the train.

This was, without doubt, the worst piece of Chinese rolling stock we'd seen on the whole trip. The windows were caked with greasy coal grime, the toilets were unspeakable, and the roof leaked. This became apparent when rain began to fall heavily just after we'd clambered aboard. I thought I had gotten used to the worst China Railways had to offer, but here they'd managed to surprise me again. At a minimum, you expect to stay dry inside a railway carriage, but the constant drips from the shattered roof had most of the bedding wet already, and pools of noisome water collected on the floor. There was evidence that someone had been keeping chickens in the carriage until quite recently. Lots of grumpy old men settled down for a long night of hawking, smoking and spitting. My attempt to open a window was greeted with geriatric hostility, and a conductor bustled along to snap it firmly shut and glare at me. This was not going to be a fun night.

We got the children bedded down as best we could, wrapped in multiple layers of clothing and tucked up with the good, heavy wool blankets supplied on all Chinese trains. We would need them, because the outside temperature was dropping rapidly towards zero. Winter was starting to bite as we got further north and west. It would be colder still in the Gobi.

TEN

Lanzhou had been described by someone as a garrison town, a Han outpost in a hostile sea of Muslim tribesmen, but on first sight it looked like any other regional city in central China, a combination of 1950s Soviet Federal architecture, wide avenues and crowded buses. We'd rolled in early in the morning, after an uncomfortably cold, damp night on the train. The first job was to find a hotel.

I found a taxi, and managed to argue the price down to something like four times the local rate, so we climbed in and set off on the now familiar morning hotel hunt. The first place had a nice reception desk, signs clearly spelt out in English, and prices that would compare with the Mandarin Oriental in Bangkok.

'Are you serious? You have nothing for less than $100 American?'

'Sorry, sir,' said the wonderfully polite girl on the desk. 'You might try the Lanzhou Hotel. It's not far from here.'

We let the taxi go, and hoofed it around the corner to the Lanzhou. This was a large hotel which occupied a whole city block, the sort of place built as a Russian enclave in the convivial era when Soviet engineers, scientists and advisers were posted to China to help out with the reconstruction after the war. At the gate, a small shop sold bottles of orange juice, cigarettes and packets of biscuits. A wide courtyard, big enough to spin a few limousines, was enclosed by iron railings, and several buildings flanked the main hotel. We walked up the grand steps and through a clever double-door air-lock designed to keep the heat in and the riff-raff out. The lobby was magnificent: wide marble floors, a spacious reading lounge, a long reception desk and a full set of those clocks that tell you what time it is in Paris, London and New York.

'Excuse me, I'd like beds for five people. Do you have dormitories?'

In the tangled world of Chinese euphemism, 'dormitory' is the code word for a room with more than one bed in it. These are let by the bed, to Chinese people who have no objection to sharing a room with a stranger. If we could get a hotel to admit the existence of dormitories, the five beds we needed often took up the whole room anyway. If they refused to let on about the dormitories, we'd be shoved into double rooms at ten times the price.

'No dormitories. Only double rooms.' The gentleman at the reception desk was polite, but firm. He quoted a rate for a double room that would keep a Chinese family in food and clothing for two months.

'But I was told you had dormitories. The CITS office in Xi'an said that you had dormitories for Y20 per person.' This was not precisely true. In fact, I'd just made it up on the spot, but it did seem to worry the desk clerk. He frowned and looked uncomfortable.

'You will have to wait. No dormitories available until afternoon.'

This was no problem. It was a very nice lobby, and the kids had already taken over the reading lounge. They were playing gymnastics on the leather cushions. Our distinctly riff-raff luggage was already spread all over the floor. Dorcas was reading the *China Daily*, and I was content to have a nice snooze while we waited. I drifted off for a little while.

When I woke up, it was nearly ten o'clock. Dorcas had broken out packets of biscuits, and the kids were having a game of 'tigger' which involved racing across the lobby and squealing. I thought I'd check in with the reception desk.

'Any sign of those dormitories yet?'

'Dormitories not available until the afternoon.'

'No problem. We'll wait over there.' I couldn't imagine the demand for rooms was all that great, since we hadn't seen anyone else in the place for the last two hours. We decided to go and have breakfast.

The hotel restaurant was empty too. A waitress seated us at a table, then ran away to find her supervisor. A well-dressed woman arrived and asked us if we would like the Chinese or the western breakfast.

'Dad, Dad, can we have the western breakfast?' the girls chimed. They had not taken to rice gruel and sour pickles as quickly as I thought they might. They were delighted when the woman brought back glasses of warm milk, slices of toast and a fried egg each. There

Dorcas enjoying the relative luxury of the Pujiang Hotel,
Shanghai.

The girls meet an old cadre in the Mandarin Gardens,
Shanghai.

Hanging out the back window of the Jiefang Hotel, Xi'an.

Clare and Kerry at the Qin Shihuang Tomb, Xi'an.

Aislinn between visits to the doctor in Lanzhou.

A street market in Lanzhou with more varieties of tofu
than we ever knew existed.

Crossing the Gobi Desert on the Beijing–Xinjiang Express.

Fresh bread from the Muslim bakery, Ürümqi.

The spice market at Ürümqi.

With our friendly conductor on the Ürümqi–Alma-Ata
Express.

The view from our hotel window with the mountains of
Alma-Ata rising steeply behind the city.

Smoked pork and 40 kinds of sausage at a street market
in Budapest.

With Kay in Ireland, on our way down to the west coast.

The free-for-all market on the Trans-Siberian Express.

The bare necessities of life on the Trans-Siberian Express.

Kerry, Clare and Aislinn spending their pocket money
in Beijing.

was even coffee, a rare beverage in China. The children finished quickly, and asked if they could go and play in the lobby again. Apparently the marble floors were 'excellent slippery', and they were pretending to be Olympic speed-skaters. Dorcas and I lingered over coffee.

When we got back to the lobby, the speed-skating had given way to a game of running-up-and-down-the-stairs-giggling, and the desk clerk was signalling frantically at me.

'Dormitory rooms ready, OK, sir. Ready now.'

'But it's only 10.30.'

'OK, never mind, ready now.'

'Really, we don't mind waiting.'

The girls had discovered the bannister was also excellent slippery, and were sliding down it with great whoops of excitement.

'Children please take to rooms, sir.'

'How much are the rooms?'

'OK, 20 yuan per person.'

I had to drag the girls off the bannisters, but we were all glad to get into the rooms. They were on the third floor of a large building set to one side of the courtyard. There were stout iron beds, and a sink in each room. Bathrooms were down the hall. Housemaids chattered over cups of tea in the pantry. Surprisingly, the heat was on, so we spread half-damp socks to dry on the radiator and made ourselves cups of coffee. Outside, on the little concrete ledge in front of the window, it was cold enough to chill the bottles of juice we'd bought at the shop.

Aislinn still wasn't well, and the antibiotics were nearly exhausted. She was a brave little sausage, but the exertions in the hotel lobby had clearly worn her out, and she was reduced to shivering under a coverlet.

'She doesn't seem to be getting better,' Dorcas said.

'Shall I try to find more antibiotics?'

'No, we'll let her finish these and see how she gets on. I'll keep her in bed. Will you go out and see about some food?'

I crossed the courtyard behind the hotel and strolled down a long alleyway full of market stalls. Farmers offered beetroots, spinach, wizened carrots and chilli peppers. Further down, there were tofu stands and spice shops, fishmongers and fruit sellers. I was surprised to see good apples, plums and even bananas for sale. It was, after all, February in northern China, and there weren't a whole lot of apples on the trees. I learnt that the distribution of food within the country had improved out of sight once the central government relaxed the central planning restrictions. Communes were given the opportunity to negotiate independently with transport collectives and send their produce wherever the market would take it. As a result, fruit from the southern provinces, near the Vietnamese border, was reaching every part of the country. I bought some fried tofu balls, some fruit, and a loaf of lovely flat *naan*, fresh from the oven. All the bakers were Muslims, and most of the butchers *halal*.

When I got back, Clare and Kerry tucked into lunch, but Aislinn was listless and weak. Dorcas was worried about her.

'I've taken her temperature, and it's very high. We should see about a doctor. I think there's one in the hotel compound.'

I had noticed the glass door with a red cross on it when we came in. It was across the courtyard, in a row of low buildings that included a billiard parlour and some offices. I found the door and went inside. In a chilly corridor, public health posters encouraged the masses to have only one child, and to refrain from spitting on the floor. A woman in a white coat came out to see me.

'My daughter sick. Little girl. Seven years.' I was struggling in very bad phrasebook Chinese and that peculiar form of baby-English we native speakers reserve for foreigners. It wasn't working. The woman beckoned me to a telephone and rang the front desk. The telephone operator translated for us, and I learnt the doctor would be back later, and that I should bring Aislinn down at two o'clock.

I did. The doctor was a large woman with gentle hands and a starched white coat. She examined Aislinn thoroughly and took her temperature again. Aislinn was pretty sick, she explained, and the course of antibiotics we'd given her had not been enough to knock down the chest infection. There was a danger of pneumonia, and it would be best to give her a course of penicillin, certainly before we travelled further. Where were we going? Into the Gobi, I said, on the train to Ürümqi. The doctor looked at me as if we were mad. Why would anyone go to Ürümqi? She could start a course of injections immediately, but it would take at least three days to complete. I agreed, and explained to Aish that the doctor had to give her a needle to get her better. She didn't look too sure about that, but reluctantly agreed.

I had to fill a few chits and pay for the penicillin (it was very cheap), and then take a script across the road to buy a box of disposable needles, which the doctor would use. So far, I was impressed with our first contact with medical care in China. It was straightforward and competent; certainly easier than buying railway tickets. Aislinn held her breath and winced when the jab went in to her backside, but she was plucky, and held back her tears bravely. It did seem to be a very big needle. The doctor and nurse congratulated her, and I took her hand in mine to walk back across the courtyard.

We stayed in the rooms for most of the day, making occasional forays out for food or business. I could not find a foreigner's ticket window at the railway station, so I went in search of a CITS office. I found it just around the corner, but it was closed every time I went back. Eventually, I located the Gansu Tourism Service, a provincial government office which arranged group tours. They told me that tickets on the train to Ürümqi were difficult to get, since few travellers broke their journey in Lanzhou—most seats were booked straight through from Beijing to Ürümqi. They offered to get us the more expensive soft class tickets, but I thought I'd try the railway station once more. This time I found the right window, and learnt that spare tickets were released each day at 10.00 am. We'd just have to try our luck every morning.

Back at the hotel, Aislinn was a little improved. I took Clare and Kerry out to find some dinner at a little café in the market. We had *niu rou mein*, a local specialty made with fried beef, cabbage, chillies and noodles. Pork had almost disappeared from the menu now, since most of the customers were Muslims. Kebab-sellers were common; on small charcoal stoves they grilled scraps of fresh mutton, sprinkled with dried chilli and salt. The smell was delicious in the winter air.

Aislinn was due for a second shot that evening, so while Dorcas went out to find herself some dinner, I marched the patient down to the doctor's office. She buried her head in my jumper while the doctor stabbed the needle in. Her lip trembled, but she held the tears back again. She was a tough little kid. She suffered bravely through her course of injections, but I began to feel like an executioner, marching her across the long, grey courtyard each morning and evening for her jab. She improved visibly, though. Her fever went, and she played happily all day in the room, until the dreaded appointment came around again. On the third day, we had good news. We could get tickets for the train to Ürümqi the next evening, if we were willing to pay for 'soft class' berths. By this time, we were wondering if we'd ever get out of Lanzhou, and the days were ticking away on our Russian visas. We decided to take the offer. If there were any leg of the journey on which we could treat ourselves to some comfort, we reasoned, it might as well be this one: three days and two nights on the train across the Gobi.

The Gansu Corridor is the name given to the long chain of oasis towns that stretches from Lanzhou to Hami. The railway line, which was only completed in 1963, follows the line of the Great Wall, built during the 3rd century BC to keep out the wild nomadic horse-tribes of Mongolia immediately to the north. To the south-west, the crumpled and folded mountain ranges of the Qilian Shan rise up to the Tibetan Plateau, and the headwaters of China's two great rivers, the Yangtze and the Huang He.

We looked at several different maps. The confusion of place names was almost impenetrable. For every town, it seemed, you had the choice of at least four names: the ancient Chinese name (usually with one or two variations), the modern Chinese name (with a choice of Wade-Giles or pinyin spellings), the old local name (in Uighur, Tadzhik, Tibetan or Mongolian) and the modern local name (often written in Arabic script). Thus, Gansu province had taken its name from its two principal cities of Gan-chow and Su-chow. Unfortunately, Ganchow could also be written Ganzhou, or Kanchow or Changye or Zhangye, according to which map you read. Likewise, Suchow was recognisable as Suzhou, but as Chichuan or Qiquan or Jiuquan it was easily lost, and so were we. Just to round things off, some geographic features still carried the names bestowed upon them by 19th century European adventurers. The Qilian Shan was marked on older maps as the 'Richthofen Range', for the German explorer who, in 1877, first gave a name to the ancient trading route that connected Imperial China with Rome. He called it the 'Silk Road'.

For more than 2000 years, caravans had assembled in Xi'an for the long and dangerous journey across the hostile wastes of the Gobi, prey to bandits, evil spirits, starvation, shifting tracks, hallucinations induced by the semi-poisonous springs and the ever-present threat of death. Few would complete the whole journey from east to west; vigorous markets sprang up at Dunhuang, Hami, Kashgar and Yarkand, where traders from India and Central Asia would do business with Chinese merchants for precious silk, amber, silver, medicines and religious objects. The Silk Road was, in fact, not one route, but a series of trade routes that branched across the desert, following the line of mountain-fed oases where precious water could be found for beasts and men.

We would travel with a speed unimaginable only 60 years ago. The Chinese government had pushed to complete the railway line for more than one reason. As early as the 1930s, prospectors had looked closely at the Gobi, and the surface pools of 'stone-oil', which for centuries the locals had collected for cooking and for greasing the axles of their carts. Drilling revealed rich reserves of oil under the desert, and with the help of their Soviet socialist brothers, the Chinese tapped oil fields from Gansu to Ürümqi. If the Chinese railways could be connected with the Soviet main line from Novosibirsk to Tashkent, then export of this valuable commodity would be that much easier. The railway line would also provide for rapid movement of troops, in case they were needed again to suppress Muslim uprisings in the notoriously unstable western provinces. Serious rebellions in the 1930s and 1940s had been put down with terrible ferocity, and as recently as 1990, Muslims in Kashgar had butchered as many Chinese officials as they could lay hands on. When the fraternal relations with the Soviet Union degenerated into active hostilities in the 1970s and 1980s, the ability to move military equipment and troops to Ürümqi and beyond became even more important. All this kept Xinjiang province strictly off-limits to outsiders until very recently, not least because of the Chinese nuclear testing grounds at Lop Nur, south-west of Hami.

We still weren't sure, but the persistent rumour of an open rail line between Ürümqi and the Russian railhead at Aktogaj still intrigued us, and we had to go there to find out. We presented at the railway station at four o'clock the next afternoon, ready to board the Beijing –Xinjiang Express.

The afternoon departure allowed us a great view of the countryside, which was already flattening and turning dry as we left Lanzhou. Mud-brick villages grew further apart, and the yellow and ochre colours of harvested straw and old earthen walls merged into the background. We saw fewer animals now, and the single highway which crossed and re-crossed the railway line was used only by a few lorries and long-distance buses. Our compartment was the last word in Chinese luxury. Four berths were provided, complete with satin pillow-covers and frilly cotton trim, and two folded up during the day to allow plenty of sitting room. The table had a lace cloth and a little jar of plastic flowers. The rarest privilege of all was the door, which could be firmly closed when we wanted a respite from China and the Chinese. After five weeks in China, I had to admit that it was wearing on my nerves. I remembered some gentle advice I'd had from a traveller in Shanghai. He said, 'When you're beginning to feel like you hate the place, leave as quickly as you can. If you do, you'll want to come back. If you stay, and burn out on China, you'll never want to set foot in the place again.'

We slept well, in our cosseted compartment, and were woken by a smiling conductor, who brought us fresh flasks of hot water. Our fellow passengers in soft class were prosperous-looking businessmen in western suits and high-ranking cadres who had hung their immaculately tailored uniform jackets on the pegs in their compartments. Our tickets, although reasonable by western standards, had cost an unearthly amount of money to the average Chinese. The girls were unusually subdued, and spent their time playing word games or drawing in their notebooks.

Dorcas and I gazed out the window as the Gobi rolled by. 'Gobi' is not actually the name of the area, although it was described that way on all our maps—it is a Mongolian word for a flat, gravel-strewn pan between outcrops of mountains. There are many 'gobis' in the Gobi Desert, and in fact the landscape was changing rapidly as we tracked west. To the north there was a low line of dark hills, very far away, to the south a tall range of mountains topped with snow. For a great distance on either side of the line, the dry, barren plain extended under a porcelain-blue sky.

Late in the afternoon when the shadows were lengthening across the desert, we saw a remarkable structure just north of the railway line. Standing out of the dry plain was a gigantic fort with high watchtowers and curling Chinese roofs. This was the Ming fortress of Jiayuguan, built in 1372 to serve as the western terminus of the Great Wall. It looked massive, imperial and forbidding, alone in the desert, commanding the narrow corridor between two mountain ranges, which any would-be invader must use. But the Ming emperors had retreated from the ancient boundaries, for the Wall once extended well beyond here to what the Han Dynasty called the 'Gate of Sighs', the uttermost end of the empire. From the train, we could see the low, crumbling remains of the ancient wall, stretching further west from the Ming fortress, finally disappearing into baked dust and shattered stones.

Between the Jiayuguan fort and the oasis town of Hami, we entered the Black Gobi, one of the most desolate regions on earth, and the most remote from any ocean. It takes its name from the black, fine gravel that stretches to the limits of vision in all directions, broken only by low outcrops of bare rock and crumbling escarpments. It is harsh, but it has a sere and stony beauty of its own. I tried to imagine what it must have been like to travel with slow, heavy carts drawn by mules across the endless stages, enduring terrible nights in which animals simply froze to death, and violent dust storms which could suck the breath from a man's lungs. The Black Gobi is part of a vast inland basin which includes the Taklimakan desert, the Turpan depression and the Mongolian wilderness. In the rain shadow of the massive Himalaya-Karakorum mountains and the Tibetan plateau, the region is desperately dry. Only the *kerez*, the underground irrigation channels which carry water great distances from the mountains to the oasis towns, allow for any agriculture at all. Aside from the line itself, and the occasional mud-brick oasis village, I saw no mark of man on the landscape for hundreds of kilometres.

The atmosphere in the dining room was cheerful and busy, and the familiar clatter of soup bowls and chopsticks welcomed us to dinner. The cooks worked in a narrow, cramped kitchen that took up one-third of a carriage and half its width. An open door allowed them to chuck vegetable scraps and waste water straight out the side of the train, but they paid for it with a whistling 5° wind, so that they were all wearing thick woollen jumpers under their white jackets. A stove for three woks, a soup boiler and a couple of rice steamers were all the equipment they had, but they managed to cope with three services every day, and a reasonably long menu. As well as serving the restaurant car, they prepared hundreds of packed meal-boxes, which were wheeled down the length of the train for sale. We had a thin soup with shredded egg, stir-fried chicken with green beans and a crispy dish of fried fish complete with bones. I noticed that rice was still the staple, as though the kitchens, like the clocks, were run by some Central Planning department in Beijing. The time difference was becoming silly: all over China, there is only one official time, that of Beijing. But the country stretches across more than three time zones, so that no one in Lanzhou would dream of reporting for work at the 'official' 9.00 am, since it was still pitch dark and freezing outside. On the train, the restaurant car stayed more or less open all day, and meals were served when there was some sort of unspoken agreement that it must be time for lunch.

Perhaps the harshness of the surrounding landscape made me realise how dependable these dirty green trains really were. Apart from the struggle to get tickets and the appalling grubbiness of the rolling stock, they did actually get where they were going reliably and on time. In all the thousands of kilometres we travelled, we were never held up by mechanical breakdowns or accidents on the Chinese railways. Now our paired diesel locomotives, blazoned with the big red star of the People's Republic, chugged away steadily towards the west.

Late in the evening, near the town of Hami, I saw the first signs of cultivation, as farmers prepared for spring. Small mounds of dirt marked the melon fields, and seedlings were already started under plastic frames beside mud-brick dwellings, weighted by hayricks and piles of fodder. We spotted donkeys and horses, and caught our first glimpse of the shaggy, dark brown Bactrian camels which look so strange in zoos, and yet fit perfectly well in this freezing desert. Hami is famous for its melons, and the fresh ones were shipped, in season, as far away as Beijing. Turpan, several hours further along the line, was renowned for its grapes and apricots, and both towns dried their fruit for export. The desiccating, hot summer winds were perfect for this job, and we saw open brick-work drying sheds scattered on the edges of the town, waiting for next summer's harvest.

At daylight, we pulled into the station for Turpan (the town was actually some distance south of the track). There was frost on our window, and occasional patches of wind-blasted snow along the line. The mountains were much closer, and we could feel the train dragging as we climbed towards the high pastures of the Tien Shan range. Over the next few hours, the landscape became more broken and dangerous, as the rail snaked along dry scree-lined valleys under jagged peaks of bare rock. As we neared Ürümqi, we levelled out on to a high, cold plain. To the north, a shadowy range of impossibly high mountains seemed to rise straight up from the wet, gravelly plain to block out a quarter of the sky. Soaring to more than 5000 metres, they are called the Bogda Shan, the Mountains of God.

In the confused rush of people and luggage pouring off the train, Clare and I were separated from Dorcas and the younger girls. Since we all had to leave by the same gate, I was not concerned, and knew that we'd find each other outside. Clare tapped my arm.

'Dad, look, Mum's waving at you from over there.'

I could see Dorcas at the barrier, with two Chinese officials. She was vigorously waving me over, but a struggling crowd was between us, and it took several minutes to get near her.

'What is it?' I called over a few dozen heads. 'What's wrong?'

'It's Kerry. She's been arrested!'

'She's what?'

'They've taken her away to that room over there. I don't know what they want. Go and see!'

I pushed my way into a grey, cluttered room bristling with posters and regulations, where two uniformed women had Kerry up against a wall and were staring at her grimly. Kerry did not seem to be unduly concerned about her arrest. She was, in fact, giggling.

'What's going on?' I demanded.

'They're measuring me,' Kerry said.

'What?'

'Measuring me. You know, they thought I might be too tall for the kid's fare, but I'm kind of scrunching down and I think I'm going to be OK.'

'Mum thinks you've been arrested.'

'Well, they did sort of grab me off the line, but they're nice.'

The two railway women agreed that Kerry was just barely under the 1.4 metre limit for children's fares, and that she could be released. We walked out of the station into bright, cold sunshine. Dorcas, Clare and Aislinn were standing to one side with our bags.

'Free,' I shouted, 'free at last!'

Dorcas glared at me. 'Oh, do shut up and go and find a taxi.'

ELEVEN

Now, Ürümqi really was a garrison town; there were soldiers and military vehicles everywhere, and no one had a good thing to say about it. Our Lonely Planet guide grumbled about the 'concrete-block architecture' and Mildred Cable waxed on at length, in an unusually uncharitable tone of voice:

> The town has no beauty, no style, no dignity and no architectural interest. The climate is violent, exaggerated and at no season pleasant. During the winter there are constant heavy snowstorms, but the snow must not be allowed to lie on the flat mud roofs, lest at the first thaw the water should leak in to the houses. It is therefore shovelled wholesale into the streets, and trodden by the traffic to a hard, slippery surface which makes walking extremely difficult for several months of the year. The summer heat is even worse than the winter cold, and the dirty, dusty roadways are filled with jaded, unhealthy looking people. (*The Gobi Desert*, pp 283–4)

On the other hand, Ürümqi had some of the liveliest and most colourful markets we'd seen anywhere in China, an extraordinary jumble of Muslim and Chinese cultures, and the most interesting food I'd seen since Guangzhou. It was a rough, noisy, dirty town with some very nice people, and an outstanding regional museum. Within an hour of our arrival, we had a piece of news that made our whole day. It came from a young man who approached me while I was negotiating room rates at the front desk of a slightly seedy hotel.

'Can I help you with anything in Xinjiang Autonomous Region while you are visiting?' he said, in excellent English.

'No, thank you, we've just got here.'

'I can arrange tours to places of tourist interest, or act as interpreter.'

'No, we don't need anything just now, thanks.' I was trying not to be rude, but while this fellow was distracting me, the woman behind the desk was chewing her pencil, struggling to think of a few more 'special charges' she could slap on our bill.

'I can also arrange tickets, for bus tours or trains.'

'Did you say trains?'

'Certainly. The Bogda Travel Service arranges all types of tickets for railway or air travel.'

'Do you know anything about trains into Russia?'

'Of course. The international train to Alma-Ata leaves on Tuesdays and Saturdays. We can reserve tickets for you, no problem.'

'You little beauty, you.'

'Excuse me?'

'I said we would be happy if you could arrange some tickets for us. To Alma-Ata.'

I gave him my name and our room number, and he promised to look into the train bookings for us. I realised I hadn't asked his name yet.

'I am Mr Xie,' he said, offering a formal handshake.

'I am very pleased to meet you, Mr Xie.'

I related the good news immediately, and we were so pleased that we hardly noticed the cramped, damp, horrible little room to which we had been assigned. There was hardly enough room to step around each other. Much of the floor space was occupied by a strange spacecraft-like shower/toilet/bathroom module modelled out of orange plastic and bolted to the floor in one corner. You had to sort of strap yourself in to it to take a shower. It emitted odd hisses, leaked water into the carpet and filled the room with smelly steam. We decided to make do for the one night and find another hotel in the morning. First, we'd have a walk around the city.

Outside, it was warm enough to set some of the icicles on the roofs melting, and walking along the icy, slippery footpaths was an exercise in careful balance. The air was cold, and drifts of old snow, overlaid with grimy coal soot, lay in the parks. We caught the aroma of grilled kebabs and fresh bread, drifting out of tiny cafés, where old men in Muslim caps sat on rickety metal chairs. We walked past the unlikely apparition of a Holiday Inn, complete with coffee shop, foreign currency store and a discotheque. There were plenty of buses and taxis, and the amount of traffic made it clear that this was a large city, not some remote oasis town with six camels and a tea shop. It was easy to imagine that we were somewhere in central China, rather than five days away by train from Beijing.

Out of curiosity, we followed a stream of people descending what looked like the entrance to a Metro. We discovered a sprawling underground market, full of clothing shops, electronics stores, housewares and bicycles (I had been surprised to see people negotiating the icy, treacherous lanes above on two wheels, laden with packages). In here, safe from the elements, the whole population of the city seemed to be on a huge buying spree, haggling over radios, bed quilts and electric toys. Driven by the oil boom, the population of Ürümqi had risen from 140 000 in 1954 to nearly a million in 1993, and they all wanted to buy something.

The faces in the crowds were a mixture of Han Chinese and the pale, Caucasian features of the Uighur people. Uighurs are a scant majority in Xinjiang. There are also Kazakhs, Kirghiz, Uzbeks and Mongols in the province, although most of these 'minority nationalities' are still semi-nomadic pastoralists. The Uighurs are of Turkish stock, farmers who settled here from the 8th century onwards, as the Persian and later Turkish empires expanded eastward. They brought with them the Manichaean religion, and the Uighur town of Turpan became an important centre for this antique faith, long after it had been hunted down and destroyed in the Christian and Muslim west. The Uighurs were not converted to Islam until sometime after the beginning of the 12th century, just in time for a Mongol invasion under the warlord Temujin, who would later call himself the Universal Ruler, the Genghis Khan.

It felt strange, after weeks of standing out so obviously in the crowds of Han Chinese, to be somewhat less obvious in the mixed-race bazaars of Ürümqi. The market women were apple-cheeked and round, the girls shy and pretty. The older men wore the white cap of the hajji, but most Uighur men wore the uniform we first saw in Xi'an—a black suit coat and trilby hat, layers of woollen cardigans and a button collar. The strict rules of Islamic law sat pretty lightly on their shoulders; women went unveiled, and beer was sold freely in the shops, but pork was definitely off the menu. All the butchers wore white caps and bled their carcasses of mutton on the hook. In the spice markets, sacks of vividly coloured cinnamon and dried chillies crowded for space with sesame and poppy seeds, ground turmeric and ginger, asafoetida and fennel, cardamoms and corianders.

The dried fruit merchants sold almonds and walnuts, dried apricots and pomegranate seeds, and the most beautiful array of dried grapes I'd ever seen. Pale amber sultanas were plentiful, others were dark gold or almost purple, but the choicest and most expensive were the translucent jade-green grapes from Turpan. These were counted precious as far away as Beijing and Tehran. Mildred Cable had quoted an old Chinese rhyme:

With East Sea crabs and West Sea *hsia* [prawns]
Stand Turpan grapes and Hami *gwa* [melon]

We bought ourselves dried melon, apricots and Turpan grapes to taste. They were headily perfumed with the aroma of the fruit, soft and chewy, full of intense flavour and natural sweetness. These were fruits that had been grown for their flavour alone, rather than their suitability for machine harvesting or extended shelf-life. I'd never tasted anything like them.

We moved the next day to a more comfortable hotel, and Mr Xie called to say that we could obtain tickets in five days' time. This would shave one day off the precious ten on our Russian visas, but we were not disappointed to spend a few days exploring Ürümqi. We set off on the bus to find the Xinjiang Regional Museum, and had a long and interesting ride through the busy suburbs of the city. The girls were fascinated by the luxurious drifts of snow on the ground, and were chafing at the bit to be let loose to have a roll in it. The museum was a grand building with a wide courtyard and a gilded Islamic dome that made it look like a mosque (which, indeed, it could have been once). We were the only visitors that morning, but the Han caretaker was pleasant, and sold us tickets for the Silk Road exhibition, which had only been opened, he said, the previous year.

The collection was remarkable by any standard. Well thought out and presented, the exhibition explained the history of the Gobi and Taklimakan areas from the palaeolithic era to historical times. A clever three-dimensional model showed the ancient caravan routes that criss-crossed the desert, and displays of funerary objects, manuscripts, clothing fragments and weapons helped illustrate the history of the region. It was all the more impressive because we could understand it without being able to read a word of the captions—they were all in Uighur Arabic or Chinese. The 'minority peoples' displays were great; full-scale recreations of a Uighur household and a Mongolian yurt, complete with costumes, brass kitchenware, silk carpets and wonderful embroidery. In the parched high deserts, buried in sand or hidden in dry caves, thousands of rare objects and manuscripts had been preserved for centuries. The remnants of twenty different cultures had washed up on these dry shores, and even the archaeological pillage carried out by British and German explorers in the 19th and early 20th centuries had not found it all.

I had read conflicting opinions on the work of men like Sir Aurel Stein, who in 1908 had taken 29 crates of priceless Buddhist scrolls and paintings from the sealed caves at Dunhuang and removed them to England, where few of them have ever seen the light of day since. The Chinese government has described this as imperialist looting of national treasures, and many of our more politically correct friends at home would agree whole-heartedly with the Chinese demand that the British Museum return the treasure immediately. On the other hand, Sir Aurel Stein left behind far more at Dunhuang than he took away. In the ensuing years, virtually every last scroll, statue, painting and artifact had been destroyed by fanatical Muslims or Red Guards, sold off by corrupt government officials, stolen by tourists or allowed to crumble away to dust by careless preservation. What had taken the monks at Dunhuang twenty centuries to accumulate piece by precious piece, hand-carried across the terrible wastes of the Taklamakan desert, has taken less than one century to destroy.

Outside the museum, the girls started a vigorous snowball fight, and I was the first to collect a couple of icy hits in the neck. Clare took particular delight in creeping up behind me and stuffing handfuls of frozen snow down my collar. Aislinn had read in some forgotten children's book about snow angels, and proceeded to lie down in the dusty drifts and fan her arms and legs about until she had left the proper imprint behind her. Wet, sooty and bedraggled, she had to be hauled out of the snow giggling, and taken off to lunch.

In a busy marketplace across the road, we found two teenage girls, one Uighur and one Chinese, serving from a makeshift table braised Chinese pork in a pocket of fresh naan bread—a perfect cross-cultural lunch.

'Do you understand, iron rice bowl?'

'No, what's that?'

I was talking to Mr Xie in the office of the Bogda Travel Service. I'd come to give him our passport details for the Russian tickets. The office was a converted hotel room with three desks, two telephones and a lot of maps.

'Iron rice bowl means a government job which you cannot lose. A job for life. Most people have an iron rice bowl here. They don't want to lose it.'

'But people who sell postcards are making more money than university lecturers.'

'I know, I used to be a university teacher! But the pay is terrible, so I started to work for this company. It's still state-run, but at least there's an opportunity for change. The best jobs now are with the joint-venture companies. Everybody wants to work for the Holiday Inn, but you must have very good English.'

'But how is the government going to keep doctors and teachers and engineers working, if they are not paid enough to keep up?'

'It's a big strain, but Deng Xiao-ping has the right idea. He wants to change things slowly. When we look across the border into the Soviet Union, we can see what happens if you try to change everything at once.'

We had time to walk around the city a little together. Xie told me that he was born in Kashgar, the old Uighur city near the Pakistan border. He described it in glowing terms, and said that when we came to Xinjiang next, we must visit there.

'You'll think it funny, but I don't like Chinese food,' he said.

'Really?'

'I grew up with Muslim food, you see? That's what I like best.'

The crowd of Uighur bankers around the Bank of China was something to see, and I had to fight off an army of young lads brandishing pocket calculators just to get inside. Competition for hard currency made it a seller's market, and I negotiated a good rate with two teenage brokers before I'd even left the foreign exchange counter. Ürümqi is the centre of an elaborate cross-border trade in people, currency and consumer goods. Chinese radios, running shoes and cigarettes are popular on the Russian side of the border, and I'm not quite sure what flows in the opposite direction, but American dollars were clearly the medium of exchange, judging by the fat rolls of US currency brandished by the money-changers in the foyer.

I was walking back to the hotel when I witnessed an amazing scene. In front of a nondescript office building, a man with a bicycle had spread out a small selection of magazines and comics on a groundcloth on the icy footpath. He didn't seem to be doing much business, when suddenly, three army vehicles and two motorcycles squealed to a halt in the road. A dozen soldiers and a couple of officers jumped out, leapt across the snowbanks, and began shouting at the man. They tossed away his groundcloth and started tearing up his magazines. He was backed against a wall, literally shaking with fear, while one of the officers screamed in his face. Stunned by the sudden violence, I was left standing, speechless, ten metres away. The second officer caught sight of me, and nodded to his companion. The first one glanced at me, then kicked the bookseller's bicycle to the ground. Ten seconds later, they had all climbed back in their vehicles and roared away.

The hotel we were staying in, Mr Xie explained, was owned by a general in the People's Army. How a general came to be in the hotel business I was unable to grasp, but it was a very nice hotel. We had a comfortable room, and a variable crew of housemaids to look after us. As in most Chinese hotels, they had a room of their own, where they filled the vacuum flasks with hot water for tea, folded laundry, and slept on camp beds whenever their duties allowed. We were used to going along the corridor and calling politely at the door when we wanted an extra towel or a bar of soap, rousing a sleepy housemaid from her cot. Children in a Chinese hotel were a rarity, and three foreign children even more so. Our girls were often whisked away, to be entertained in the maid's room for hours at a time. One or the other would come back from time to time, to assure us that they were having great fun. They were fed sweets, had their hair combed and plaited, were given small presents. That they had no language in common didn't seem to matter; the Chinese fondness for children overcame such petty obstacles, and there were times when we wouldn't see the girls from breakfast until dinner.

The hotel had a communal dining room, as well as a more expensive restaurant. We filed in to the dining room on the first night, for a meal that was served at 7.00 pm promptly. In a cavernous banquet hall, a half-dozen round tables were set with ten places each. You sat where you were put, and platters of food were delivered to the table to be shared. We had a bowl of steamed rice and one of steamed bread, some greens with oyster sauce, a dish of spinach with scraps of pork and some tofu noodles with ginger and chillies. It was pretty uninspiring stuff, but at Y3 a head, it was cheap enough, and an echo of what the communal dining halls must have been like during the Cultural Revolution, when even cooking was regarded as a revisionist threat to the new order, and chefs, along with university professors and Buddhist monks, were forced to work as toilet cleaners and road-sweepers.

In the streets, the cooking was vibrant and interesting. Onion-cake men set up their griddles on every market corner, and there seemed to be a bakery on every block. I made a nuisance of myself, hanging around these bakeries, watching the method of production. From a covered bowl of dough, the baker would pull a lump of the right size and flatten it with the heel of his hand. A heavy stamp evened the dough and perforated it with a decorative pattern. Sprinkled with salt water, and sometimes a little minced onion, the flat bread was lifted on to an unusual mould—a sort of bowl with an internal handle, tightly covered with a wet cloth. This the baker used to reach into a deep clay oven and stick the fresh dough to the inside wall. With practised timing, the baker would fetch the bread out again with a pair of iron tongs just as it was cooked, and about to fall. The bread was crisp and at the same time chewy, slightly salty and so delicious that it could easily serve as a meal on its own. Each fresh loaf was added to the stack on a small table outside the bakery. They hardly had time to cool before they were sold.

In a covered market near the hotel, the blue-grey smoke from a dozen kebab-sellers drifted towards the tin roof overhead. The butchers' stalls were handy just behind them, so there was no question about the freshness of the meat. My favourite delicacy was the sheep's kidney, cut into tiny cubes and threaded on a steel skewer. You took a place on a low wooden bench in front of the brazier. The skewers were dusted with salt and chilli and set to grill over the charcoal fire. When they were almost cooked, they were set in front of you to finish cooking as you liked. Hot and crackling, slid off the skewer with your teeth, they were superb. Steaming bowls of boiled noodles with chilli sauce could be had for as little as Y1, and there was a rough version of the Cantonese *wan tun* made with ground lamb, served in soup. A few stalls kept simmering cauldrons of stewed lamb, enriched with carrot, onion and cubes of cooked rice starch. Chillies were served with everything. Outside, in the sunshine, a bicycle man was selling bright red toffee apples and water chestnuts. If you bought one, he'd give you a little paper twist of chilli to sprinkle on your sweet! I was surprised by this endemic use of the capsicum plant, because it is a native of South America, and could not, by most accounts, have reached China much before the 17th century. On the other hand, the Chinese sometimes took to new foreign products with a vengeance: the British had introduced opium in Guangzhou in 1773, and within 50 years it was a plague all over China.

Even at this enormous distance from the sea, the Chinese merchants still managed to keep seafood on the menu. Parboiled squid of impressive size and rubberiness were sold in the market, along with frozen prawns and salted fish. Only the freshwater varieties were available fresh: writhing tubs of brown, slippery eels stood on the pavement and live carp were despatched to order with the broad side of a cleaver.

We were preparing ourselves to leave China, and start the next part of the journey, into central Asia. Mr Xie jokingly advised us to stock up on food. 'All you can buy on the other side is black bread and more black bread,' he said. Like the students we met in central China, he wanted to see the wider world, but the cost of travel was far beyond what he could afford. In some ways, he seemed content to let the world come to Xinjiang, and he was enthusiastic about the opening of the area to tourism. We knew each other for only a few days, but we'd made a close friendship. He was embarrassed when we presented him with a bottle of *mao tai* as a gesture of thanks at the railway station.

At various times, we had been driven up the wall by China. At worst, it is cold, dirty, noisy, over-priced, over-crowded and clearly could not give a damn whether you live or die. The arrogant rudeness of sales clerks, ticket sellers, desk clerks and every other sort of petty bureaucrat is enough to make you grit your teeth and wish you'd brought a gun. This is made worse by the language problem, so that you often don't even know why you can't get what you desperately need. Employees of any government-run shop or office can be expected to shout at you, spit on your shoes, slam their little windows closed or pretend you don't exist. The blatant official overcharging (foreigners pay anything up to twenty times the normal price for museum tickets) is bad enough, but they also insist that you pay with FEC, which amounts to nothing more than a government-run racket to confiscate money from foreigners. The petty dishonesty of sales clerks can make you into a waspish pain-in-the-ass after the fifth time you've been deliberately over-charged, short-changed or even refused change for a purchase. The standard advice is that you must keep smiling, retain face, stand your ground and maintain the patience of Job. While this is true in most cases, it's interesting to note that when you do occasionally thump the desk, raise your voice or walk straight through a barrier, things start happening around you. This must be used judiciously, and you cannot afford to really lose your temper, but it can get things moving when you're faced with a blank wall of non-cooperation, or some obtuse official who simply wants you to go away.

The recent policies of 'opening to the West' and 'encouraging market socialism' have spawned a whole army of hawkers, restaurateurs, taxi drivers, touts and 'change-money' men who are only too happy to have your business, and will climb over each other to secure your custom. This makes buying meals and taking taxis a breeze but unfortunately, these people do not yet run the Chinese railways, the hotels or the banks. Given a little time, though, they probably will.

Once out of the government offices, things are different again. Individuals met on the train or the boat, bus conductors and students, 'Serve the People' cadres and even policemen can be absolute sweethearts. They are open, friendly, amused with your attempts at spoken Chinese, and are genuinely pleased to have you in their country. These are the real idealists, the working people of China who believed in Mao Zedong and the communist State, and still do. They agree with Deng Xiao-ping's reform policies, and if you are touring China as a result, then they're very pleased to see you, and will offer a warm welcome. We blessed their proletarian hearts, because it was these flashes of genuine warmth and friendliness that restored our faith, and make us glad that we came to China in the first place.

There are sights to be seen in China that would draw us even if the conditions for individual travellers were twice as hard. The civilisation is so old that it puts events outside China into a different perspective. Xi'an's buried army was already old when the emperor Tiberius sat on his throne in Rome. Chinese imperial records reach back to the time of the Egyptian pharaohs, and the graves of well-dressed and interred Chinese nobles have been dated to 4000 BC. It's impossible to look at the ancient landscape of Shannxi without feeling the weight of millennia, and the connection is direct; people have been living and farming there continuously since the earliest ages of mankind. Areas like the Gobi are so remote that nomadic pastoralists and oasis farmers have been able to preserve many of their old ways, even in the face of so aggressive a colonial power as the Han.

We shook hands again with Mr Xie, and hefted our bags to board the Russian train to Alma-Ata. Our route would take us north of the Tian Shan range, along the southern edge of a vast marshy grassland that extends north to the Mongolian border. As we travelled west, two mountain ranges would converge, forcing us into a natural funnel and a single high pass over the mountains. In 1219, Genghis Khan, wild with rage after a Mongol embassy to the Turkish governor of Samarkand had been captured and murdered, led an army of 30 000 horsemen through this narrow gap and exploded into Central Asia. He sacked Bokhara and Samarkand, and finding them easy prey, carried on to take Afghanistan, Persia and southern Russia. The pass is still there, of course. It is called the Dzungarian Gate.

TWELVE

The train was a revelation. On the platform, a conductor with broad
Kazakh features, a trim blue overcoat and a furry Russian hat inspected
our tickets and directed us to the right carriage. Like children on
Christmas morning, we couldn't believe our luck as we explored the
shiny woodwork and the clean windows, the neat rows of coathooks,
the gleaming samovar and the tidy carpets. After six weeks of grubby,
filthy, broken trains, this looked like heaven; smart four-berth compartments with clean tablecloths and Russian-style tea-glasses in metal
holders. The carriage carried a brass-maker's plate near the door, with
the name of an East German factory, and that year's date. The captain
of the train, an impressive figure in a crisp uniform, actually introduced
himself and welcomed us aboard his train. If he noticed the stunned
expressions on our faces, he was far too polite to mention it.

As far as we could see, we were the only foreigners on the train.
The other passengers were a mixed group of Kazakhs, Uighurs and
Chinese, carrying great truckloads of baggage, television sets, track
suits and running shoes. The train left promptly, and we gazed out
the windows as we passed through the outskirts of Ürümqi. A fresh
coating of snow made everything look pretty, the industrial sprawl of
the city giving way to a familiar landscape of mud-brick houses, with
sheep and chickens running loose. Inside the train, a group of Chinese
had started early, throwing melon seeds and orange peelings out into
the corridor. The conductor descended on them like the wrath of
God, and told them to use the rubbish bins. Smoking was also banned
in the compartments, making a welcome change from the dense fog
of cigarette smoke we were used to on Chinese trains.

We were hopelessly confused by the train timetable, which had to cope with the change from Beijing time to Moscow time, neither of which had any relation to local time. As far as we could determine, the trip to Alma-Ata would take about 30 hours, including a change of bogies at the border, since the Russian and Chinese railways run on different gauges. We'd also have to pass through customs and immigration control, so I took some time to go through our passports and visas. Each of us had more than one passport, a legacy of the several different countries we've lived in. For simplicity, the children travelled on my Irish passport, while Dorcas had her own British passport. At the bottom of another bag, we had a neat set of Australian passports, which we had obtained before leaving home, and would need re-entering the country.

As the light faded over a wide, snowy landscape, I could see the single-lane highway which ran west of Ürümqi and followed the railway line at a distance. Traffic was sparse, and more than half the lorries were tankers, carrying fuel to outlying settlements. Just on sunset, we passed a great pipeline which led north to the oilfields of the Junggar basin. We were quickly running out of map, since I'd been unable to find an accurate map of the CIS in Hong Kong. We'd also have to do without a guidebook, because nothing of any use had been published since recent changes had allowed individual travellers inside the CIS. Once over the border, we'd be on our own.

We had an early dinner in the Chinese restaurant car, where everyone seemed to be making the best of it while the food and the beer lasted. There was definitely a party atmosphere, but we returned to our compartment to enjoy the luxury of clean sheets, soft pillows and reading lights that actually worked. The kids played word games until it was time to sleep. Dorcas and I sat up a while longer, then turned in for a few hours' sleep before we reached the border.

We woke when the train slowed to approach the new Chinese station at the Alatau Pass, a grand architectural effort which boasted a huge two-storey immigration hall, wide concrete plazas and a flight of steps that would have done good service in the Forbidden City. Why all this floodlit concrete was necessary, we couldn't work out, since for the next six hours, all the immigration and customs control would be done on the train. Crews of Chinese railway workers toiled outside in the freezing, foggy night to jack up the train carriages and change the bogies, a process that involved tremendous banging and thumping underneath our feet. Somehow, the children slept through it. Sleepy passengers, poking their heads out into the corridor to see what was going on, were suddenly galvanised by the arrival of the Chinese border guards, who swarmed aboard the train like an invading army. In minutes, the sleepy train was transformed into a loud Chinese shouting match, as the aggressive guards demanded to see papers, inspect luggage and empty compartments for more thorough inspections.

Our turn came with a violent rapping on the door, and I opened it to a squad of three guards in crumpled PLA uniforms. They seemed to be in a state of high excitement, and barked unintelligible instructions in Chinese. I offered our passports, which were snatched away abruptly. The presence of foreigners on the train evidently alarmed them, and they sent for reinforcements. Two more guards arrived, a man and a woman, dressed in extraordinary black leather uniforms, bristling with straps and epaulettes. I tried to indicate that we had three sleeping children, but they insisted on barging in and sitting on the lower bunks to interrogate us. Our exit visas and passports were in order, I knew, so I had a hard time understanding what it was they wanted. We struggled along with scraps of English and Chinese, until it dawned on me that they were demanding money.

We learnt later that this was a regular procedure—the Chinese border guards were running a sort of racket, extorting cash from Chinese nationals who were crossing the borders with quantities of consumer goodies for their relatives in the CIS. You either made the appropriate payment, or were turfed off the train in the middle of the night, to find your own way back to Ürümqi. Our hosts clearly saw a family of rich foreigners as something of a yearly bonus, and opened negotiations with a demand for Y100 each, to be paid in US dollars. Chinese currency was out of the question, it appeared. Since it was illegal for Chinese nationals to possess foreign currency, I thought I had a reasonable chance of refusing, and replied with an offer of Y10 each, payable in Renminbi. Leather Jackets One and Two thought this was hilarious, and repeated their demand for US dollars, immediately. I told them we didn't have any US dollars, which drove Leather Jacket One into a rage. We must pay, he screamed, or we would be taken off the train. I tried to keep my voice calm, and upped my offer to Y100 for all of us, payable in FEC.

All the shouting had finally woken the girls, who peered sleepily down from the upper berths to see what the fuss was about. Leather

Jacket One jumped to his feet and stormed angrily out into the corridor, uttering dire threats in Chinese. The small crowd of green-uniformed lesser ranks who had gathered curiously at the door scattered before him. Leather Jacket Two, the female half of the dynamic duo, now stood at the door making eyes at Kerry and Aislinn, who were playing peekaboo with the blankets. Dorcas and I discussed the situation.

'Are you trying to get us shot?'

'What do you mean? Our papers are fine. This is extortion!'

'He's probably gone away to get a machine gun.'

'Relax, we just have to negotiate a little.'

'I do not want to get off this train in the middle of the night.'

'Don't worry, it'll be fine.'

Ten minutes later, another guard arrived, in a green officer's uniform. Leather Jacket One was probably lying down somewhere with a wet cloth on his head. This officer was serious, and insistent. US dollars, now, or things might go badly with us. Can we discuss how many US dollars, I asked. This was possible, he indicated. There followed an intense twenty minutes of offer and counter-offer, bluff and protest. We eventually struck a deal for US$1 each, cash. I produced a billfold, and ten necks craned forward to see. I slipped the notes out carefully, thinking this a bad time to be flashing our travelling funds around wildly. The officer accepted the notes and left. I felt in need of a drink.

The train lurched forward into no man's land, and there was an excited atmosphere of relief among the passengers. One Chinese 'businessman' in the next compartment boasted that he'd had to pay US$100 in cash, but that they had not even looked in his luggage. We didn't know what he had in there, but he seemed to be well pleased with the deal.

The next hurdle was the Russian side of the border, and I was not looking forward to it. As the train slowed to a stop, I heard the unmistakable sound of soldiers boarding the train. Let's get it over with, I thought, so I opened the compartment door wide, and stuck my head out into the corridor. Four men, unmistakably Russian in heavy grey winter uniforms and huge furry hats, were walking along from compartment to compartment, inspecting passports. They all seemed to be seven feet tall, and blue-eyed. One of them appeared in our doorway, and said 'Good evening' in Russian. I offered our passports, and our Russian visas. He checked them silently, raising his head briefly to count heads. He handed them back to me courteously, and said, 'Thank you. Welcome to Russia.' He was gone before I realised he'd said it in English.

In the next hour, we were visited in turn by a man from immigration (who looked at our visas again), another from customs (he made a perfunctory check, careful not to wake the sleeping children), a third from agriculture (were we carrying any fresh fruits or vegetables?), a fellow from currency control (would we please declare how much foreign currency we were carrying) and finally, a doctor, who spoke good English in a soft, cultured voice. Was everyone feeling well, he asked? Any illnesses or complaints? We assured him that we were all fine, and we chatted for a few minutes about our plans to see his country. When he'd left, we looked at each other. Could that really be it? They'd been efficient and polite, they were very thorough, but considerate about the children, and they said 'thank you' as they handed our passports back. For our first brush with the KGB, it hadn't been too bad at all.

The whole train slept late after our overnight exertions. I'd given up trying to work out what time it was, but it felt like ten o'clock or so when I got up and went for a wash in the wonderfully clean bathroom at the end of the carriage. Our conductor was friendly, and showed me how to use the samovar to make tea. Through the windows, the landscape was almost without feature, an undulating plain of snow under a curdled sky. At the horizon, land and sky merged in a white fog, but so far away that a sense of vast distance remained. As the morning lengthened, the rail line curved gently north, and we lost altitude. The continuous snow fields gave way to rough pasture and marshy boglands, high and wild and untouched by any sign of people. Before noon, we reached the junction at Aktogay, and turned south on the main Novosibirsk–Alma-Ata line. For the first time, we saw sand desert, rolling low dunes sparsely thatched with dry grasses. In the distance, to the west, we could just catch glimpses of the salty marshes of Lake Balkash.

Our first stop on the Russian side of the border followed: cold sun, no crowds, a bare station platform on which stood six *babushkas*, stout country women wrapped in greatcoats, scarves and shawls, their feet planted in thick, furry boots. Passengers piled off to buy what they were selling from their little wooden carts. I swapped some Chinese currency for Russian roubles with the conductor, and bought us lunch. I found *piroshki* (large fried dumplings with a filling of potato and cabbage) and *pyel'meni* (boiled dumplings with a ground meat filling). There were glass bottles of cold *smyetana* (soured milk with a tangy yogurt taste), and boiled potatoes seasoned with paprika and onion. All of it was delicious, not least for the complete change of texture and tastes.

The journey to Alma-Ata was hours long, and the conductor agreed cheerfully that we were running late. We arrived, at last, in darkness. The railway station was huge and forbidding. We wandered around in a crowd of Caucasian faces, no longer standing out like visitors from another planet. Dorcas had learnt some Cyrillic, years before in Bulgaria, and used it to decode a few of the station signs. Someone on the train had told us there was a hotel in the station building. With some difficulty, we found it. A woman asked us for our passports and US$15 each, for a bare couple of rooms with spindly cot beds and no blankets. We declined the offer, and I left the station to negotiate for a taxi.

'Mistre. Hello, taxi?' The grinning Kazakh in a flat cap had an uncanny knack for knowing when to use English. Perhaps we weren't blending in as well as I thought.

'Hello, taxi?'

'Yes. Taxi . . . five people,' I said.

'Where go?'

'Hotel. Hotel Kazakhstan.' I named the only other hotel I'd ever heard of in Alma-Ata, courtesy of the train conductor.

'5000 *roubli*,' he said, holding up mittened fingers.

'Forget it.' I made a show of looking for another taxi.

'Hello, mistre . . . OK, five dollars, OK?'

'Two.'

'OK, two.' He grinned.

The taxi was a clapped-out Lada that had seen hard service for the last 20 years or so. When we piled our luggage and ourselves into it, it sank on squeaky springs. We'd been through three gears before we got out of the car park. The driver looked very intent now, hunched over his steering wheel, the better to see the road without the lights on. He punched a badly dubbed cassette into the dashboard, and Elvis Presley launched into 'Heartbreak Hotel'. In-flight entertainment.

We drew in to the courtyard of a big, shiny Soviet-modern hotel which soared to eighteen stories above the street. 'Hotel Kazakhstan' was lettered across the entrance in metre-high Cyrillic characters. The lobby was wide, echoing and chilly. The woman at the reception desk spoke English, and checked us into a double room for US$60. Again, there was no mention of roubles—US dollars were the preferred currency, and the little signs on the cashier's desk invited you to use American Express, Visa or Mastercard. The girls stared around at the unaccustomed luxury of the carpeted lifts and the mirrored hallways. Our room was small, but we'd had plenty of practice at re-arranging hotel rooms to make up four beds, and the luxury of a bath was welcome. In half an hour, we were all asleep.

In the morning, we found the hotel café, and breakfasted on thick sour milk, poppy seed pastries and black tea. As we stepped in to the lift, a well-dressed Russian businessman hurried up and tipped his hat to Dorcas.

'Congratulations to you, madame,' he said in English.

'I beg your pardon?'

'Congratulations. Today is International Women's Day. This is very important holiday in Russia.'

'Well, that's very kind of you. Thank you.'

'You are welcome.' His hand slipped in to his inside pocket and produced a sleek black leather wallet.

'Now, would you like to change some money? I can give you very good rate for US dollars, German marks, English pounds . . . ?'

Dorcas smiled sweetly and jabbed the button that closed the doors.

The view from our window was spectacular. Beyond the imposing, modern buildings of the business area, the high, sharp mountains were close enough to see the frozen snowfields near the summits and the deeply eroded glacial valleys that scarred their flanks. This was still the Tian Shan range, but we were looking south towards its 5000-metre peaks. On the other side of this range was Lake Issyk-Kul, a great salt lake 1600 metres above sea level.

The city was surprising; a very Russian town serving as the capital of an independent Kazakh republic. But Russians made up nearly half the population, we learnt, the result of mass migration in the 1960s, when Khrushchev had been intent on transforming Kazakhstan into the second grain basket of the Soviet Union. In any case, it was not an ancient city (the nomadic Kazakhs didn't have many cities), but had been founded as a military outpost by the Russian czars during the late 19th century, when Britain and Russia vied with each other in the Great Game for influence in Central Asia. It had been destroyed by an earthquake in 1887.

We saw wide, tree-lined avenues and handsome buildings in the Soviet Federal style. A good bus and tram service made it easy, even on a public holiday, to get around the city, and being able to walk across open squares and wide, leafy parks without overpowering crowds of people was a relief. We set out early to find the train station, leaving the girls behind at the hotel, watching an incomprehensible Russian children's program on the television.

The station looked a bit less gloomy by daylight, but our inability to speak Russian was not going to help us get tickets out of Alma-Ata. We planned to go to Tashkent and Samarkand, about 900 kilometres south-west, into Uzbekistan. I spent a fruitless hour in a long queue, only to discover that without an internal Russian passport, I wouldn't be allowed to buy tickets, and would have to go to a special foreigners' office somewhere upstairs. The ticket-seller, a red-faced woman with Turkish features, was shouting and waving her hands at me, while several of my fellow-hopefuls in the line helpfully translated for me into Turkish, Uighur and Chinese. Somehow, I got the message and left the line.

Dorcas and I wandered around on the second floor of the building until we found the foreigners' ticket window, which was closed. We waited. After some time, we were joined by a group of young Czech students carrying backpacks. They were on their winter break, it seemed, and we managed to exchange a few words in a jumble of German and English. The ticket clerk arrived, a severe, stylishly dressed woman in her mid-forties. I had written down our destination, Tashkent, and the number of tickets we needed. I passed the slip under the glass partition, and exercised my very few words of Russian. Two adults and three children, please, overnight sleepers to Tashkent.

Nothing in Russia is that straightforward. There followed a close examination of the age of each child. Did we have visas for Tashkent? Where were our passports? No, we certainly could not pay in Russian roubles, only US cash dollars would be accepted. With every question and answer, the woman made it clear that we would be allowed to buy tickets only as a singular and very great favour, one which was in her absolute power to grant or withhold. Like some horrible school-mistress, she demanded submission. The Czech students, fluent in Russian, came to our rescue. 'Don't be such a bitch,' one girl called out, 'just give them the tickets.' Another said, 'They're guests in your country, so charge them the right price.' She-who-must-be-obeyed looked quite put out by this unwelcome democratic participation, and made short work of the stamps and receipts. We left with our tickets, and a grateful smile for our Czech champions.

On the way back to the hotel, we remarked on the absence of shops. A few signs announced the Ministry of Internal Affairs or the Kazakhstan Museum of Fine Art, but there wasn't a market to be seen. A few stalls were open here and there, selling cut flowers or newspapers, a basket of oranges or packets of cigarettes. We decided to get off the bus and walk the last bit, buying what we could for lunch. Dorcas had been told, years ago on a visit to Bulgaria, that if she should ever see a queue on a Bulgarian street, she should instantly join it; whatever was at the other end would doubtless be in short supply and worth having. Accordingly, when we saw a busy flow of people going in and out of an unremarkable door in a building near the hotel, we walked over to see what it was.

We were delighted to find it was a bakery. Fresh loaves of bread lined the wire shelves, and a woman in a white coat collected payment at the door. We chose an armful of crisp rolls and a loaf of fresh, chewy rye bread. Next door, we found a general grocery, where we got cooked sausage, smoked cheese, butter and milk. These self-service shops were barely utilitarian, but pleasantly clean, and if the range of products available was limited, there seemed to be no shortage of supply. We paid in roubles, and prices equated to about a tenth of what me might pay at home (although they were, by local standards, high).

The girls fell upon this bounty like wolf cubs, tearing off pieces of bread with their fingers, smearing them with fresh, salty butter, lopping off bits of cheese and sausage with my Swiss Army knife and chewing contentedly. We weren't far behind. The taste of cheese was one we'd missed, and the familiar spices of the meaty sausage and the smell of fresh bread were luxuries, after weeks of rice and sweet buns and strange pickles.

Now we were pressed for time. The visas we had obtained in Shanghai were simple transit visas, intended for passengers taking the Trans-Siberian train from Beijing to Moscow. They allowed us ten days before we had to be out of the country, and we'd already used up three. It began to dawn on us that there was quite a lot of Russia to get through. From Tashkent to Moscow was 4000 kilometres, from

Moscow to the Hungarian border another 2000. We considered the southern route, across the Caspian Sea to Baku, but two things were against it: the difficulty of getting tickets for this complicated route, and a shooting war in Azerbaijan. We pored over railway timetables, trying to match up one train with another, but the Russian railway system, like many others, was centred on the capital—all roads led to Moscow. If this was the way me must go, we'd have to go quickly. I'd met our friend, the train captain, on the platform at the railway station. He told us that the Tashkent express to Moscow was a good train, and that it took three days and two nights to get there. He intimated that the overnight train from Alma-Ata to Tashkent was not such a good train, and in any case, we should get off at Chimkent and take a bus, 'Much faster', he said. If we took the Moscow train, we would miss Samarkand, which Dorcas dearly wanted to see, but there seemed to be no other way, so we agreed to press on north.

We packed up, and left our luggage at the train station. We had hours before our evening train. We decided to have a look around Alma-Ata, and boarded a bus at random, intending to take it to the end of its line, then return to the station. The bus wandered through the modern apartment buildings of suburban Alma-Ata, picking up and letting down passengers every few blocks. A pretty girl carrying a 'cello was evidently off to her music lesson. *Babushkas* with full shopping baskets struggled on and off the bus. Eventually, we reached a kind of park, a botanical garden with a gaggle of kebab-sellers and beer stalls outside then gates, where the bus route ended. We walked into a well-kept public amusement park, where pony rides and ice-cream shops amused a few dozen families out with their children. Our heads turned to the jingle of saddle bells, and a brown-faced Kazakh in a sheepskin jacket led a string of four Bactrian camels into the square. Bearing ornate saddles and richly decorated harness, these great brown shaggy beasts maintained their haughty dignity while excited children were hoisted on and off their backs. Kerry and Aislinn were delighted, but Clare had to weigh up the conflicting demands of excitement and her 14-year-old dignity (she'd passed her birthday on the train to Alma-Ata). She finally decided a ride on a Bactrian camel was too good to pass up, and clambered up with the other two to sway off into the distance, clutching a wobbly, woolly hump.

In the station forecourt, a couple of cafés were open, selling black tea and boiled dumplings to a crowd of men in blue jackets. Tiny government stalls offered cigarettes, chocolate and orange juice.

'Get some of that orange juice, will you?' Dorcas said.

'Good God, have you seen the price of it? It's dearer than vodka!'

'Fine. We'll let the children drink vodka, shall we?'

'Well, I . . . oh, all right, how many do you want?'

We stocked up with bread and sausage, cheese and orange juice, since the train did not have a dining car, as far as I could determine. Outside the station entrance, a long line of people stood, holding various items of food or drink in front of them. This was our first introduction to the informal Russian food market. Someone would put six jars of home-made pickles in a bag and carry it down to the station. With the bag between their feet, they would hold up one jar for inspection. Customers paused to enquire the price, and an exchange might be made. Another jar of pickles came up out of the bag. There were no hawker's cries, no hand-lettered signs, no proud displays of shiny vegetables. There wasn't even any bargaining that I could hear. When I offered one woman a package price for three bottles of home-brewed beer, she seemed astonished. No, she indicated, she was selling *one* bottle of beer, for 100 roubles (about 20 cents at the time). If I bought *one* bottle of beer, she might have *another* bottle of beer to sell, but there would be no connection between the two transactions. After three generations of Soviet central planning, they were a little rusty on the laws of supply and demand, but I supposed they'd pick it up as they went along.

By far the best-selling item on the station forecourt was vodka. Half-litre bottles were disappearing into jacket pockets at an alarming rate. I made a couple disappear into my rucksack, just in case of a chilly night.

THIRTEEN

The overnight train was a bit of a nightmare. The carriage was grubby, broken-down and packed with a noisy assortment of Uzbeks, Tadzhiks and Kazakhs, bristling with vodka bottles. Within an hour, the whole train was beastly drunk. Dozens of villainous Genghis Khan look-alikes were weaving up and down the corridors, slapping each other on the back, singing emotionally and practising their kung-fu moves. There were no doors in the carriage, so it was one big party. The fellows in the next bay were doing experiments with vodka, beer and apple juice. One would proclaim loudly that only he knew the secret proportions for the perfect drink, then slop about with bottles for a while. They'd all have a taste. 'Rubbish!' the other four would cry, so they'd polish that lot off, and another one would have a go at being Mr Mixology. They were mostly too pissed to pour liquids, and eventually settled down to sucking vodka straight out of the bottle.

We fed the girls and packed them off to bed. By now the Kazakh cowboys had discovered the presence of foreigners on the train, and one of them had attached himself to me, declaring loudly that I was his one, his only true friend in the world. 'Ahztraylia good!' he shouted, repeatedly, while hugging me violently around the neck and taking long pulls out of my vodka bottle. When I'd wrenched it back out of his hand, I had a few more pulls myself. 'Kazakhstan good!' I announced, to universal acclaim. We were getting along famously, and staggered off to the smoking department together. By the time I came back for the second bottle, Dorcas had rolled herself up and was firmly asleep, her head on her rucksack and her back to the world.

I crept into bed at 2.00 am, my head spinning with Russian vodka and Tadzhik tobacco. At 3.00 am, we stopped at some godforsaken town, where my drinking buddy had to get off, something he couldn't do without waking me up, kissing me on the ear and swearing eternal brotherhood. He was replaced by a muttering nutcase, who climbed into the berth opposite us and thrashed and turned for the next hour. I had drifted off nicely, when Dorcas woke me.

'Kerry's in tears,' she said, 'I'm going to swap places with her.'

'Why?'

'The fellow in the the opposite bunk is a nuisance. He keeps pulling the covers off her bed.'

'What?' I mumbled. My tongue was not operating correctly.

'Just keep an eye on her.'

'Right. OK.'

I would have gone off again, but for renewed muttering and thrashing from the opposite bunk. Our odd companion in the upper berth was twisted up with a blanket over his head, talking to himself as if in a dream. Every so often he would flop an arm or a leg out, so as to rest upon another bunk. This seemed a little contrived to me, so I stayed awake to watch him. The next time his flailing arm touched down on Dorcas's berth, I watched his hand slide surreptitiously under the bedclothes, guided by a beady eye under his blanket. I got up, and he instantly withdrew it. I shook Dorcas gently.

'Change places with me.'

'What for? He's not bothering me.'

'Humour me.'

'Oh, all right.' Dorcas slipped down to the lower berth and I took her place, but slept this time with my head towards our strange bedfellow. As I thought, it wasn't long before his hand was casually tossed over towards me, and I waited until it began to forage. When he was leaning well out of his own berth, I gave his arm a little tug and he crashed down in a very satisfying manner to the floor, where he lay moaning even louder. The conductor came along to see what had happened and chided him for being drunk. If he couldn't stay in his berth, the conductor seemed to say, he'd have to sit up all night. This he did, muttering Uzbeki curses in my direction for the next two hours, until he finally got off the train, and I could curl up to get some sleep. An hour later, we arrived in Chimkent.

Buses would meet the train, our train captain had said, and they were in front of the station as the train pulled up. Several buses, in fact, with enterprising touts hustling passengers aboard for the two-hour trip to Tashkent. This, at least, seemed to be some sort of private enterprise, because it was strictly no waiting: fill the bus, hit the road, next bus. We were helped on to the crowded bus, and found room at the back with an Uzbek couple who smiled at us. The drive took us through the back streets of Chimkent, and here it was much more like the Central Asia we had imagined. Dusty mud-brick houses, children in the streets, donkeys laden with bundles and the occasional mosque—it looked more like Turkestan than the industrial Han cities of Xinjiang.

The climb was long and spectacular, as the bus followed a good highway up in to the hills, passing woolly herds of fat-tailed sheep and wide fields of thin pasture. We reached a high pass, marked by a beautiful trio of stone lions, vaguely Turkish or Persian in design. From our vantage point, we could see the close range of mountains that marked the border with Uzbekistan and Khirgizstan, and beyond them, floating in the blue haze of great distance, the jagged white peaks of the Pamirs. Somewhere in that range was Pik Kommunizma, 7.5 kilometres high and the tallest mountain in the old Soviet Union.

We had been looking forward to Tashkent, a city that had a fine romantic ring to it. It lay on a tributary of the Syr Darya, the ancient river that Alexander knew as the Jaxartes, one of the borders of the Persian empire in the 4th century BC. The city had changed hands many times: first founded by the Sasanids, it was threatened by Chinese expansion during the Tang Dynasty (618 to 907 AD) then overtaken by the Seljuk Turks in the 12th century. Timur the Lame ruled his Mongol empire from nearby Samarkand in the 14th century, to be displaced in turn by local warlords who established a Turkic-speaking khanate with capitals in Tashkent and Ürümqi. The Russians had taken it in 1865 as part of their expansion towards Afghanistan and the borders of British India.

The bus rolled to a stop in what looked like the industrial edge of a large city, and everyone piled out with their baggage and bundles. We stayed on, thinking the bus must go further in to the centre, but the driver made it clear that this was the last stop. I looked around with the sinking feeling that we might have a very long walk ahead of us, but our Uzbeki comrades pulled at our sleeves and indicated a flight of steps leading down under the road. I thought this must be a pedestrian underpass, but when we tottered down there, we discovered the Tashkent Metro.

Tashkent, we learnt in short order, was a modern city of two million people, and we might have been in San Francisco or Paris, sitting on the tidy seats of a fast underground train. Smartly dressed women in gorgeous leather boots and Russian men with neat suits and briefcases sat all around us, making us feel distinctly scruffy after six weeks' travelling on trains. We peered at the Metro map, trying to work out where the city centre might be, and decided to try the main railway station as a likely start.

We staggered up the stairs with all our bags, into the open air. Bright yellow trams snickered along on steel rails, lumbering buses passed us by. A lone kebab-seller on the corner looked at us hopefully. Guideless and mapless at this point, I really didn't know where to start.

Dorcas and the girls sat in the railway station while I made a fruitless expedition to find a cheap hotel nearby. There were hotels, all right, but they weren't about to let rooms out to foreigners, and I hadn't enough Russian to argue the point. After my fourth try, I had to go back to the station and admit defeat. We decided to have lunch and gather our strength.

In a courtyard of the station building, a busy café was gearing up for the lunchtime rush. A line was forming outside, and three sturdy cooks in white jackets were dishing up mutton kebabs, pilaf rice studded with sultanas and chickpeas, and slices of chewy rye bread. The girls looked at the gristly kebabs with mixed emotions, but brightened considerably when they discovered icecream for sale at another stall. We gave them money to go and buy some. Dorcas and I shared a plate of food and a bottle of local beer standing at a counter inside the café. It was filling fast, and although we couldn't understand a word, there was an easy familiarity of gesture and tone of voice that seemed very European. We realised that much of the difficulty we had in China was caused by an entirely different set of signals used by the Chinese to convey meaning. It wasn't just the language—it was the wordless communication of the shrug, the tilted head and the grimace which we suddenly found ourselves understanding in a busy pub in Tashkent.

I managed to collar a dishevelled policeman on the street, and in a difficult exchange in six words of English and four of Russian, he pointed us at the right tram for the only hotel he could recommend.

We managed to get off at the wrong stop or walk in the opposite direction, because this turned into a 3-kilometre hike, asking passers-by frequently for directions. Just to make things more cheerful, it began to pour with rain as we trudged along seemingly endless avenues in search of the Hotel Uzbekistan. When we found it at last, I wondered how we were going to pay for it, because it was a huge, gloriously expensive-looking place with three reception desks, four restaurants and a concierge desk. We collapsed in the lobby and dripped for a while.

The receptionist was charming, spoke perfect English, and wasn't backing down from the asking price of more than US$200 for a triple room. At this rate, we would be broke before we got to Moscow. The problem, it seemed, was that our visas did not specifically mention Tashkent as a destination, and no other hotel would let us in without the proper stamps and paperwork. In the end, I had to grit my teeth and pay the nice lady the money. For this huge sum (about three months' wages for a Russian bus driver), we got a large comfortable room on the 11th floor, and a lovely view of Tashkent in the rain.

I'd been told terrible stories about the 'floor ladies' in Russian hotels, supposedly a mixture of jailer, headmistress and guardian of public morals. Ours was an elegant woman in her mid-thirties, fluent in French and German, seated at a smart desk near the lifts. She was wonderfully helpful with extra linen and wake-up calls, and apologised profusely as she informed us that the hotel hot water system had just broken down. They were working on it, she said, and it should be back on in time for evening baths. We made do with dry towels and a change of clothing. The girls fastened themselves to a television program about Russian gymnasts, while I went to see about tickets.

There are certain advantages in staying in expensive hotels, even in Russia. I discovered that the hotel had its own travel desk, and surprisingly, it was open for business. The woman behind the counter said that she could certainly arrange tickets for the train to Moscow, and when would we like to go? I calculated that we could afford an extra day in Tashkent for a bit of sightseeing, but the trains were heavily booked and I was left with a choice of staying three days or leaving in the morning. Plotting a spin through Russia in ten days was becoming an exercise in taking what we could get. I was more surprised to learn that she would accept part-payment in Russian roubles and the balance in US dollars, and that the fare was somewhat less than I had expected for the three-day run. I accepted readily, and counted myself lucky to have escaped at least one station ordeal.

We were looking forward to a good dinner, and all that remained was to find somewhere to get it. The hotel had a number of restaurants, most of which accepted nothing but western currency, at western prices. Happily, there was also quite a posh (and cavernous) restaurant on the ground floor which accepted payment in roubles. The current exchange rate for roubles wasn't making life any easier for the locals, but at 600 roubles to the dollar, we were throwing the stuff around like Saudi princelings. I booked a table for an early dinner, and went upstairs to deliver the good news about tickets.

The hot water had sputtered into life, and everyone was enjoying the luxury of a bath. We scrubbed ourselves and every bit of spare clothing, hung it all up to dry, and went down to the dining room.

The maitre d' was a thin, gaunt man with a fine Turkish moustache. He showed us to a table, where we enjoyed the novelty of cutlery and napkins. A waiter rolled up a sort of travelling bar and dispensed mineral water, beer and softdrinks all round. A menu, mercifully translated into English, listed dozens of Russian and Uzbek specialties at the sort of prices that would encourage you to order everything, so to keep things simple, I did.

The meal was wonderful. Dishes were prepared with ingredients we had sorely missed: sour cream and paprika, cheese and butter. Fresh bread rolls disappeared faster than the waiter could keep up with them, and we savoured the tastes of pickled beetroot, cold roast chicken, spiced beef and caviar. An excellent soup of mutton and vegetables was followed by plates of fresh tomatoes, vinegared red cabbage and potatoes with mayonnaise. Fried veal chops and chicken Kiev, smoked pork and turkey breast vanished off the plates. We descended on the feast like starving men. An hour later, we were all sitting back in our chairs, burping contentedly, already half asleep. The Russian dance band struck up a few old Beatles numbers, and the restaurant began to fill with Turkish businessmen, Russian bureaucrats and the occasional American spook.

The departure for the station came early, with a taxi ordered for us by our obliging 'floor lady'. It was still dark when we bundled into the Russian sedan for the short trip to the station. 'Vagzhall, pazhalsta!' I said with a flourish, showing off my newfound mastery of the Russian language. I quite liked the sound of it—I tucked my chin into my chest and did my best Khruschev impersonation, like something out of an old *Get Smart* episode. The driver looked at me strangely, then showed me a grin full of gold teeth and Russian dentistry. 'Amerika?' he asked. 'Nyet. Afstralii-a,' I replied. This was going terrifically well, chatting casually with the locals in their own language. 'I have a brother in Melbourne,' he said, 'he drives a taxi, too.'

The station was busy at 5.00 am. The sixteen-carriage Moscow express stood at the platform, and dozens of passengers were loading great bagfuls of Chinese electronics and running shoes on to the train. The station buffet was serving breakfast, small glasses of hot sweet Turkish coffee, cold fried chicken and bowls of steaming broth with meat dumplings. The shelves of food looked spare after the Chinese station stalls, but passengers were loading up with tins of sardines and packets of biscuits. There was a dining car on the train, we'd been assured, but we put a few provisions by just in case. The only thing you couldn't buy at the kiosk was booze, a mark of the official government campaign against alcoholism, a chronic problem in the CIS. The black market provided what the official one could not, and the shopping-bag ladies were doing a brisk business in bottled beer and half-litre bottles of Stolichnaya.

We found our compartment in good shape, a newish East German carriage with all the bits in working order. I noticed there'd be no question of opening the windows; they were stoutly double-glazed against the Russian winter. It was cold enough in Tashkent, and the Russians considered this the steamy tropics. The heating was obviously working, though, and we had plenty of warm blankets and pillows. Our conductor was a cheerful, raffish-looking Kazakh in a smart blue uniform, and we settled in happily for the 60-hour trip. The first grey lights were appearing in the sky as the train pulled out of the station, heading north.

I had tried again to find a map of the CIS, but even in the expensive luxury of the Hotel Kazakhstan, I'd been unable to find one. We had to be content with tracking our progress along the railway timetable, and the names themselves were romantic enough; the train called at Turkestan, Kyzil-Orda, Aral'skoe More, Orenburg and Samara. The railway generally followed the course of the Syr Darya towards the Aral Sea, across a flat landscape of winter fields, under which were buried the bones of ancient Greek, Persian and Mongol invaders. The native Kazakh and Uzbek herdsmen, descendants of the Golden Horde, had been encouraged to settle into Soviet-style co-operative farms, and much of the land was put to irrigation, growing water-hungry cotton and wheat. This had made one part of the desert bloom, but also carried a disastrous environmental price tag, as the Aral Sea shrank from its shores, and the unirrigated grasslands withered, starved of their natural water supply. To the east and south, the great deserts of the Khyzlkum and Karakum grew a little bigger each year.

We made ourselves a picnic lunch of sausage and cheese, bread and oranges, and settled comfortably into our cabin. The girls had already begun to explore, bringing back reports of how many of our fellow passengers they'd met. The compartment next to ours was occupied by a trio of Pakistani gentlemen who had changed into baggy long-johns as soon as the train got under way. This was evidently their preferred travel wear, since we never saw them in anything else for the next three days. Most of the Russians preferred the ubiquitous blue track suit, worn with slippers, others sported Gucci shirts and Adidas running shoes of doubtful provenance. A couple of young Russian athletes, on their way back to Moscow, tried out their limited English. We met an Afghani teacher named Mahmoud Abdul, whose English was excellent. He told us he shared a cabin with an older man, a Mr Ibrahim, who was already wearing him out with long and colourful stories of his cross-border business dealings between Pakistan, China, Russia and Afghanistan.

'He is drinking all the time, and he is already drunk. This is not good for a Muslim, and it is not good for me,' he said.

'Perhaps we'll meet him later.'

'You will meet him, I can guarantee it. He will meet everyone in the train. He is drinking with everybody. There is no sleeping at all in my cabin, it is always full of people.'

I wandered down to the dining car in the afternoon, and found it almost deserted. A few of the staff were at one table near the kitchen, playing cards. I took a window seat to smoke a cigarette, and watch the bright, harsh scenery rattling past. One of the stewards wandered down to my table and asked in Russian what I wanted. I didn't know what he had, so I tried the basics.

'Coffee? *Kofi?*'

'*Nyet. Sok.*' I had no idea what *sok* might be.

'Tea? *Chai?*'

'*Nyet. Sok.*'

'*Piva* (beer)?'

'*Sok.*'

'OK, *sok.*'

'*Sok,* OK.'

The *sok* turned out to be a rich apple juice, dark and thick, which was dispensed from a warm tin on the kitchen counter. It was awful; cloyingly sweet and sticky. I let it sit on the table after my first taste, smoked another cigarette and read my book. Two Kazakh men came in and took a table near mine. I watched them go through the tea, coffee, *sok* routine with the steward. They got two glasses of brown apple sludge just like mine, but the steward returned with a bottle of vodka, and topped up their glasses at a ratio of 1:1. This looked like a much better idea, so I lifted my chin at the waiter. I pointed at my glass. 'Vodka?' I asked. He gave me a knowing look, and gestured for me to come with him quietly. He stopped at one of the bench seats and lifted the lid. In the storage compartment underneath, 60 bottles of vodka were neatly stacked in alternating rows.

'*Skol'ka stoit?*' I asked. How much is it?

'*Pyat' sot roubli.*' Five hundred roubles, a reasonable mark-up.

'*Spasiba.*' I'll have it.

'*Pazhalsta.*' No problem.

The taste of my *sok* was much improved by a liberal addition of vodka, and the afternoon took on a pleasantly warm glow. I was to get quite fond of the stuff over the next few days.

We tried the dining car for dinner that night. The menu, like the beverage list, was pretty limited. The waitress patiently explained in single-syllable words what there was to eat. Salad. Pork. Rice. Soup. Bread. We nodded at everything, and what arrived was very good. The cooking was definitely Russian, with no concessions to Muslim sensibilities. We had chopped eggs with beetroot and green salad, chewy rye bread and butter, a good soup and a braised meat dish with potatoes. We had to order another few platefuls to keep everyone going. The staggering bill in roubles worked out to about A$3.

Back in our carriage, things were warming up as the vodka bottles emptied. I was taken down the corridor to meet Mr Ibrahim, who was holding court like a Turkish pasha in a crowded compartment. I was invited to sit down. The Pakistani lads squeezed up a little tighter. The Russian athletes dangled long legs from an upper bunk. Mahmoud Abdul bustled around like a fussy housewife, and Mr Ibrahim had his arm around our conductor.

'He is like son to me!' he exclaimed, pinching the poor man's cheek.

'Ha! You are Afstralia! Very good, sit, sit, here!'

I was in the place of honour, scrunched into a bottom berth directly opposite Mr Ibrahim. He poured me tea. He was a man of about 60, I guessed, round and prosperous-looking, dressed in the waistcoat of a good suit and an open-collared business shirt. He was very drunk, but this did not stop him from keeping up a complicated and continuous story. How he managed to keep the thread, as he slipped in and out of Kazakh, Russian, Farsi and English, I couldn't imagine.

'Afstralia good country. Very good!'

'Yes, it is.' I wasn't about to complicate matters by telling him that I'd been born in another country, and raised in a third.

'English I speak very well.'

'Yes, your English is very good.'

He smiled a sad smile and rolled his head. 'Ah, I speaking many languages. Many languages. But I am drinking, forget words.'

'I get that way, too.'

'Ha!' he laughed. 'You have drink with me.'

'I will.'

Mahmoud Abdul was summoned to unearth another bottle of vodka from the baggage, and Mr Ibrahim made long, sloppy pours all around. I got half a pint of warm vodka in a tin cup. While Mr Ibrahim had an armlock around our conductor, the ban on smoking in the compartments seemed to have been temporarily lifted. Everyone lit up with contraband English cigarettes, presumably smuggled in from Pakistan.

'I am businessman. Many, many businesses. In Afghanistan, in Pakistan, many businesses.'

We diverted into several other languages for a while, as Mr Ibrahim explained the scope and breadth of his business interests to the gathered audience. Mahmoud Abdul translated for me.

'He says he is from Afghanistan originally, from a family of merchants. He says his family was broken up by the Russian invasion of Afghanistan. Now, he has brothers in Pakistan and in China, and in Moscow. He's going to visit one of them.'

'What sort of business . . . ?' I enquired gently.

'Obviously, he is a smuggler. Pooff!' Mahmoud Abdul blew out his cheeks to indicate exasperation with black marketeers, lapsed Muslims and fellows who kept him up all night.

'Afstralia!' I was back in the limelight of Mr Ibrahim's attention.

'Kazakhstan!' We clanked tin cups and drank a toast to internationalism. I had a feeling Mr Ibrahim knew a bit more about it than I did.

'All my monies losing, Afstralia, many many monies losing when Russians come.' His eyes were sad, his shoulders slumped.

'You had to leave Afghanistan?'

'No. I am already live in Tashkent, but my brothers sending me things.'

'What things?'

'Televisions! Televisions very many, very good. Best televisions, Japanese, best colour televisions. All gone, Afstralia. Russians come to mountains, shoots camels. Bang bang bang!' He riddled me with automatic rifle fire. I gulped my vodka.

'Camels? They shot your camels?'

'Camels carry televisions, Afstralia. All camels carrying televisions. Trucks no good in mountains, break televisions. Camels good.'

'How many televisions did you have?'

'Three hundreds televisions, Afstralia. Three hundreds televisions all gone. Bang bang bang!'

FOURTEEN

In the morning, everyone had a sore head, including me. Mr Ibrahim had succumbed to drink and exhaustion some time in the early hours of the morning, and was now snoring so loudly that Mahmoud Abdul could not sleep through it. For a man who didn't drink or smoke, poor Mahmoud Abdul was looking pretty rough himself. Kerry and Aislinn were up early, running up and down the corridor in their long-johns, and were soon joined by the Pakistanis, emerging to take the morning air, in their long-johns. It looked like the Extended Care Wing in some hospital for people with Dress Sense Disability. The day was bright and cold, with snow lying on the ground; patchy, but getting deeper as we went north.

We reached Turkestan station at about 10 o'clock, and everybody got off the train for a little fresh air and calisthenics. The *babushkas* were out in force, selling dried fish, onions, beer and packets of soft cheese wrapped in paper. I crossed the tracks to a tiny stall which sold cigarettes and chocolates. The queue was already long, so I had to wait, stamping my feet for warmth and regretting that I'd left my overcoat on the train. Finally I reached the counter, and fished out enough roubles to pay for some cigarettes and sweets. As the woman handed me my change, there was a bit of commotion behind me and I turned to see the train pulling out of the station, slowly gathering speed. In a panic, ten of us leapt and tripped over the icy rails and sprinted full stretch for the opposite platform, spilling coins and cigarettes in all directions. A thoughtful conductor had left a few doors open. We grabbed at the hand-rails and dragged each other up on to the now briskly accelerating train. The conductor was all smiles, clapping us on the back and congratulating us on our race. He looked pleased enough to be a man who had won a bet.

The train rattled along at a steady rate, the view unchanging as we traversed hundreds of kilometres of central Kazakhstan. It was well dark by the time we reached the salty marshes of the Syr Darya delta, and we had no glimpse of the Aral Sea into which it emptied.

At dinner that night, our waitress sombrely repeated the menu. Pork. Salad. Rice. But we enjoyed it all the same, and the girls experimented with bottles of fizzy pear and cherry drinks bought on the station platforms. The evening was more subdued than the previous one, but Mr Ibrahim was in fine form, staggering along the corridor to greet everyone and share a few glasses of his inexhaustible supply of vodka. We got him out of our compartment with some difficulty, late at night, after he had assured us of his undying brotherhood a dozen times over, and promised that if we should ever visit Afghanistan, we need only mention his name at the border, and the whole country would be at our disposal.

I woke once, in the small hours of the morning, when the train stopped at some remote little station on the steppes. The night was crystalline; deep drifts of snow covered the fields, and the station lights sparkled with frost. In front of a wooden station house, a woman in a thick, belted greatcoat and stout boots saluted the train as it pulled away into the deep-frozen night. We were in Russia.

We pulled in to Moscow's Kazanski Station in the early afternoon. There was a lot of excitement on the train, as everyone changed into their best city clothes. The Pakistanis became elegant in leather jackets and expensive shoes. Mr Ibrahim, apparently sober, was finely turned out in a pin-striped suit. We didn't have much of anything to change into, so we settled for brushing down our coats and repacking our bags. One of the Russian boys gave us detailed and complicated instructions for the Metro, which I attempted to memorise, and promptly forgot. I had no idea at all where we were going to stay, or how to go about getting tickets for the train to Budapest.

We descended the steps into the Moscow Metro with the three Pakistanis in tow. They looked a bit stunned by the noise and the busy crowds of people thundering along the passages, pouring down staircases and crowding the platforms. I tried to convince them there was no point in following us, since we hadn't a clue where to go, but they seemed reluctant to turn us loose. The station was a complex warren of overpasses, tunnels, escalators and staircases. We tried to follow the signs in Cyrillic lettering, aiming for central Moscow. The Pakistanis, for reasons we couldn't clearly understand, wanted to reach the Central Post Office, and kept repeating this like a mantra. The girls thought all of it great fun, and they pointed at the ornate chandeliers, the heroic statuary and the vivid frescos that made the whole Moscow Metro look like a museum for the collection of Socialist Realism. The Pakistanis met an English-speaking Muscovite who told them where to get off for the Central Post Office. They looked doubtful, but followed his instructions. The last we saw of them, they were standing on the platform as the train drew out, waving bleakly at us.

We found what seemed to be a main station, and rode a very long, antique escalator up to the daylight. The day was bright and bitterly cold. We huddled inside the glass doors of the Metro entrance, reluctant to face the city. Outside the girls found, of all things, an icecream vendor and returned triumphant with blocks of sweet vanilla icecream. I offered to go and look for a hotel, if Dorcas would mind the children and the bags. A huge sign announced 'Hotel Metropole' on the building across the street. It seemed a start, at least.

Inside the revolving doors, the Russian Empire of Czar Nicholas I had never faded. A string quartet played Vivaldi in the corner. There were rich people everywhere, sipping tea from elegant crystal glasses in silver filigree holders. Uniformed bellhops and porters glided over the oriental carpets as if on tiny electric wheels. The receptionist was poised, impeccably dressed and spoke four languages. Play this cool, I thought. Seasoned, sophisticated, wealthy traveller returns from darkest Central Asia, desires comfortable accommodation.

'Ah, have you got any rooms?'

'Certainly sir, and for how many people?'

'Well, there are five of us, actually.'

'And would you prefer a suite, or adjoining rooms?'

'Well . . . could I see your rates?'

'Of course. Here you are.'

She passed a printed card across the counter and waited indulgently while I read it. Single rooms at the Hotel Metropole started off conservatively at US$300 a night, warmed up around $500 for a double, and went straight off into the stratosphere for suites. I coughed. The receptionist smiled pleasantly.

'I, ahh. I was looking for something a little more . . . '

'They are a bit expensive, aren't they? Would you like me to help you find something a bit more reasonable?'

'Yes, please.'

She led me to a desk off to the side, and gave me a chair, while she rang around a few of the other hotels. They did not offer this kind of service in London, New York or in Sydney, I thought. More likely a boot in the pants and an escort to the trade's entrance. She was wonderful. On the fourth call, she looked up and smiled at me, then wrote something down.

'It seems this hotel can do a triple room with an extra bed. It's not too expensive. I'll show you how to get there on this map.'

'Is it far away?'

'No, just a few stops on the Metro.'

'I don't know how to thank you.'

'Please. It's no trouble. Enjoy your stay in Moscow.'

I puzzled over the Cyrillic writing on the little card she gave me, but the directions on the Metro map were clear enough.

'Excuse me, but what's the hotel called?'

'It's the Gorbachev Fund Hotel. For his retirement, you see?'

We left the Metro at Leningradsky Prospekt, and trudged a little further along the icy pavements. Banks of thick, white snow lay on either side of the wide road, and a set of tram lines ran up the middle. With the winter sun dropping behind the buildings, it was becoming frighteningly cold very quickly. I was keen to get the children inside, somewhere, before their little fingers started falling off. The Gorbachev Fund Hotel was a great barn-like building, with a high-security court-yard, iron railings and an alert guard, who telephoned the desk before allowing us to pass. Once inside, though, our room was great: two adjoining bedrooms, lots of hot water and a bathtub. We scrubbed and washed and hung up t-shirts to dry on the heated bath-rails. With hair combed and shoes cleaned, we went in search of dinner.

It was a big hotel, but curiously empty. It looked as if it had been designed for large groups—all the lounges were cavernous, and the cafeteria on the second floor could have seated several hundred. I discovered that they took roubles, unlike the more expensive restaurant next door, which announced plainly that only US dollars were considered. We chose the cafeteria. Business was slow, with just a few tables of American and German guests. Two waitresses served food to the tables, and although they spoke no English, we had little trouble ordering a meal in simple Russian and broken German.

* * *

'Russian service', in the rather old-fashioned terminology of the hotel trade, once meant food served directly from the kitchen on a plate, in a succession of courses. It's now so familiar to be served your soup, followed by a hot or cold entrée, then a main course with vegetables, then dessert, that we've quite forgotten that there's any other way to do it. But in the early 19th century, it wasn't the proper thing at all, because *service a la française* was still the rage. This meant that all the food was served at once, placed on the table on platters, so that diners could admire the fantastical decorations and elaborate garnishing. If you were sitting at a formal dinner table, you were expected to content yourself by picking at the array of dishes nearest you, not necessarily the same dishes available to someone on the other side of the table. A little cheating was allowed (you could ask a neighbour to pass you something) but it was considered rude, or greedy, to do it more than once or twice. So, if you were uncommonly fond of roast turkey, and it happened to be at the other end of the table, it was more or less stiff bikkies. Since everything sat on the table all night, there was no expectation that the food be served hot—you just took it as it came. Whole roast peacocks and such were thought to be hugely impressive, so they would be carried in and presented entire, before they were removed, carved and returned to the table on platters. Aristocratic hosts displayed their wealth and class by serving dozens of different dishes all at once, rather like a modern buffet table.

Antoine Carême, the great French chef, visited Russia in the early 1800s, and noted that they did things differently there. 'Not suitable,' he sniffed, 'for French cuisine.' But when another French chef named Felix Dubois returned from service with the Russian nobleman Prince Orloff in the 1870s, Paris was ready for a new fashion, and took to the new 'Russian' style immediately. This meant that the *haut monde* had to hire a whole lot more servants, because getting carefully garnished, individual portions of hot food to the table all at once required more chefs and many more waiters. This was very expensive, since you had to dress them all up in the clothing of the previous century, and that suited everyone just fine, because gaudy, conspicuous over-consumption was just as popular then as it is in Hollywood today. The new 'Russian service' didn't suit everyone, of course, and some of the more intransigent aristocracy (notably the English) refused to have a bar of it, and continued with a modified version of the old French system, which came to be known as 'silver service'. The name was no coincidence, since one of the bitterest complaints from the old English gentry was that the new style did not allow them to show off the family silver and thus impress the lower orders.

At the Gorbachev Fund Hotel our food arrived in little platefuls, and it was very good. There were several choices for each course, and we had tried most of them by the time we finished. A cold salad of diced vegetables bound in mayonnaise rang a bell, then I remembered that I'd eaten the same dish as a child, and that it had been called 'Russian salad'. There was good smoked salmon (at about 50 cents a plate, we had a few of those), onion soup, fresh rye bread and braised beef, chicken cutlets and icecream with a lovely blackcurrant sauce. We could drink water, tea or orange juice, but they did not serve wine or alcohol, and looked at me askance when I asked for it.

Alcohol was not illegal. You could buy beer or vodka from any one of a dozen street peddlers, in sealed 500 ml bottles with factory stamps and fancy labels. The price was fairly standard all over the city. In government shops, you could buy vodka, but never beer. That there was an alcohol problem I could well believe, since I'd seen bus drivers standing around depots sharing bottles of vodka at nine o'clock in the morning. I could find no wine shops, and bars were rare, except in the hard-currency confines of the plush hotels, where Moscow yuppies were knocking back shots of Johnnie Walker at US$5 a pop. In the hard-currency shops, Russian vodka hardly got a look in. The brands of choice were Polish and Finnish, but for the real high-rollers, there was a bottle of Smirnoff Silver Label, imported all the way from New Jersey.

After dinner, with the girls packed off to watch television in the room, Dorcas and I went into a sort of coffee lounge next door to the restaurant, where we could have small cups of lovely black Turkish coffee and plates of rum babas or chocolate eclairs. A large, imposing woman in a severe black suit was serving behind the counter. I asked, hesitantly, if there was such a thing as an after-dinner drink to be had. She gave me a mock-stern look, then produced a bottle of vodka from under the counter and poured me a generous 100 grams with an indulgent smile.

Dorcas took the girls off the next day to explore central Moscow, while I went in search of train tickets again. I took the Metro to Kievsky Station, from which the Budapest train departed, but I was defeated by the confusing ticket windows, and the short shrift I got from the gruff ticket clerks. 'Intourist' they growled at me, as soon as it became clear that I was a foreigner. The directions were vague, but I wandered in the direction they pointed, looking for the Intourist office.

I found myself in the middle of an informal market, in the square in front of the station. It was fascinating to watch how this worked. A constant crowd milled about with string bags at the ready, keeping an eye out for whatever went on sale. A man opened a suitcase on the ground, and displayed 20 kilos of fat smoked sausages tied with string. The rush was on. People waved crumpled notes at him wildly, grabbing sausages loosely wrapped in bits of brown paper and shoving them deep into their coat pockets. In minutes, all the sausages were gone, the man packed up his suitcase and left. Some of the vendors had enough to justify setting up wooden stalls, and there was a brisk trade in home-bottled cucumbers, smoked cheese, dried peppers, fish, some very wizened apples and the occasional pile of hot-house tomatoes. One man had an amazing display of pineapples, which were selling for 1000 roubles each, a good deal more than a week's wages for a Moscow bus driver. Another had a neat plastic tray full of kiwifruit, a hopelessly exotic luxury in Russia in early March. Food, foreign liquors and cigarettes were certainly getting into the country, by whatever informal arrangement, and the farmers had discovered that a sackful of onions was worth more than a handful of roubles.

I found the Intourist office in good time, and enquired about tickets for all of us to Budapest. It wasn't a problem, they told me, but payment would be in US dollars cash only, and no discussions would be entered into. This was something of a nuisance, since we'd already converted a lot of money into roubles, thinking that we'd need them for the train. Converting roubles back into hard currency was, in theory, possible, but difficult. I paid the bill with our dwindling supply of dollars, the price very high compared to similar distances we'd already travelled on Russian trains. Intourist once had an absolute monopoly on foreigners travelling inside the Soviet Union, and they can't seem to get out of the habit of charging ten times the going rate for everything.

On the way back in the Metro, I noticed more traders, with an odd selection of goods for sale. A woman held up a pink baby suit, a man around the corner held up a telephone. Another had a box of Eveready batteries, the one beside him a handful of cheap lipsticks. A beggar-woman held out a filthy hand for a few coins. The crowds hurried by, busy as people in big cities always are.

We found some food shops near the hotel, and loaded up with supplies again for the two nights on the train to Budapest. The Russian shopping system is based on the principle that anything worth having is worth queuing up for. First you queued to have a look at what was on offer: there were reasonable supplies of butter, margarine, meat, chickens, cheese, grains and the inevitable sausage. You then queued up at the cashier, to tell her what you wanted and to pay for it. The last hurdle was the queue for service, when you handed over your receipt and got your half-kilo of sausage and your carton of milk.

The girls had some things to collect as well, but most of their business could be transacted at the little kiosks which sold chocolate, sweets and cigarettes. All along, they'd been given pocket money once a week, just as they had at home. Whichever country we were in, they received the local equivalent of a couple of dollars to go and buy what they could find. In China, they had acquired a keen interest in exchange rates, and a fine appreciation of the point spread between the official rate and the black-market rate. If the de facto currency, against which all others were measured, was the US dollar, it was the Mars Bar which set the standard for the girls. They managed to find supplies of chocolate in the most unlikely places, from the back streets of Shanghai to the bazaars of Tashkent. In Russia, the disastrous state of the economy meant that they were effectively rouble millionaires, since their pocket money translated into the average weekly wage for a shop assistant. Equipped with bundles of 5-rouble notes, they cornered the local market in Mars Bars, and returned from their shopping expedition bristling with the things.

All that remained was to find some bread, and for that I set off alone to find a bakery. There wasn't one in sight, so I pulled out my Russian phrase book and set to work memorising the words for 'Excuse me, but is there a bakery anywhere around here?' This involved sitting on a park bench and mumbling to myself, while taking regular nips from a half-bottle of vodka which had somehow found its way into my coat pocket. No one took any notice, since the park benches were full of hairy, scruffy-looking people muttering to themselves and drinking vodka. At length, I had it. I accosted the first *babushka* who came along, popped my question in a stage-Russian accent heady with vodka fumes, and was inordinately pleased with myself when the woman understood me perfectly and pointed me in the right direction.

The train ride from Moscow was comfortable and interesting, as we passed through the more populous part of the country, and had a look at dozens of small towns. Most of them consisted of a train station, a school, a shop or dispensary of some sort and a few dozen wooden buildings, then the huge fields of the collective farms. Many of these seemed to be lying fallow, while bare-chested farmers tilled small private plots of potatoes or onions in the weak spring sunshine. I saw horses hitched to old wooden ploughs, while giant tractors stood idle on the collective's land. Women in headscarves, thick and red-armed, loaded fodder onto wooden carts or cleared irrigation ditches with long-handled shovels.

Smoking was banned in the carriages, as on all Russian trains, so a sort of club formed in the small connecting compartments between the carriages. Here, it was permitted to smoke, and the dense fug of cigarette smoke would put anyone off who did not have reason to be there. On the other hand, I found some of the most interesting conversations happened in the 'smoking compartment' since the men I met (I never saw a woman once) were not the ones who would introduce themselves to foreigners willingly. They spoke no English. I spoke no Russian. But standing chest to chest with someone, puffing thoughtfully on a cigarette, it was almost impossible to avoid some kind of an exchange. This would often begin with a tap on my chest. 'Amyeriki?' they'd ask. 'Nyet, Afstralii.' This aroused great interest, because Australia, it seemed, was a popular country, and if Americans were common enough in the big cities, Australians were not.

I learnt that not all Russians spoke the same language, and that they were inclined to identify themselves first as Ukrainians, Carpathians, Tadzhiks or Georgians, and only Russians as an afterthought. Nor were they shy about telling me their own biographies in their native language. Sometimes, another would join in to translate into Russian or smatterings of German or English. There was a lot of talk, demonstrative and intense, but none of us could understand one word in twenty. Surprisingly, this didn't hinder the conversation, and I found myself understanding quite complicated stories about how someone's brother had been caught on the other side of the border after the Great Patriotic War, and now lived comfortably in Vienna or Melbourne. We made jokes about Australian kangaroos and told each other what we did for a living. We swapped cigarettes constantly, an essential piece of social exchange in Russian society, and one that I would have reason to use before much longer.

We slept comfortably and got up in the morning for a good wash in the mercifully clean bathrooms, put away the bedclothes and prepared a breakfast of bread and jam, cheese and oranges. We were aware of passing the Ukranian border, because the train stopped briefly to pick up a squad of Ukranian soldiers, who had been pressed into service as border guards, following the declaration of independence in 1992. These were no scruffy Chinese border guards in shabby uniforms; they were serious-looking soldiers in camouflage battle-dress, carrying Kalashnikov rifles and walkie-talkies. They were, however, polite and well disciplined, and when one of them knocked on the door of our compartment, I was ready with our passports and Russian visas. The soldier examined these carefully, then looked up at me.

'Ukraine visa?' he said.

'Russian visa.' I pointed to the grey cardboard folder with our photographs on it.

'No Ukraine visa?'

'Russian visa. See, here it says Moscow, Kiev, Budapest.'

He shook his head doubtfully. He gestured for me to come with him. I expected to go along the corridor to the conductor's compartment, but he stopped me with a hand on my chest. He indicated I should put on my shoes and take my coat. I wasn't all that pleased with this development. Where were we going that I would need my overcoat? I swapped a glance with Dorcas, shrugged, and went off with him.

The commanding officer was a tough, spare man in his forties. He had set himself up in the conductor's compartment, and listened to the soldier's account while I stood around uncomfortably. The officer asked questions through the conductor, whose English was patchy but serviceable.

'You have no Ukranian visa for yourself or your family?'

'I didn't know we needed one. Look, these visas were issued in Shanghai. No Ukraine embassy in China.'

'This is a problem. You have no visa.'

'Can I get one?'

'This is not the point. You are already in the Ukraine without a visa.'

'But we're going straight through to Budapest.'

'I am sorry, you must get off the train at the next stop. We must speak to Kiev on the telephone, do you understand?'

'Yes, all right.'

I went back to Dorcas and told her the news. She was taking it very well.

'Yes, dear. Well, don't do anything silly, will you? We'll stay here.' What did she think I was going to do, make a break for it? I gathered up my hat, my cigarettes, our passports and some money. Like the condemned man, I was led down the corridor. A childish voice rang out.

'Daddy!' Aislinn's blonde head stuck out of the doorway of our compartment.

'Yes, sweetheart?' I was ready to console her, tell her it would be all right, Daddy was just going away with the nice soldiers for a little while.

'Can I have your bread roll?'

When the train pulled up at the next halt, I was with the sergeant near the door. He grinned at me. *'Dyesyat minutii,'* he said holding up ten fingers. Great. We had ten minutes to sort out whatever these guys wanted, then the train would leave, with us or without us. He had the door open before we stopped moving and sprang out like a good paratrooper, landing on the run. I leapt out like a bad tourist and nearly brained myself on the door. We trotted down the platform together. He looked like he could do this for the rest of the day. I was already regretting my sedentary habits. We reached the end of the platform, and took off along a dirt track towards a squat lighthouse, evidently what passed for GHQ in this tiny Ukranian hamlet. The sergeant sprinted up the stairs, I wheezed along after him.

Upstairs, things looked grim and military. A hard-faced officer with binoculars around his neck glared at me. The sergeant was explaining fast. I was grinning foolishly and panting. The officer demanded my passport. Without looking at it, he barked:

'Amyeriki?'

'Nyet. Irlandii.' I wasn't about to get all complicated about country of residence. It was an Irish passport, therefore I was Irish.

'Vasha zhena. Angliski?' Your wife's English?

'Da.'

This seemed to amuse him greatly. He looked around his staff, made some sort of joke about the English and the Irish. Everybody chuckled the way soldiers do when their commanding officer makes a joke. I chuckled too, and started handing out Marlboros in all directions. We all lit up. The CO looked at me through his smoke, eyes narrowed. He'd been watching too many war movies. He laughed and slapped my arm, handed me back the passports and told us to get lost. We did, in a hurry. The sergeant and I sprinted back to the train with less than a minute to spare.

I opened the door of our compartment and took off my hat. It should have been a poignant moment, returned to the bosom of my family. They'd packed away the food and were playing word games.

'Hey, what's happened to my breakfast?'

'We've finished breakfast, you'll have to wait for lunch.'

'Mummy said you might not be back, so we should eat yours, too.'

'Thanks.'

The last stop before Budapest was at the border post at Cop, which we reached at some ungodly hour in the morning. Half asleep, we had to deal with yet more border guards, and one of them had some bad news for us. I had about 80 000 roubles left, which I'd been assured we could change at the border for the $100 or so it was worth. But the currency inspector shook his head sadly.

'There is no bank here. You should have changed your roubles in Moscow.'

'I tried to. They told me I must do it at the border.'

'I'm sorry, but there's no bank here.'

'Well, never mind, we'll be coming back through Russia in a couple of months. We'll use them up then.'

'Sorry, you can't do that, either.'

'Why not?'

'Because it is not permitted to take roubles out of the country.'

We had to settle for an official receipt, and an assurance that if we came through the same border post in two months' time, we could collect our money on demand. It wasn't something I was planning to bank on.

FIFTEEN

After two months of travel in China and Russia, we had almost forgotten what it was like to enjoy the normal conveniences of a western city, but our arrival in Budapest brought it all flooding back. There were intelligible signs and station buffets loaded with familiar foods. There were newspapers in several languages. There was a hotel booking office with free city maps for the taking. We were pathetically grateful. I stared in awe at a proper currency exchange counter, with posted rates and little national flags next to the numbers. This is bliss, I thought. Welcome to Europe. Budapest had the only Metro I'd ever seen that operated on the honour system. You bought a book of tickets at the counter and then were expected to stamp them yourself when you used a tram, a train or a bus. The tourists seemed to be the only ones cheating.

We found a cheap and cheerful traveller's hostel on the Pest side of the Danube, up near the botanical gardens and zoo. It was busy and friendly, and the young people working there were great. For the first time in months, we were talking to other travellers, from Australia and South America, Europe, the US and the Middle East. Speaking to one of the Hungarian girls in the office, I remarked on the number of red, white and green Hungarian flags flying around the city. She told me we'd arrived on Hungarian National Day, a good-natured celebration of the Hungarian rising against the Hapsburg Empire in 1848. The anniversary had a keener edge of national pride following the departure of the last Soviet military forces in 1991.

We dumped our bags and took off for the city centre. The day was glorious, sunny and mild, and the city looked marvellous. We walked along the Danube, past the 19th century neo-Gothic Parliament building, a combination of St Paul's Cathedral and Westminster in bronze-coloured stone. We looked across the river at the high rocky bluffs the Roman legions had defended when the Danube was a Roman frontier 2000 years ago. Bits of their military camps, temples and roads were still to be seen all over the city. The Celts had been there before them, and Attila's Huns over-ran the place in the 5th century. The Magyars, a tribe from the Volga area, moved in during the 10th century, which made them fairly recent arrivals by European standards. They hadn't had an easy time of it. They had only just gotten themselves established when disaster struck, in the form of the Mongolian Horde.

When Temujin, the Genghis Khan, exploded out of the Dzungarian Gate with 30 000 horsemen in 1219, his armies laid waste to all of Turkestan, then drove westward across Persia to threaten Asia Minor. Northern armies, under the Khan's generals, invaded Siberia and Poland. Temujin died in 1227, but the incredible expansion of the Mongol Empire continued with no less ferocity under his son, Ogodai Khan, and by 1236, Russian Georgia had fallen, followed by Kiev in 1240. The Hungarian King Bela IV went to war, but he was no match for the Mongolian cavalry, who slaughtered the Hungarians in a great battle in April 1241. Buda fell to the Mongols, and they gathered their strength for the push on to Vienna and the European heartland. Things were looking pretty grim for feudal Europe, and history might have taken a very different course if Ogadai Khan had not died suddenly in December of that year.

The clan-like structure of the Mongolians required all the great generals and chiefs to be physically present for the election of a new Khan. This had happened before, when Temujin died, but then the vote had been quick, and the battles had resumed under the leadership of his son. When Ogodai perished in 1241, the succession was not so easily accomplished. Political intrigue and argument kept many of the generals in the Mongolian capital of Karakorum for years, and the conquered lands in eastern Europe were allowed to fall back into the hands of local rulers. King Bela IV returned from exile to pick up the pieces of his shattered kingdom, and the Mongols never again threatened central Europe, although they retained a stranglehold on Russia for another 200 years, isolating it from the rapid changes that would lead the western kingdoms and city-states into the Renaissance.

Buda and Pest, the twin cities across the river, had only been combined in the last century, after a long and complicated history of rising and falling kings, peasant revolutions, Turkish invasion, Hapsburg domination and an unerring knack for picking the wrong side in European wars. As part of the Austro-Hungarian Empire, the Hungarians were badly mauled in World Wars I and II, then had to put up with heavy Soviet influence culminating in the bloody repression of a nationalist rising in 1956. Along the way, they managed to lose two-thirds of their country to the Ukraine, Austria, Czechoslovakia and Romania. Having finally booted everyone out, appointed their own government, and chosen for their president a famous writer who'd been in jail for political subversion, it was no wonder they were celebrating Hungarian National Day with such enthusiasm.

It was spring, and daffodils were already out in the city parks. We walked through the old sections of the city, fascinated by the jumble of architectural styles that had survived, or had been restored since World War II. Baroque and neo-Classical seemed to be the front runners, but there were fine examples of Gothic, neo-Gothic, Moorish and Art Nouveau styles too. It was hard to tell what was original and what had been rebuilt, because the Hungarians, like the Chinese, are very clever at restoration of old buildings. St Istvan's Basilica was a good example, a huge mouldering 19th century pile of blackened statuary and collapsing roofs which was being sandblasted and shored up even as we watched.

Budapest is a city famous for its food, no less than Paris, and we were looking forward to it. The Magyars have a cooking style all their own, based on rich sauces, often laced with paprika and sour cream, but the range goes much further, we discovered. The Hungarian pastrycooks insist that they taught the Viennese how to make pastries, and I was delighted to learn that they had a Museum of Pastrycooking in this city of a hundred museums. Although Hungary was in theory still a socialist state, there was nothing Russian about their food shops. They were extravagantly well-stocked with pork (smoked, spiced, cooked and made into a score of different sausages), with cheeses soft and aged, with cream, butter, liqueurs and wines, beautiful pastries and fancy breads. Even the people shopping in them looked great— elegantly turned-out women and courtly old gentlemen with gloves and walking sticks. I suspected we were suffering from post-Asian shock, but everything seemed so wonderfully civilised and clean.

The staff at the hostel told us about a good restaurant across the river in Buda, not expensive, and real Hungarian cooking. I took directions carefully, but we still managed to get lost. It was worth finding, the Markus Etterem, and we went back to it several times to taste almost everything on the menu. We feasted on *gulyás* (not a stew, but a soup), thick with beef, paprika, potato and sour cream. Another soup, made with chunks of smoked pork, sausage and brown beans, was addictive, and the huge bowls served were enough to make a meal. The *paprikas* stews of lamb, pork or beef tripe were delicious, served with the free-form egg noodles the Germans call *spätzle*. Turkey was often used, pounded flat like a schnitzel, coated in a delicate *parisienne* batter and then fried in butter. I didn't want to think about the quantities of rich goose fat and pork lard we were eating, but the Hungarians like to cook with them, and the richness of flavour was irresistible. The meatiness of the cooking was nicely offset by small fresh salads of sliced cucumber or tomato with sharp vinegar dressings. I was impressed. I caught myself stopping in the street, reading all the menus I could find.

In English-speaking countries, I was used to menus that read like a second-year creative writing class, full of 'pan-seared fillets of baby salmon' and 'crisp parcels of tender young vegetables'. The amount of effort that went into writing the menu often overshadowed the effort put into the cooking. In countries where food was enjoyed and appreciated for itself (rather than as a vehicle for social climbing), I noticed that the habit was quite the opposite. In China, a menu looked like a newspaper, full of columns of closely set type, often listing more than 100 dishes even in a modest restaurant. The number of dishes a chef could prepare was a mark of his skill, and if he prepared Beggar's Chicken, for instance, the resulting dish would be carefully examined for its faithfulness to the traditional recipe, the subtlety of the flavour and the arrangement on the platter. In France, menus tended to be lists of foods, and the better the restaurant, the longer the list. If you were served a *truite au bleu*, you judged it on freshness and flavour, not on the breathiness of the description on the menu.

The Hungarian love of good cooking was written in its menus. It wasn't unusual to see 30 or 40 dishes listed, followed by a dozen or more desserts. They went by simple names: stuffed peppers, hunter's salad, mixed grill, chicken with paprika—but the flavours were superb.

The girls fell in love with Hungarian pancakes, either savoury (pancakes *Hortobágyi*, made with minced beef and sour cream) or sweet (they discovered the luscious *Gundel* crêpes, filled with nut and raisin paste, topped with chocolate sauce). They also announced that we didn't need to go loping off halfway across the city to find funny little restaurants, they were quite content with the 'Non-Stop Buffé' straight across the street from the hostel. This was the Budapest equivalent of the fast food joint, a small hot-food counter that dispensed coffee, strudel, fried chicken, pizza bread and icecream at any time of day or night. Even at this level, the Hungarians were discerning eaters; most of the food was prepared on the premises in a tiny, clean and well-organised kitchen. A similar place in Australia would be serving frozen hamburgers and dried-up meat pies; here they were stuffing mushrooms and roasting turkey. Prices were about the same, but the quality of the food was much better.

The downstairs lounge at the hostel was a proper travellers' club, and every night there was a long round of conversation, card games and travel stories in six languages, fuelled by frequent trips to the shop for more bottles of good Czech beer and Hungarian wine. Four of the staff were Palestinians, and I struck up a conversation with a fellow the Hungarian girls called 'Danny De Vito', a roly-poly little guy who worked as the night manager. He told me that he and his friends had come to Hungary as refugees, after Israel invaded Lebanon in 1982. When he heard that I was a chef, he became very excited, promising that he would make me his favourite dish, Palestinian chicken, as soon as he could get hold of the ingredients. He was as good as his word, and the following evening, I followed him into a tiny kitchen to watch him make it.

He heated a pan of oil and fried slices of potato, aubergine, onion and cauliflower, lifted them out when they had browned slightly, and left them to drain. He was a meticulous cook—every piece had to be cooked just so, and he kept up a continuous description of what he was doing. When he had finished the vegetables, he layered them in another pot, starting with the potatoes. The chicken followed, cut into joints, but not sealed. He scattered a handful of rice between each layer, finishing with a thicker layer of rice. He unwrapped a twist of paper. 'From the Palestine shop,' he said, significantly. This was a mixture of ground spices, which he dissolved in hot water, then added to the pot. I could see saffron, and smell cinnamon, cumin, pepper and other, more elusive ingredients. He added salt, then closed the pot and left it to steam. He called his friends together and they set a table, all the Palestinians and me. When 'Danny' brought the dish to the table, he had turned it out of the pot, upside down, so now there was a great mound of yellow, spice-fragrant rice, topped with steamed chicken and slices of tender vegetables. We went at it with spoons and fingers eagerly. For me, it was an interesting new dish, and a method I hadn't seen before. For the Palestinians, it was a taste of home.

We left Budapest reluctantly, but we knew we'd have a second chance, because our route back would start from here—north again to Moscow, then across Russia on the Trans-Siberian Express to Beijing. We spent a day wandering around the brilliant museums in the old Castle District (I was disappointed to find the Museum of Pastrycooks closed), then had dinner in a very fervent vegetarian restaurant (brown rice, homespun table mats, and a resident folk singer). The following morning, we caught the train for Prague, an easy day trip from Budapest.

The Czech and Slovak republics were in the process of splitting up, the formal declaration having been signed in January 1993. The rules regarding visas and border control were still a bit confused, but in the end, we had no problem at all; the immigration control was as perfunctory and casual as it would be in the rest of Europe. We were pleased to be able to use the Eurail passes we'd bought before leaving Australia. Not only were they good for any train (without the necessity of buying a ticket), but they also entitled us to camp out in the first class compartments—a lovely luxury, since they were seldom full.

Prague looked like a well-preserved cuckoo clock, full of medieval buildings and ornate facades. It was certainly beautiful, but in a severe, Germanic style that I found a little chilly after the romantic atmosphere of Budapest. We got the address of an inexpensive pension from a booking agency, and checked into a quiet, extremely clean place that looked like it once might have been a bürgermeister's mansion. It had a cool, well-scrubbed, somehow Lutheran air about it. Every door had a key, and silence was the rule. No late-night pool games or boozy travellers' parties here, I thought.

We found dinner in a busy, smoky local pub, where we squeezed on to a long table between stout Czech housewives and their husbands. The food was plain, German in style, leaning heavily towards sausage, sauerkraut and fried potatoes. The beer got far more attention than the food. Half-litres of excellent Pilsener were disappearing down the collective throat at a rate of knots, and I felt obliged to defend the honour of Australian beer-drinkers, to the point where I was weaving pleasantly as we walked home.

Prague supported two English-language publications, a daily newspaper and a weekly magazine, which were entertaining and interesting. There had obviously been a wave of immigration in the wake of Vaclev Havel's 'Velvet Revolution' in 1989 and the Soviet dissolution that followed it. From the articles and the many advertisements, we gathered that a lot of the new arrivals were American college students, clutching freshly minted MBAs and looking for business opportunities in newly liberated eastern Europe. The Czech Republic, and Prague in particular, had gained a new social class of English-speaking yuppies almost overnight. In between the ads for late-night dance parties, second-hand Porsches, English teaching posts and ski equipment, there was some biting satire on social habits in the new Czech society.

We walked down Václavské námestí, the central avenue that runs from the gloriously ornate National Museum down to the Old Town. The traffic was brisk and the pavements full of Italian and German tour groups, filing in to expensive restaurants. The prices on the tourist menus outside were ferocious, and I could understand why the American Express office and the McDonald's restaurant looked like the busiest places in town.

In the Old Town Square, a marvellous 14th century clock tower was faced with its original clock, a beautiful medieval treasure with painted apostles, phases of the moon, intricate gears and gilded arms. A plaque to the side explained its history, adding the rather depressing information that when the master clock-maker had finished this, his life-work, his grateful aristocratic patron had the craftsman's eyes put out, so that he could never make another.

The kids were getting a little bored with my enthusiasm for old buildings, but they soldiered on bravely through Prague's winding lanes. We visited the strange, dark Old Synagogue, built in 1270, and Prague Castle, high on the hill overlooking the river. I was entranced by St Vitus's Cathedral, a huge High Gothic masterpiece, crusted with gargoyles and illuminated windows, but all my gabbling about fan vaults and tracery screens, I could tell, was falling on deaf ears. By the time we reached the National Gallery, the kids were becoming mutinous, and flatly refused to be shown the priceless collection of medieval woodcuts and religious statuary.

'They're exhausted,' Dorcas said. 'So am I. You go in by yourself.'

'But they might never see this stuff again!'

'They might never speak to you again if you drag them around museums and churches for another four hours. Go on, I'll buy them some icecreams, and we'll wait for you out here.'

'All right, but . . . '

'I'll come with you, Dad.' Clare took my arm.

'Great! Wait 'til you see, they've got Dürers, and Breughels, and . . .'

'But you have to buy me an icecream, too, when we come out.'

'OK, it's a deal.'

On our last evening, I insisted on tracking down a small Czech restaurant on the other side of the river, which had been extravagantly recommended in one of the English-language papers. Dorcas was resigned, but the girls couldn't understand why I went to the bother, when there was a perfectly good McDonald's right downtown. We took the Metro, then a tram, finally getting off in an industrial neighbourhood miles from the river.

We trudged around the streets, quite baffled by the Prague street signs, which seemed to change their minds every 200 metres or so. I tried asking questions, but this was clearly not a tourist neighbourhood, and my attempts at broken German got me nothing but blank looks. Speaking Czech was out of the question, since it is one of Europe's more unpronounceable languages, slightly ahead of Albanian and just behind Polish on the incomprehensible scale. It got dark. It was getting colder, but I still couldn't find the place. We retraced our steps to the tram station and started again. This time, I found the right street, and the restaurant, which looked warm and cosy and fine.

We were shown to a table. The waiter shook his head and raised his hands with a smile when I tried him on English, French and German. We had to be content with menus all around. I obtained beer and lemonade by leaning over the bar and pointing at the stuff.

The menu presented a few problems, as it was entirely in Czech, a language even more baffling in print than in speech. 'Very authentic cooking' the newspaper had said, 'Prague specialties that are getting hard to find these days.' Could these be the *parék v rohliku*, or possibly the *cuckrárny zmrzlina*? No help from the waiter, who looked on indulgently. Maybe some *pivnice ve skorepce*, with a side plate of *knedelky*. I had never seen a menu so utterly untranslatable; I could see why they hadn't bothered trying. The Chinese used the same four characters all the time for rice, chicken, beef and fish. If I couldn't read Russian, at least I could sound out 'kuttelet' or 'bifstek', and wave my hand to indicate vegetables, bread, trimmings, whatever comes with it. Most countries have slipped at least a few of their dishes on to the international menu, so you can order a kebab, a lasagne, a tortilla or some sushi without too much trouble. But *smízelny syr* hadn't exactly made it on the international stage.

I waved the waiter over and made a bold front of it, pointing at random to half a dozen dishes. From the quizzical look on his face, I suspected that I'd just ordered 'please check your coat at the door' and 'no dogs allowed'. With an expressive shrug, he wrote it all down and went off to the kitchen.

'What did you order, Dad?'

'It's a surprise.'

First came the Hawaiian toast with the tinned pineapple rings, followed by the curried rice and the banana omelette. Then we had chicken and chips, fried cheese and a beetroot salad. The boiled sausage with mustard was nice, but it clashed slightly with the flavour of the icecream and the beer. It was not a happy group I escorted back to the city centre to catch the overnight train to Stüttgart. They could have had dinner at McDonald's.

We were on our way to Switzerland, where friends of ours lived outside Zürich. We consulted railway timetables and worked out the smartest way of getting there. The first class compartments on European trains were more than comfortable enough to sleep in, so if an overnight train was available, we'd take it, and save the cost of a hotel. The girls loved the luxury of climate control and piped music, reclining seats and towels in the loos. I was getting pretty fond of it myself.

SIXTEEN

Stüttgart, at seven o'clock in the morning, left us in no doubt that we'd arrived in the West. The station buffet would have won restaurant awards in Australia, and it was only one of six restaurants competing for the honour of serving you breakfast. They were baking fresh croissants in front of us and grinding coffee to order. An immaculately clean chef cooked tiny veal sausages and new potatoes in a giant copper pan. The fruit and vegetable shop looked like a prize display at the Royal Melbourne Show.

I went off to the currency exchange and got the unwelcome news that our battered Aussie dollars were worth about the same as Deutschmarks, which made the gorgeous displays of food frighteningly expensive, but we enjoyed breakfast anyway. In plenty of time we found the Zürich express, and spread ourselves in the first class compartment as if born to the manor.

The neat fields and tidy farmhouses looked as if someone had been over them with a vacuum cleaner and a brush during the night. Even the rubbish bins were clean and brightly painted. Gentlemen farmers delivered bales of hay in the boots of their BMWs to herds of well-mannered cows, and the tiny railway stations reminded me of the scale-model train sets I'd played with as a child. With our dusty baggage and travel-stained clothes, we felt quite the untidiest blots on the landscape.

Zürich station was an introduction to the Swiss passion for technology. Intelligent vending machines dispensed local train tickets. The waiting rooms were equipped with climate control and air-locks, lest you be disturbed by the noise of the trains outside. The telephones offered instructions in a choice of five languages. We rang our friends and got directions for the local train. While we stood on the platform, I noticed a yellow metal box on the wall with a speaker grille and a single button. I walked past it a few times, but finally couldn't resist the temptation. I looked around me quickly, then gave it a firm push. I nearly leapt out of my skin when a smooth, female voice said 'Yes sir, can I help you?' in English. I babbled something about the time of the next train and was calmly informed that it would arrive in four minutes. How do they do things like that?

We'd known Terri and Erich for years. Erich was a chef, and we'd worked together at the Sheraton Auckland in New Zealand. We'd met his American wife, Terri, when they came to live in Australia. They had moved back to Erich's native Switzerland, and now lived in a small dairy-farming village outside Zürich, where they were raising three multilingual daughters. Terri drove to the station to pick us up, and there was a busy exchange of news for the next couple of hours, while our three met their three and got to know each other. They shared a large, two-storey Swiss farmhouse with another family, but in a uniquely Swiss way. Each family had their own rooms, opening off a central corridor, but shared the corridor, the stairs and a front door. In the three days we stayed with Terri and Erich, we never clapped eyes on the other family, who seemed to move about their business through secret passageways and hidden stairwells. How they reacted to four adults and six noisy children banging around in the other side of the house we never learnt, since Swiss decorum insisted that they wait until we had *finished* using the corridor, before they emerged to use it themselves.

The village was idyllic. Only 20 minutes from the city, it was as rustic as an old farm tractor, but of course in Switzerland there aren't any old farm tractors: they're all brand new and have Mercedes-Benz engines. A tiny shop sold the rich milk and wonderful cheeses made locally, and a meticulously punctual bus collected the village children each day and took them off to school. Our girls loved the brown-eyed calves and the chickens wandering about the place, and if they began comparing them unfavourably with Bactrian camels and Mongolian ponies, a fierce look was usually enough to shut them up.

Terri, with the wisdom shared by all mothers of three children, knew that our packs must contain weeks' worth of grubby clothing, and insisted that we empty everything into her computerised washing machine, including the packs, our cotton shoes and every garment we owned. We padded about in borrowed socks, blissfully clean and comfortable.

Erich was home by mid-afternoon, and had already started planning dinner. It was to be *raclette*, the Swiss melted cheese dish that had begun life as mountain picnic food. The cheese came originally from the French-speaking Valais district, and was carried along on outdoor expeditions. With a fire well lit, the wheel of cheese was propped close to it, and the melted cheese scraped off with a knife as it softened, to be eaten with potatoes or bread. Erich showed me a *raclette* grill suitable for the dinner table, a clever little appliance with individual trays. You put in your slice of cheese, topped it with a little sliced raw onion or gherkin according to taste, and grilled it yourself. We ate the rich melted cheese with new potatoes and veal sausages, crisp bacon and a local white wine. It was lovely, and no one was in a hurry to leave the table. As the evening wore on, Erich produced a bottle of village-made schnapps and the children were packed off to sleep. We stayed up late talking about our travels and friends in the trade.

'You got to have the three cheeses,' Erich explained, 'got to have the Tilsiter for body, and the Gruyère for the flavour and the Emmenthaler for the creaminess, otherwise your fondue is no good.'

Erich was cooking again, the second night of our crash course in traditional Swiss cookery. We were not complaining.

'First you wipe a little garlic in the pot, then a splash of white wine. Then you put the grated cheeses in, and you stir them slow while they melt.'

He matched action to words, stirring with a wooden spoon. As a novice chef, I'd been taught never to let a cheese sauce boil, but Erich kept the pan on the heat until the mixture was bubbling gently. It was the high fat content of the cheeses that kept them from curdling, he explained, as he poured in a bit more wine and a splash of schnapps. With a touch of salt and pepper, the fondue was ready for the table, and the ten of us gathered around the pot eagerly. We speared bits of crusty bread on long forks and prepared for battle.

'Hey!' Erich barked, glaring fiercely at seven-year-old Aislinn. 'You know if you lose your bread in the fondue, something really bad gonna happen.' She stared at him, her eyes wide with fright.

'What?' she said in a small voice.

'You gotta take your shoes off and run around the house three times in the snow.'

'Really?'

'Yep, that's the rule. Three times, and no cheating.'

'OK.' She fastened bread firmly to her fork, and started first.

I'd never much liked the stale bread dunked in cheddar cheese sauce that passed for fondue in England or America, but this was a revelation. Nutty, creamy and chewy all at once, it was delicious. Twenty minutes later, we were scraping the very last bits from the bottom of the pot. Aislinn had managed to hang on to her bread every time.

Erich was head chef at a busy restaurant overlooking Lake Zürich, catering mostly for locals at lunch and dinner. Split shifts were still the norm, and Erich went in twice a day to supervise a kitchen brigade of Swiss, Italian and German cooks. When he mentioned a big cocktail party he was preparing for, I offered to go in and give him a hand. It would be fun to get into a kitchen again, if only for a night. We drove in to work in the company car.

'New car next week.'

'Why? This one still looks brand new.'

'Wrong colour.'

'What? What's wrong with yellow?'

'Nothing, but if the boss doesn't change the colour, then nobody's going to know it's a new car. And if he doesn't get a new car, then everybody's gonna think he can't afford one.'

'That's crazy.'

'No, that's Swiss.'

The cocktail party was for 150 guests, and it was nicely busy, since we were running à la carte service at the same time. The waiters were all Swiss as far as I could tell, but the chefs were talking to each other in a jumble of German, French, English and Italian. George, the kitchen hand, was from Liberia. We got along fine. After the rush, Erich prepared his orders for the next day, and the two of us slipped down to a local pub/brewery, where they make their own weissbier, a yeasty wheat beer with a sour tang.

Erich told me that it's getting harder to find chefs every year, even in this country which makes an industry of training them. They don't want to work the hours any more, he said, the split shifts that require a cook to work from 9.00 in the morning, through lunch service until 2.00, then back again for dinner service from 5.00 until ten o'clock or later. He said the Swiss don't want to do any of the service jobs that keep the country running, which accounts for the influx of Turkish and Yugoslav workers. This is creating racial tensions in a society known for its implacable reasonableness.

'Where do they live?' I asked.

'Who?'

'All the Turkish workers. I don't see very much new building going on, so where do they live?'

'You know about the bomb shelters?'

Under every Swiss house, by law, there must be a fully equipped bomb shelter, big enough for the whole family and stocked with tinned food, water and a gun. It's been the cornerstone of the Swiss national defence policy for decades.

'Yes. What about them?'

'Well, since the end of the Cold War, the government says you can use the shelters for housing. So that's where they live.'

'You mean underground? The Turks live underground?'

'Yep. It's cheaper than building new houses.'

I thought of the German term *untermensch*, and decided that it had been given a new lease on life.

Clare, Kerry and Aislinn regarded Switzerland as one of the high points of the trip, if only for the wonderful chocolate, sold in every corner shop and supermarket in 10-gram bars, wrapped in packets of five. This was eminently sensible, the girls thought, since you didn't have to go to the shop so often. In the chocolate shops along the Banhofstrasse, the art of the confectioner was displayed like jewellery at Tiffany's—velvet trays and museum lighting in glass and gold cases. Sixty varieties of hand-moulded bon bons, dipped biscuits, chocolate cakes and petits fours were offered for sale in the Lindt shop, and a very well-dressed and well-heeled clientele was doted upon by counter assistants in white gloves. I had never seen a group of people who looked quite so extremely pleased with themselves.

Why the Swiss should turn chocolate into a national treasure was something of a curiosity, since there is no obvious connection between this landlocked Alpine yodel-park and the sweaty jungles of Central America, where chocolate comes from. The Swiss didn't have any colonies in the area, and really didn't get into the chocolate business until 200 years after the stuff first arrived in Europe. The Dutch and the English made all the running at first, but failed to raise it to the art form developed by the Swiss. Inventing milk chocolate around

1876 certainly helped, but cornering the market on very high quality beans, and perfecting the mechanical kneading and tempering of sweet chocolate, has kept them at the pinnacle of the chocolate-maker's art ever since.

Dorcas had been speaking to Terri, who said that while her *Schweitzer-Deutsch* was improving, she was still finding some difficulty in adjusting from the free and easy Californian lifestyle to the more rigorous standards expected of a good Swiss *hausfrau*. We complimented her on the pretty garden beds around the house, bright with flowers even in March. Terri said that the village ladies would take a dim view of any slacking in the garden department, and that this was but a minor detail in the catalogue of socially acceptable behaviour in a Swiss village.

When we'd poured out our thanks for their hospitality and packed our (considerably cleaner) bags, we caught the village bus to the railway station. The schedule said 8.17 am, and it was precisely that when the gleaming clockwork bus pulled up in the village. I paid what seemed a lot of money for five tickets to the station, but I put it down to the high cost of living in the Alps. Standing on the station platform with a crowd of commuters waiting for the Zürich train, I saw the bus driver come marching down towards us in a high state of agitation. He was distraught. He hadn't understood that we had rail passes, and had incorrectly charged us the inclusive fare into the city. He made sure we understood this, then went on to say that he had no authority to issue refunds and had no intention of giving us any money back. It wasn't charging us too much that upset him, it was charging us *incorrectly*.

We detoured slightly to include a ride on the Glacier Express, a cog-assisted railway that runs over the Alps from Chur to Brig. It was memorable for the spectacular scenery (although often obscured by blizzard-like conditions) and for the walloping $150 surcharge which the conductor relieved me of along the way. It was all correct and highly efficient (it was, he explained smoothly, a private section of the line—cash, credit cards or traveller's cheques were most acceptable) but it left me muttering into my beard about the insufferable Swiss. We did get to pass through the tiny village of Neiderwald, near the sources of the Rhine and the Rhône, notable as the birthplace of Caesar Ritz, the little Swiss boy who came down the mountain, met up with Auguste Escoffier, and went on to invent the modern art of hotel-keeping.

The French chef and the Swiss hotelier rose to fame when they were persuaded to come to London and, in 1890, to open the Savoy Hotel, then the largest and most luxurious in the world. They went on to further glory at Claridge's and the Carlton Hotel in London, then to the Paris Ritz. The modern arrangement of the professional kitchen, with separate sections for the preparation of cold foods, of vegetables, of meats and of pastries, was invented by Escoffier and meshed perfectly with the elaborate, showman-like service developed by Ritz. Escoffier's golden rule *'faites simple'* and Ritz's eye for dining as entertainment were the progenitors of modern *nouvelle cuisine* and 'themed' banquets.

Coming down out of the mountains, we were suddenly in French-speaking Switzerland, and all the signs changed as if by magic. Our school French was limited, but a vast improvement on our Chinese, Russian or German. We could actually read notices, comprehend directions; even ask questions with some hope of understanding the answers. It was a refreshing change, and we had a good time reading each other billboards for a while. It's amazing what will amuse you after sitting on a train for two and half months.

We changed trains in Lausanne, for the sleek, spacey French TGV, the *train à grande vitesse*. This rocket on rails would whoosh us up to Paris in four hours, but we decided, on impulse, to get off at Dijon and spend the night. I was resigned to racing across Europe pretty quickly (the whole point now was to get to England and Ireland for a few weeks' rest), but I was loathe to pass up all of France without a pause.

I'd never visited the capital of Burgundy before, but I'd been in love with its wines and its cooking for years. This is the heartland of great French food. Dijon was the ancient capital of the Burgundian kings, who made their court the rival of anything in 12th century Christendom. The towns and villages on our map sounded like a catalogue of my favourite wines: Gevrey-Chambertin and Bâtarde-Montrachet, Nuits-St Georges and Côtes de Beaune.

We arrived late in Dijon, missed the last bus from the centre of town and had to call a taxi. The hostel was of the large French type, much used by school groups and sports clubs, with a very noisy disco in the basement and an enormous restaurant, unfortunately closed at that hour. The only food to be had was instant chicken soup dispensed from a machine.

'This is horrible, Dad.' Coming from Kerry, it was a major complaint.

'It tastes like school glue,' said Aislinn.

'You said the food here was going to be great,' from Clare.

'Look guys, I'm sorry, there's nothing open. We'll just have to wait until breakfast. I'm sure they do great breakfasts here.'

They retired, grumbling darkly, to check the bottom of their rucksacks for stray Mars Bars. Fortunately, French youth hostels have a very enlightened policy about wine, and I was able to buy a nice bottle of Chambertin at the reception desk, so that Dorcas and I could console ourselves.

Breakfast put them back in good spirits, as we introduced them to the pleasures of crisp baguettes and wide bowls of hot chocolate, sweet French butter and soft cheeses. We set out on a walking tour of the old city, visiting the extraordinary gargoyle-fronted Eglise de Notre Dame and the Romanesque St Philibert's. By ten o'clock the girls, sensing the onset of another day of medieval church architecture, bolted for the shopping precinct, where the cake shops and the clothing stores held far more interest for them. I was content, poking around in the 11th century crypt beneath the Church of St Bénigne, imagining the whispers of monks and soldiers, discussing the news of the bastard William of Normandy's daring invasion of England in 1066. We met for a *prix fixe* lunch in a small restaurant off the town square, where the roast spring lamb and the delicious *vin du pays* suited me very well. The pizza and chocolate icecream, I gathered, were OK too.

There was little enough time, but we enjoyed Dijon very much. We had a meal at the youth hostel (very good and very cheap), loaded up with a few of bottles of Burgundy and one of *marc de bourgogne*, bought some Opinel pocket knives for gifts and packed for Paris.

We hadn't been in Paris for fifteen years, Dorcas and I, and whenever we'd been there before, we were broke. I remembered sleeping rough in the Gare du Nord, walking all over the city to find a 12-franc menu, surviving on baguettes, rough Algerian wine and endless slices of *pâté de campagne*. It is a beautiful city, but it had always been, for me, blighted by the need to make 50 francs last for three days. We still weren't rolling in cash, but I was looking forward to enjoying Paris a little more, if only for a day or two.

Clare wanted to see the Eiffel Tower, Dorcas wanted to go shopping at Galleries Lafayette, and I wanted to spend a whole day to myself in the Louvre. Kerry and Aislinn had never heard of Paris, but were open to suggestions. The TGV had us there in two hours, whispering through the green fields of France at more than 200 kilometres an hour.

The Gare du Nord was a mess. Heavy machinery was tearing out great chunks of masonry, and there was a bulldozer working near Track 12 which rather got in the way of the streaming crowds of passengers trying to get to the trains. They were renovating the place, and the cacophony of diesel engines, departure calls, police sirens and hammering workmen made it seem like a nightmare. I enquired about tickets for the Calais train, and learnt there were seats available that afternoon. We had a quick family conference and decided to keep going, straight for England.

SEVENTEEN

The man in the lounge bar was wearing a circlet of condoms on his head. His ears were stuffed with tissue paper and he had two drinking straws up his nose. An almost-empty bottle of cheap gin stood on the table between his knees. He was dead drunk, and sound asleep. His mouth was open and he was snoring fitfully. His friends, who were also drunk, but wide awake, thought this was hilarious, and stuffed more bits of tissue paper between his fingers before taking out a flash camera and snapping a few photographs for posterity. They got bored with him after a few minutes and staggered away to buy some more gin from the duty-free shop.

All around him, the tables were packed with working class Britons out on the cheap day-ticket to Calais, where they could, under the new Common Market regulations, load up on inexpensive French wine and cigarettes. Cartons of Stella Artois and French *vin ordinaire* were stacked between the chairs, the tables a forest of pint glasses and overflowing ashtrays. None of them seemed to be paying any attention to the man with the condoms on his head.

'My 'usband's got the boot of the car full of beer,' a woman confided, 'but the whisky's cheaper on the duty free, so he's gone away to get as much as he can carry.'

This was a real treat, being suddenly able to understand the conversations going on all around us, and speak to strangers.

'Did you come on the day-ticket as well?' she asked.

'No, we've come from Australia overland.'

'Have you really? Lovely, lovely. Brought your kangaroos along, have you?' She slapped her knee and wheezed with laughter. 'Mind you,' she said, suddenly serious, 'I've got a sister in Melbourne . . . '

We were on a cross-Channel ferry bound for Dover. These had changed quite a lot since I'd last taken the overnight 'cattle-boat' to Paris. The ferries were now floating supermarkets, laden with duty-free goodies, casino slot machines, multiple bars and restaurants. The trip took less than two hours, so the passengers had quite a bit of frenetic buying, gambling, eating and drinking to do before we got to Dover. Most of them had gotten a good head-start on it back in Calais. The Common Market regulations, which provided for free importation across EC national boundaries, had changed the habits of a generation used to hoarding the single carton of cigarettes and the two-bottles-of-wine-or-one-of-spirits that the English customs had previously allowed. Cigarettes and wine were cheap in France, so why not pop over and buy a carful? Through a quirk of the laws, the stuff bought on the ferry was free of EC duty as well, so the trip would easily pay for itself, and provide a good old booze-up as well. Return tickets were so cheap that I suspected the shipping companies were making more than enough out of duty-free sales to cover the cost of eighteen sailings a day.

We stayed in London for a few days, rented a car, and drove off north to visit Dorcas's mother and see a bit of the country. London had been horribly crowded, and the traffic was a ridiculous grid-lock for most of the business day. Getting from north London into the centre could take more than an hour on a bus, and I lost patience with the scrum. I'd been into the West End to visit some of what I remembered as the best Cantonese restaurants on the planet, and they did not disappoint, even after our adventures in Guangzhou. London's large and active Chinese population kept up the demand for high quality, sophisticated Cantonese cooking, and I was reminded that however good the cooking out in the kitchen, it was useless unless you were able to get at it. Even in cosmopolitan Hong Kong, this had been a problem. In London's Chinatown, I could reassure a waiter that yes, we really did want the steamed beef tripe with chillies and the braised chicken feet, and no, we would not run screaming into the street when we found out what was in the claypot special.

I slipped down to buy the papers one Sunday morning and stopped into the local 'caff' for a spot of workingman's breakfast—sausage, egg, bacon, chips, beans, mushrooms and tomatoes washed down with over-sized mugs of strong brown tea. This, evidently, had not changed in fifteen years, and probably not in the last hundred. But the eating habits of the young and rising middle class certainly had changed. On the television, in magazines, and most clearly in the supermarket, there was evidence that the English had at last discovered food. The roast beef of England had become a strictly working class dish, while upwardly mobile housewives stood around in the food court at Marks & Spencer, wringing their hands with indecision: should they drink the Bulgarian cabernet with the *saucisson sec* tonight, or should it be the Muscadet with the fresh goat's-milk cheese?

Predictably, the English had turned the enjoyment of good food into yet another way of distinguishing their social superiors and inferiors—by peering into each other's shopping trolleys. This fit neatly into the system which determined that some automobiles were horribly unfashionable (Fords and Toyotas) and others (Saabs and BMWs) were 'quite the business'. I was told in all seriousness by an English friend that houses on *this* side of a particular suburban street were considered smart, while the poor souls on the *other* side of the street were somewhat down-market. Food had become a new weapon in the battle for class distinction. Only bus-drivers and hereditary earls would eat the common British sausage anymore, united in a blind indifference to what went into their mouths, as long as there was brown sauce on it. Everyone else was jockeying for position with hand-raised game pies, imported salamis, scallop terrines and clever French cheeses.

I saw a program on the BBC which summed it all up—a sort of foodie game show, in which contestants are invited into the television kitchen to prepare their favourite dishes. There were three: a Sloane Ranger woman and two elegant young men, who tossed their locks and told us in impeccable tones that they'd be preparing menus full of things like char-grilled lamb with grapefruit jus, confit of sweet peppers and carpaccio of fresh tuna with pink peppercorns. Robert Carrier, dressed as a country-club gourmet in a red blazer and a silk cravat, acted as judge, while the host, someone called Lloyd Grossman, emitted 'oohs' and 'aaahs' in a strangled accent. 'Fabulous, just fabulous,' he cooed over the shoulder of a contestant whisking egg whites, 'I just love it, don't you Robert, when people whisk things? Fabulous.'

We took our first flight since leaving Australia, a short hop from Liverpool to Ireland, and made our way straight to the little town of Dalkey, just south of Dublin. There we had an introduction to my business partner's family, who kept a busy pub on the high street, and we were greeted at McDonagh's like lost relations. I fell easily into the rhythms of Irish speech and manners, because I'd grown up with them, but it remained a little strange: I was born in this country, but did not grow up in it, a qualifier I had to tack on quickly in conversation, when asked where I was from. Drink flowed easily, not so much for the purpose of getting drunk as to loosen the tongue. Quick wit, sideways humour and the ability to tell a good story are the currency of the Irish pub, freely exchanged over pints of Guinness stout.

Dalkey itself was acquiring a reputation for its gourmet restaurants, and there was certainly no shortage of them in the kilometre-long main street. The food shops were excellent, and the habit of shopping daily for meat and vegetables reminded me of France. The bakery sold the rich, mealy Irish soda bread made from wholewheat flour, as well as croissants and white loaves. The greengrocer was busy, as was the fishmonger, and both kinds of Irish butcher—one for beef and lamb and poultry, the other specialising in pork, cured bacon, sausages and ham. The traditional black puddings were a treat, much better for moistness and flavour than the French *boudin noir* or the German *bluttwurst*, I thought. These, with the white pudding made from pork offal, thickly sliced rashers of green or smoked bacon, fresh eggs and fried bread, made up the traditional Irish breakfast. I'd heard it called, with mordant Irish wit, 'a heart attack on a plate', but it was irresistibly good.

Irish cooking had seldom won praise for its sophistication, but the ingredients were superb: the best butter in Europe, fine cheese, grass-fed beef, excellent shellfish and salmon. If the variety of home-grown vegetables and fruits could not compare with France or Italy, the quality, at least, was impressive. Berry fruits, spring greens, healthy root vegetables and dark green spring cabbage were all good, the flavours strong and fresh, quite unlike the taste of factory-farmed produce. Ireland has made the potato its own since the 17th century (which proved, in the pinch, a disastrous reliance on a single food crop), and remains one of the few countries where potatoes are bought by variety: fine, floury potatoes for boiling and steaming, red-skinned waxy potatoes for the best chips and for cold salads, tiny new potatoes for eating hot in their skins with slices of cold salted butter.

The foodie renaissance had come to Ireland, with the influx of European tourists and the rising wealth of the Irish middle class. Like most agricultural countries, Ireland had done well out of the Common Market, once cheap imported foods from Australia (lamb), New Zealand (butter) and the Caribbean (sugar) had been restricted, and tariffs were put in place to encourage the Germans, British and French to buy their foodstuffs inside the Community. Almost completely self-sufficient in food itself, Ireland was making a good living out of tourism and food exports, and the standards were rising. Several country hotels had lifted their game to the point where they were competing for the elusive Michelin stars, and places like Ballymaloe House in County Cork had expanded to include home farms, cookery schools, publishing and television enterprises.

A visit to the Guinness Brewery at St James's Gate, Dublin, was for me more of a religious pilgrimage than a tourist attraction. I had been drinking the stuff since I was sixteen years old (which, in part, explains why there is rather more of me than there might ideally be), and had tracked down bottles of the black beer in places as remote as northern Thailand and Lubbock, Texas. Although the giant brewery (the largest in Europe) no longer conducted tours through the working areas of the operation, they had set up a fascinating museum in an old hop store, a building that still held the strong aroma of hops impregnated in its wooden floors. There were displays of equipment, historical records and paraphernalia dating back to the beginning, when Arthur Guinness had taken over a ramshackle brewery in 1759, and begun to brew the dark, hoppy beer known as 'porter', so named because the porters in Dublin's several markets were exceedingly fond of it. Arthur's stroke of genius had been to develop a cask-conditioned beer which would travel—along the rapidly expanding network of rivers and canals that came with the industrial revolution in Georgian Ireland. Although famous for producing an oddly old-fashioned drink of unvarying quality, the Guinness family owed much of their continuing success to their readiness to take advantage of new technology as it came along. They were the first to 'go big' with steam-driven machinery, very large copper brewing vessels, bulk transport and automated bottling. As late as the 1950s, Guinness still had an enormous cooperage, where wooden barrels were made in astonishing numbers by skilled craftsmen. But when reliable metal casks were developed, the brewery lost no time in changing over. Almost overnight, an ancient art was discarded for high-speed handling that allowed the company to despatch more than four million pints a day from the Liffey-side plant.

Guinness was inextricably part of Dublin, and the ceremony of watching the black, creamy beer settle in the glass, was reverently observed in hundreds of pubs all over the city. Passing up, for once, cathedrals and Norman crypts, I wandered in and out of Dublin's drinking houses, delighted with their individual eccentricities. The ornate etched-glass and polished wood taverns near Trinity College were full of young business types at lunchtime, wolfing down beef and oyster pie and sipping gins and tonic. The working class pubs on Dublin's north side were playing country and western music or MTV on the television, and the scruffy watering holes around Moore St Market were notable for the most impenetrable Dublin dialect I heard anywhere in the city. Around the Law Courts, the drinking houses were particularly comfortable, and there was no bother about sitting quietly over a book for a couple of hours, with a pint glass at your elbow. Each one of these places had built up its own personality over the past 100 years or more, like the patina on a well-polished bar.

The inexhaustible hospitality of the McDonaghs had led to the offer of a 'cottage' on the west coast of Ireland, and we piled into a rented car for the drive down to Kerry. The green fields of Kildare and Laois slid past as the sun shone unexpectedly on a lovely spring morning. We stopped at Cashel to climb the great rock, clumping through cow pastures up to the well-kept 13th century castle. Nearby, the more atmospheric ruins of a 12th century monastery stood in a boggy field, tended only by the cows and the black rooks.

My mother, Kay, had joined us for a two-week holiday, and the six of us packed in a car made frequent stops to top up on icecreams, find a toilet or simply stretch our legs. The towns along the route were lovely: stone-built warrens of narrow streets, unmarked by neon signs or fast food restaurants, looking much as they had for the last 200 years. While the women explored the shops and tiny lanes, I'd slip into any one of a dozen small pubs for a quick restorative, then meet them back at the car. In a small town somewhere west of Tipperary, I opened the door of a dark little pub to find no one in the place. I called out, and a red-faced man of 60 appeared from somewhere out the back.

'Would you have a pint of Guinness, please?'

'God bless you, I would. Will you come out to the back bar, now, and I'll pour it for you, sure.'

I followed the publican along a narrow passage, from which he opened a glass door and showed me into another room, empty but for a small bar and a tweedy gentleman perched on a bar stool. He introduced himself, the publican did the same, and I explained that we were on our way down to Kerry. I admired the pint as it settled in the glass. The publican spoke.

'Would you not have a good pint, then, where you come from?'

'In Australia? Yes, there's good beer, but not as good as this.'

'You would drink the Foster's Lager, that class of thing?'

'They're brewing Guinness in Australia now, too.'

'They're not.'

'Mmmm, they are. Again, not as good as this.'

'Did you hear that, Michael,' the publican said to his only other customer, 'they make the stout now in Australia.'

'That's a great thing,' Michael said, 'and they'll be making the poteen next.' Poteen (pronounced potch-een) is Irish bootleg whiskey, still actively produced in illicit stills in country districts. Carefully aged for as long as a week, it had a reputation for severe effects.

'Is that the truth, now, would you get a drop of the poteen in Australia?'

'I don't think so. At least I've never come across it.'

'Listen to that now, Michael, not a drop of it in Australia.'

'I understand it is a terrible dry country,' Michael said. There was a pause, while I sipped my pint. A look passed between Michael and the publican. There was the hint of a nod.

'Would you take a taste with us now, for the health?' the publican said.

'Just a small one, then.'

The publican produced a recycled Cinzano bottle from underneath the bar and poured three healthy measures in clean tumblers. We toasted each other.

'Good luck.'

'Good luck.'

I drained the glass, surprised to find it quite smooth, clear as vodka, with a pleasantly hot aftertaste. I thanked them for the honour, and said I must be off. I finished my pint, and got up to go. We all shook hands, and they wished me fine weather for the journey. As I walked down the passageway, one of my knees gave me trouble, just a slight buckle that righted itself in a moment. When I opened the door, the sunshine seemed very bright, and there was a faint buzzing in my forehead. I found the car and let myself into it. The women had not returned yet. I thought I'd have a little snooze, with the sun so pleasant and warm.

'Dad, you were snoring,' Aislinn said, in my ear.

They had all miraculously reappeared in the car.

'What?'

'You had your mouth open and you were snoring.'

'How long have you been back?' I asked Dorcas.

'About an hour. Have a nice lunch, did you?'

We passed through Kilmallock, Killarney, Killorglin and a lot of other places that began with K, the country getting wilder and more windswept as we neared the sea. The villages were smaller now and dark, made of wet grey stone, against which the brightly painted shopfronts made an effort to look cheerful. Cahersiveen was a long street of shops and cottages, with muddy tractors and farm machinery parked outside the pubs. Dorcas, Kay and the girls went off to stock up on groceries. We'd been warned there were no supplies in the house, so they bought food and toilet roll, soap and batteries. I was sent to find a bag of coal and a couple of bottles of wine. These I dumped in the boot of the car, and, left with half an hour on my hands, I made a tentative survey of the town. Cahersiveen was not a big place, but within sight of the car, I counted one church, one post office, two tea shops and seventeen pubs. There's nothing like sound town planning.

We drove on another 20 kilometres, on a narrow road through wet, rocky fields and peat bogs. Great piles of the dark brown mud-bricks were stacked for drying, and we passed a small electricity-generating plant, run entirely on this soggy fuel. At Portmagee, a short bridge took us on to Valencia Island, a ragged fingernail on the shaggy coastline of Kerry.

We found the house after enquiring at the village pub. It was a fine, square Georgian farmhouse, which belonged to a couple who were living in Canada. They were working to make enough money to pay for the repairs it badly needed. The house was more or less in one piece, but the outbuildings and kitchen garden which belonged to it were long since overgrown in a tangle of vines and briarwood. We fetched the key from Mrs Murphy, who lived next door, let ourselves in and explored the two-storey building. We'd been given directions for turning on the water, switching on the electricity and connecting the gas bottle. I did all that, while Dorcas sorted out beds for the girls. Kay was settled in the front room with a coal fire and portable radio belting out Irish country and western, interspersed with mass times and cattle prices. She had an edgy look on her face that said this was not quite what she'd had in mind when we'd offered a two-week holiday in a cottage on the west coast. I asked her to break out the duty-free whiskey and poke the fire occasionally. I went off to see what Dorcas was doing and met her on the stairs.

'OK?'

'It's fine. There's plenty of bedding, and the girls can sleep in one room.'

'Great. Shall I bring all the stuff in from the car?'

'I'll get that, if you'll see about the hot water. We need baths.'

'Right, coming up.'

The absent owners had left a sheet of instructions for starting the peat-burning stove in the pantry, which would, in theory, heat the water tank through some complicated arrangement of pipes buried in the wall. There were all sorts of flues, levers, grates and knobs which had to be adjusted correctly to keep it going. I put in some coal and half a dozen firelighters, then gave it a match. The coal caught readily enough, but there was a small problem with smoke, which began to billow merrily out of the wall. I studied the instruction sheet for guidance, but there was nothing on it about smoke, so I left the whole thing going, to warm up a bit. I went back to the front room to see about Kay. Her nose was wrinkling.

'I can smell smoke.'

'It's the stove. I've only just started it. Where's the whiskey?'

'Here, you open it. Shouldn't you be watching it? The stove, I mean.'

'It's fine. Are there any glasses?'

'They're very dangerous, those coal-burning stoves. People have been asphyxiated in their sleep. I read it in a magazine, just last month.'

'Don't worry. Have a whiskey.'

I'd been driving all day and the whiskey tasted wonderful. Kay took one reluctantly, casting glances at the door every few seconds. Johnny Cash was singing about Folsom Prison on the radio. There were two sheep in the front garden.

'Please. Go and check the stove. I'm sure it's getting worse.'

'OK, I'll go. Just relax, it's fine.'

I went out into the corridor, where the smoke was, indeed, a bit thick. I opened the door to the pantry, where it was worse. The stove was happily belching out great clouds of the stuff. I tried more of the levers and flues, but it wouldn't stop doing that. I opened the back door, the front door and all the downstairs windows, which helped a bit, although it left the place a fraction breezy. Dorcas looked in on me fiddling with the stove, then retreated with eyes streaming, deep coughs racking her chest. This is nothing, I thought, you want to try the smoking compartment on a Russian train.

Dorcas got the girls lined up for baths, but Kay refused to budge from the front room, convinced that she'd be overcome by fumes before she reached the stairs. She had the headlines all worked out in her head: FAMILY OF SIX DEAD IN HORROR BLAZE. She stuck it out bravely for one night, but by ten o'clock the next morning, she'd moved in with Mrs Murphy.

Driving along rugged hillside tracks more fit for goats than shiny red rented cars, we passed abandoned cottages, their slate roofs long since blown off, their granite walls crumbling slowly as the winter rains ate away at the foundations. Here and there, a whitewashed stucco house sported a television aerial and a curl of peat smoke from the chimney, but the hills had an empty look, as if most of the people had wandered away. And indeed, they had.

In 1845, subsistence farmers living on tiny plots of wet, barren land in the west of Ireland, lifting the season's crop of potatoes, noticed they were affected with small patches of scale and black spots. It didn't look too bad, so the potatoes were put in storage as usual, to provide food for their families through the year. Potatoes had only become a staple food in Ireland in the previous century. Their suitability for poor soil and their fast rate of growth made them the single most important food crop for a desperately poor peasantry, living in conditions little changed since the Middle Ages. Supplemented by wheat, milk, seaweed, barley and cabbage, they provided an adequate survival diet. But within weeks of lifting the crop in 1845, the potatoes began to blacken and liquefy, making them useless as food.

The disease called 'blight' was the result of a virus in the soil, and it was extremely contagious. It had first shown up in Europe as early as the 1830s, but it wasn't until it reached Ireland that it found the cool, wet conditions in which it thrived. In 1846, the entire potato crop in Ireland was destroyed, and in 1847 it happened again. Two years without sufficient food will kill anyone, and more than a million Irish peasants starved to death. Another one and a half million fled the country on disease-ridden ships for America or Australia. The population of Ireland in 1840 was something over eight and a half million. By 1861, scarcely six million were left alive. It was a devastating lesson in food economics from which the country never really recovered.

EIGHTEEN

Dorcas and I took the car to the western end of the island, parked it in a cul-de-sac and set off over the fields towards a distant tower on top of the cliffs. Off to the left, the long ocean swells were rolling into the inlet, crashing on to the rocks and throwing great heaves of spray into the air. Sea birds wheeled over our heads and the sheep, tucked into hollows in the lumpy pasture, bounded away in alarm when we approached them. The track climbed at a tangent up the side of Bray Head, beyond which lay the open Atlantic. We reached the tower, and looked cautiously over where the springy green grass ended abruptly, and the sheer cliffs plunged 150 metres into the sea. We stood in the stiff wind, our hair blown across our faces, and looked out to sea. This was the end of the line, the western edge of Europe.

'We haven't long, have we?' Dorcas asked.

'No. I'll try to call Budapest tomorrow.'

We'd found an agent in Budapest who would purchase tickets for us on the Trans-Siberian, by post. The German agencies charged a fortune, and made the journey sound like the twelve labours of Hercules. If we could get the tickets held for us, it would cut a week off our travel time.

'Right, well, let's go back then, shall we?'

'Let's.'

We turned our backs on the sea, and walked back down to the car.

We gave the car back in Dublin, saw Kay off at the airport and thanked the McDonaghs for looking after us. The first leg was a gentle train from Dublin down the Wicklow coast to Rosslare Harbour. The ferry was a 20-hour trip to France, reaching Le Havre late in the afternoon. We'd use the Eurail passes to get us back to Budapest as quickly as possible, then pick up the tickets for Moscow and Beijing. The girls were ready for the trip.

'Are we going all the way back by train?' Clare asked.

'Yes, that's the idea. Maybe a boat trip at the end.'

'It'll be fun. Russia was crazy!'

We were in Paris for just a night and a day, just long enough to squeeze in a few meals (a great little restaurant near the Louvre, which served lovely *andouillettes* and *pommes frites* done in olive oil) and to attend (unwittingly) a fascist rally. I was walking back to our hotel near Les Halles when the crowd became thicker, and I saw a stage being set up. There were roadies coughing into microphones and '*testing un, deux, trois . . .* '. I stopped to watch people buying sausages at the food stalls and handing out leaflets. An honour guard of skinny bike-boys with leather jackets and and blue scarves formed up, as a long black limousine arrived on the rue de Rivoli. Jean-Marie Le Pen was the guest speaker, and the crowd went wild when he marched up to the stage, flanked by medal-decked heroes of World War II and shadowy OAS types with bulging jackets and wires in their ears. I stayed for only a little of his speech, during which he said '*La France*' about six times, to roars of approval from the crowd. Le Pen was the leader of the National Front, a neo-Nazi party which had taken 14 per cent of the vote in the previous year's election.

The youth hostel in Budapest was much busier this time. The early tide of students was on its way over from America, and the French and English were swapping countries for spring holidays. The trains had been busy. We needed visas for the Ukraine (I didn't want to test my luck again) and for Russia. We'd already picked up the Chinese visas in Dublin, from a stiffly formal Chinese Ambassador to Ireland, who seemed to be the only occupant of a chilly embassy house near Merrion Square.

I found the Museum of Pastrycooks open this time and it was fun: the early Hungarian advertisements and menus made the rivalry with Vienna seem quite reasonable. We took the children to the zoo, where a beautiful Art Deco-Egyptian gate led into a park full of elephants and tigers, orangutans and kangaroos. Next door, we pressed our noses against the windows of the superbly plush Restaurant Gündel, with its waiters in full evening dress and and the Bohemian glass shining like fire. The markets were bright with flowers and yellow peppers, smoked sides of pork, bottles of fresh grape juice and country wines. Young couples were kissing on buses and street corners. It felt like being in a Gene Kelly movie: spring had sprung in Europe. Even the embassy staff were chirpy: the Russians handed over fresh visas with hardly any fuss, and the Intourist lady was almost motherly.

Wherever the sap was rising, though, it was not doing so at the new Ukrainian embassy, a converted house in the suburbs of Buda. Here, the new government was just getting its grip on bureaucracy. We joined a two-hour queue for the visa window. At the front of the line, women were bursting into tears and businessmen were threatening violence. The woman behind the counter was a first class horror, obviously taking much pleasure out of refusing visas to Ukranians wanting to go home, or cancelling travel permits issued by the old regime. An old woman pleaded to rejoin her family in Kiev, an executive brandished an expired permit, threatening to close down the entire tobacco harvest in the Ukraine. We were small beer, and too far back in the line; they snapped their doors shut firmly at 2.00 pm and refused to issue any more visas. We'd have to take our chances at the border.

We took a short day trip out to Eger, a quaintly medieval city rich with gaudy Baroque cathedrals and the occasional Turkish minaret. The surrounding vineyards were showing signs of new growth, next year's harvest of *Eger Bikyaver*, the famous Bull's Blood wine. We found bottles of rich fruit syrups and new wine in the markets, and stocked up for the trip to Moscow. Back in Budapest, there was time for a last meal at the Markus Restaurant, and a quick look around the Museum of Fine Art on Hösók Ter. We were glad to get on to the train at Keleti Station, anxious to be away. Europe was too seductive, too easy to fall in love with. We were all looking forward to the sparer, simpler routine of long-distance travel. When the train left Keleti Station at 9.00 pm, we were on our way home.

At 3.00 am, the border post at Cop was cold and foggy. I had to go and get Ukraine visas, which involved waking up an irritable official to stamp a chit and make change for US dollars. I presented the receipt for $100 that we'd collected on the way out to a plain-clothes policeman who showed great interest in it. He took it from me and disappeared. I waited, I enquired and I thumped the counter, but after an hour had to admit defeat and run for the already moving train. It was the only time in the entire trip we were robbed, predictably by a policeman.

In Moscow again, we had a 12-hour wait for the train. We put our things in storage and went for a wander in in the city. We were able to get into Red Square (on our previous visit, it had been heavily cordoned off by the military) and visited the GUM department store, which was not far away. All the snow had gone, and the Moscow parks were green and pleasant in the warm spring sunshine.

The Trans-Siberian route actually carries three different trains, the Trans-Mongolian (which cuts off a corner through Ulan Bator), the Trans-Manchurian (to Beijing by way of the old White Russian capital, Harbin), and the Trans-Siberian, which goes as far as Vladivostok (Nakhodka), and connects with steamers for Japan. The latter two were about the same length, at just over 9000 kilometres, the longest continuous express runs left in the world. The trip takes six or seven days, depending on the weather conditions and the state of the rails in western Siberia. We had tickets for the Trans-Manchurian train via Harbin, scheduled to leave Yaraslovsky Station a little before 11.00 pm.

The atmosphere on the station platform was cheerful: groups of Chinese students and families were clustered around great piles of baggage, and a crowd had gathered around the huge departures board. Dozens of trains were listed, to Perm and Ekaterinberg, to Kirov, Novosibirsk and the remote Arctic port of Archangel'sk on the White Sea. Moscow punks flitted through the crowd, elaborately decked out in motorcycle jackets and facial jewellery. The beer stall operating from the back of a truck was doing a roaring trade, popping the tops off half-litre bottles as fast as they could work the crowd. A long line of marketeers offered sausages, flowers, bread, wristwatches and vodka, each item held up for sale as if on the shelves of an impromptu supermarket.

The evening was turning cold, so we took refuge in one of the crowded waiting rooms, where the girls made instant friends with some Chinese students carrying small puppies tucked into their coats. In quite fluent English, they explained that there was a market for Russian dogs in Beijing, where local laws forbidding the keeping of pets had recently been relaxed. The problem, they said, would be getting the animals through the Chinese border, but if they were successful, the animals bought for US$5 or US$10 in Moscow would sell for twenty times that in Beijing. This was a new use for the Trans-Siberian Railway: a sort of travelling supermarket, a black-market bazaar on wheels.

The train was three hours late (not a remarkable event, I was told). We were all half-asleep when it finally pulled into the platform, through a freezing fog, eerily lit by the station lights. The green Mect-18 carriages were familiar, standard rolling stock all over Russia. The two diesel locomotives at the front of the train were already running warm, and there was no delay about boarding. We found our compartment, made up the beds and had the children asleep just as the train began to move.

The very nice bit about train travel, for the passenger, is the utter disregard you can have for the means of getting where you are going. There's no stressful take-off or landing, no one asks you to navigate from a crumpled map, there are very few things to run into, and in any case, someone else is doing the driving. You get on, you spend a given amount of time staring out the window, and then you get off. It's wonderfully simple, and I'd grown to appreciate the peaceful hiatus between one ticket counter and the next. With six days of continuous travel before us, I was a happy man. The girls amused themselves running around the train, Dorcas was submerged in a book, and the most stressful decision I was called upon to make was whether I should stroll down to the restaurant car for a cigarette, or have an afternoon snooze in an upper berth. It is a sort of travel that is fast disappearing, now that one of half the world's travellers are screaming non-stop from Tokyo to Berlin in eleven hours flat, and the other half are trying to backpack through Borneo carrying hang gliders and oxygen masks.

A train allows you to make acquaintances slowly, rather like ocean voyages did before they were taken over by rich American divorcées looking for a little Love Boat action. You may nod at someone as you pass in the corridor, perhaps lift your chin when you see them in the dining car, and let that suffice for a day or two. You are not forced into intense conversations with airline bores from whom there is no escape, other than in a toilet cubicle the size of a shoebox. With its wheels firmly on the ground, a train allows you a close, even intimate, look at the countryside, but does not expect you to scour it for road signs. You can safely ignore several hundred kilometres worth of it, and no harm will befall you.

The Trans-Siberian Railway might not have been designed with this purpose in mind, but it served remarkably well. As a feat of engineering, it was not a revolutionary development (in either sense: the project was built under the Czarist regime, from 1891–1905). It was simply very long. The idea had been to drag Russia into the 20th century with some claim to being a single country, connected from the Atlantic to the Pacific by an efficient means of transport. The Bolsheviks, and the Soviets who followed them, would probably have had to build it if it wasn't already there. As it was, they improved the line, doubled it, replaced steam with diesel locomotives and eventually electrified it. That it ran for 9000 kilometres was an achievement; than it ran all the year round, through the depths of the Siberian winter, was a miracle. During our passage, in the early weeks of May, we could still see fields of snow and ice on the wide Russian steppes.

I'd been prepared, by many travellers' tales, for the great distances involved. The steppes were endless, I'd read, and the trip dreadfully boring once outside of Moscow. But it didn't seem so from our compartment window. There were dozens of small communities along the line, where we saw broad-backed farmers, stripped to the waist, ploughing tiny fields, often with horses, while their wives planted potatoes or tended rows of skinny onion shoots. We saw the giant fields of the collective farms, many of them untilled, even this late in the precious Russian spring. I wondered if the farm workers had seen the wisdom of working for food rather than roubles, and were concentrating on feeding themselves first. I couldn't blame them if they had; the rouble was becoming more worthless every day, and the Moscow mafiosi, with their wallets full of American dollars, could hardly be relied upon to rebuild a shattered economy. A man driving a tractor might be lucky to earn 400 roubles a month, but a roast chicken, sold on the station platform, would bring 1000. Better by far to grow chickens.

We made good use of the station markets, and it became something of a sport to leap off the train briskly, scout what was on offer, and return with my pockets full of hot *pierogi*, cool *smyetana* or *kyefir* (sour milk) and a loaf of fresh black bread. There was stiff competition for beer, and bottles of lemonade, so you had to be quick, and remember your Russian numbers. It was a mark of the recent upheavals to see the Chinese passengers waving 1000-rouble notes at old *babushkas* who were so shocked that they might never have seen them before. The Chinese were not left behind in the marketing stakes. At every station, they were hanging out the windows, offering jackets, wristwatches, umbrellas, running shoes and portable radios to an interested crowd. The exchanges became comical at times, since the locals often turned up with the (presumably) pilfered products from the nearest factory. Plastic buckets were swapped for nylon tights, ball bearings for cassette tapes. At one station, a crowd of locals produced, inexplicably, a whole carton of children's plastic saxophones. The Chinese stared at these in puzzlement, until one of the vendors was inspired to give the thing a toot, and the bidding erupted with enthusiasm.

'What do they do with all that stuff?'

I was talking to Isobel, a Beijing language student returning from a year's study in Moscow. She was the one with a tiny Pekinese puppy tucked away in her coat. Another passenger had an equally small animal of unspecified breed. The two pups were allowed to run up and down the corridor yapping, with Aislinn and Kerry in hot pursuit.

'They trade all the time. Some of them take the train back and forth.'

'You mean they make their living that way?'

'Yeah, they can make a lot of money.'

'But who wants plastic saxophones?'

'Somebody will. Plenty of things are easy to get in China, but not in Russia. Some things in Russia are ridiculously cheap compared to China. Like dogs.'

'Will they let you through with him?'

'Russian side will be no problem, I think, just have to pay a little money. Chinese side will be much harder. Depends on who I get.'

'Will you sell him in Beijing?'

'I was going to, but now I think I'll keep him. He's cute.'

Isobel wanted to know all about us, and asked endless questions about Australia, and the trip. When she heard that I was a cook, she became enthusiastic about all the Beijing specialties I'd have to try when we got there.

'I can't wait,' she said, 'it's been so long since I had Chinese food. You have to come and try the real Beijing dishes with me. I'll show you where.'

'You're on. What did you miss?'

'Everything. I never want to eat sour cream again. I'm going to have a big bowl of *jia jou mein* and some Ship's Head soup.'

'What's that?'

'Jia jou mein is a special kind of Beijing noodle. Ship's Head soup is famous, real local specialty, I'll show you.'

The only Russians in our carriage were Valeri, Olga and Sasha, sharing a compartment with a young German student named Carsten. Valeri was an immensely strong young lad who was, I learnt later, the all-Russia junior wrestling champion. He looked remarkably like the Russian fighter in whichever one of the Rocky movies it was, all blond crew-cut and bunched muscles in a white t-shirt. He had a gentle, soft-spoken manner which brightened into smiles when he met Clare. The two of them spent hours playing some horribly complicated card game, drinking lemonade and bursting into laughter occasionally. Sasha, his coach, a fit-looking 40, and Sasha's wife Olga (who was a teacher) were accompanying Valeri to Shenyang in China for a five-month posting to help train Chinese athletes. They were typically Russian in the warmth of their hospitality and their eagerness to talk to us. I had met few enough Russians, other than the officials who sat behind desks at visa offices or ticket counters, but those I did meet had this same quick friendliness and generosity. I liked them a lot.

Olga was the only one of the three who spoke any English at all, and she was pressed to her limit by the number of questions that flew back and forth when we all squeezed into one compartment to share a table full of food. They produced an amazing store of tinned fish, sausages, smoked cheese, fruit, onions, butter and bread, and insisted that we eat quantities of the stuff with them. Running true to form, I produced a bottle of vodka, but Olga declined politely, and explained that Valeri was too young, even if he had not been in training. Sasha was on the point of refusing, when he decided he was Russian first and an athlete second, and joined me for a drink. We toasted Russia, Australia, *glasnost* and several other things that were later unclear to me. Even Olga got into the spirit, and accepted a demure portion, when Dorcas provided a splash of Hungarian cherry syrup to go with it.

Carsten joined us, too, and we had a good time for several hours, as the sun went down and the night grew longer. There were, I think, several trips to the dining car to replenish the vodka, each of us taking it in turn. Olga was working hard as interpreter, since we'd long gone beyond the 'what's your name and how many children do you have?' stage, and were grappling with weightier questions of international politics, the importance of sport and the essential dignity of the common man. Dorcas gave up, and excused herself to put the children to bed. Valeri went with them to play some more cards. Olga went to bed. Sasha, Carsten and I were now at the point where we were slapping each other on the shoulders, telling each other what great guys we were and insisting that the other fellow have another drink. Carsten ascended to his berth with some difficulty, leaving Sasha and I to rumble on late into the night about the really important things: Family. Country. Freedom. Motorcycles.

Sometime during the night we had passed Sverdlovsk, which had been Ekaterinberg before the Soviets, and was Ekaterinberg again, according to the new Bartholomew's map we'd found in an English bookshop. It was here, in 1918, that Czar Nicholas II and his family were executed by the State, just the first few in the terrible slaughters that were to follow. It's something that fascism and communism have in common: first, it's necessary to kill everyone, then you can explain this great idea you have for running the country. We had crossed the Ural Mountains. We were in Asia again.

The land was now boggy, flat tundra. Wide marshes stretched out for kilometres on either side of the line, marked in places with dirty drifts of old ice or snow, melting now in the sunshine. There were fewer villages, and these were simpler, often just a few buildings and one of the odd wooden towers the railwaymen built to keep an eye out for the trains. The light was pale, as if the sun were somehow diluted by the enormous distances it fell upon. I had seen such distances before, in Australia, but this was so different; not an ancient, blazing desert, but the rawly scarred surface of a land torn by glaciers and ice. The rivers were grey and full, flowing north towards the Arctic.

At Novosibirsk, we crossed the Ob River, and the country changed. The flat marshes gave way to alpine forest, hundreds of kilometres of deep green fir and pine trees, interspersed with stands of alder and birch. Now we saw more buildings—wooden houses, unpainted, closely fitted log cabins, chalets overlooking gunmetal lakes and everywhere the little glasshouses for the early vegetables. A gang of men were working on the line, heavy coats laid aside, crouched over a small fire, brewing up tea. They looked up at the train as we passed, their faces grimy with woodsmoke.

We reached Lake Baikal on the fourth day, through hilly sections of evergreen taiga. The lake is said to be the reservoir for one-fifth of all the world's fresh water, immensely deep, up to 1.7 kilometres in places, and at this time of year, still hard frozen for a distance of more than a kilometre from shore. We had plenty of time to look at it, since the train skirted the shoreline for more than four hours. In some places, the ice had melted all the way to the shore, and the water was clear and deep blue. Baikal is very rich in sturgeon, crayfish and freshwater prawns, but it is suffering badly from the industrial sludge pumped into it from the city of Irkutsk. The city lies on the Angara River, the only outflow of the lake, so the worst of it is carried away to poison the land somewhere to the north. Soon after we left Baikal, the railway line split, one track turning due south for Mongolia, Ulan Bator and Beijing. We continued east, to Manchuria.

NINETEEN

There was agitation among the Chinese traders. Bags were being re-packed, some currency exchange was going on, and we were asked more than once to 'look after' something for someone else, a favour we politely declined. The border was a tough one, placed as it was on a line of military and political stress. The Russians and the Chinese had been shooting at each other here as recently as two years ago. We would be at it for most of the day, since the border also meant a change of bogies, fitting the train out for the Chinese rail gauge. At least it would be in waking hours, instead of the middle-of-the-night imbroglio we'd put up with before. We had passed the 6000-kilometre mark (measured from Moscow) some hours before, and had left the forested hills behind. The train swayed and clacked over a bumpy pass, then rolled out on to an immense plain of parched yellow grass, rolling with low undulations to the horizon in both directions. This was our first glimpse of the Mongolian steppe and, as if on cue, a few riders on shaggy ponies appeared, sporting the jaunty long-eared Mongolian cap. The few settlements we passed were wretched dumps of broken machinery, squalid houses and scattered rubbish. A lonely road followed the railway line, but traffic on it was rare.

At length, we pulled into the station at Zabajkalskaya, the Russian border town, if indeed it could be called a town, since it seemed to exist only to service the railway and the army posts along the grim border. It was the most thoroughly tired, wasted, shattered and broken place I had seen anywhere. The railway platform and the streets were littered with the shards of broken bottles; all the buildings had their windows smashed and boarded up. A crowd of Chinese had gathered around a pair of lame dogs to torment them with sticks, and the locals were represented by a couple of evil-smelling drunks arguing over a bottle of vodka and a loaded pistol. With a few scabby children playing among the ruins, it looked like a film set for some post-nuclear saga: *Mad Max* or the *Twilight Zone*. We gathered in the spit and rubbish-strewn railway building to wait it out. We were stranded until they brought our train back. By 9.00 pm, the sun was sinking, and it began to get really cold. The children came back from their exploring, and huddled up close for warmth.

There is a sort of 'alpha' state into which most travellers can send themselves, when a long passage of uncomfortable time must be endured. On an Afghan bus or on a crowded Malaysian ferry, you must be able to absent yourself until it's over, or you would go mad with boredom or frustration. We were slipping into this state nicely, when Sasha appeared at my elbow, and gestured for me to follow him. He indicated that I should bring Dorcas and the children as well, but to do so quietly and quickly. We left the station building and walked along the tracks towards the train sheds. Olga and Valeri were waiting for us behind a battered Russian tank, mounted on a concrete plinth as a monument to some past war. We found the train still jacked up on the rails, while workers banged around underneath with giant spanners in their hands. Sasha knocked quietly at the door, and our conductor appeared. He glanced up and down, then hastened us aboard and firmly locked the door. In Sasha's compartment, a meal was already laid out on the table, and we spent the next few hours enjoying pleasant Russian hospitality.

Towards midnight, the train moved back on to the station, and our Chinese passengers rejoined us. The Russian border guards moved through the train, taking their time to inspect passports and baggage. They seemed to pay little attention to us, but the Chinese got a thorough going-over. There was a whiff of antagonism in the air between the Russians and the Chinese, and no one was smiling. Isobel had given her little dog some sort of sedative, and it lay curled up asleep in her shoulder bag. Another pup was not so lucky—I saw it carried away by a Russian soldier, carelessly swung by its two hind legs. The inspections were at last over, and the train began to move. We passed through two parallel chain-link fences, guarded by soldiers with dogs, overlooked by towers and flood-lit. There was a no man's land about 500 metres wide, then we passed under a gate bearing the big red star of the People's Republic. Our fellow passengers seemed to release their collective breath, and a great whoop went up in the corridor. We were in China.

Manzhouli was the border post, and here the train stopped for two hours. A shop, festooned with Christmas lights, was doing a brisk trade in instant noodles, Chinese sausages and sticky cakes. Everyone on the train got off, returned with armfuls of food, and started an early-hours feast, while the Chinese border guards stumbled through the train, kicking angrily at passengers camped in the corridors. There was a commotion down at Sasha's compartment, and I went down to see what was happening, but a Chinese soldier with a gun waved me back to our compartment and slammed the door firmly. I heard Valeri's voiced raised, then the sound of Olga weeping. I opened the door to see Sasha being herded down the corridor carrying his bags. Olga followed him. She stopped briefly at the door to say that they were being taken off the train, for some reason she hadn't the words to explain. She waved at us tearfully, then was pushed along by a guard. We never saw them again.

When the train moved off, I went straight down to their compartment, where Carsten, the German student, was sitting on an empty berth, looking pale and shaken.

'What happened?'

'They are bastards. They wanted money, but Sasha didn't have it.'

'What money?'

'They said US$100, to let them in. Sasha didn't have any American money, where would he get it?'

'So they took them off the train?'

'I offered Sasha some Deutschmarks, but he said it wasn't right, their papers were in order, and they'd come to work for the Chinese government.'

'What do you think they'll do with them?'

'I don't know. They were real shits, threatening jail, pushing everyone around. They'll probably hold them for a while, then let them go.'

More than a year later, we'd learn that Sasha, Olga and Valeri were all right, but the Chinese had refused them entry unless they could pay the bribe. Staunchly refusing to do so, they were sent back to Russia on the next train. China had to pursue its bid for the 2000 Olympics without Valeri's help with the wrestling team.

The railway line followed the course of a shallow river, through some of the prettiest landscapes I'd seen in China. There were neat fields and picturesque villages, clean streams and golden stacks of early wheat. This bucolic scene belied a turbulent history: Manchuria had been a battlefield for centuries. The Mongol hordes had invaded the Chinese Empire along these gentle valleys in the 13th century, deposing the Song Dynasty and placing Temujin's grandson, Kublai Khan, upon the Throne of Heaven as the first Yuan emperor. He ruled a country that was then the largest on earth, stretching from the gates of Europe to the Yellow Sea, incorporating all of Siberia, European Russia, Central Asia and China. There has never been a larger one since. It was the imposition of Mongol martial law over these vast distances that allowed trade to flourish on the Silk Road, standardised a written language, and encouraged European traders like the Italian Polo brothers to visit China, eventually to return with tales of its fabulous wealth and power. Marco Polo was only twenty years old when he first laid eyes on the new imperial city at Beijing ('northern capital') and he would serve as interpreter and advisor to Kublai Khan for almost twenty years before returning to his native Venice. Captured in a local skirmish with the Genoese, he was thrown into prison and thus given ample time to write the story of his travels to far Cathay.

The Mongols were in turn toppled off their throne by an ambitious peasant named Zhu Yuanzhang, who founded the Ming Dynasty and moved the capital south again to Nanjing, hoping to avoid further bad news from the north. It was not to be, and another wave of 'Northern Barbarians', the Manchus, eventually conquered the empire, which had lost the plot of world domination, and was gradually folding in upon itself, just as the upstart Europeans were beginning to spread their wings and set about 'discovering' the rest of the world.

Manchuria was by no means finished as a troubled northern province. The Russian architects of the Trans-Siberian Railway had secured Chinese approval for construction of the line through Harbin to Vladivostok in 1896, effectively annexing the city for the Russian imperial throne. The Japanese invaded Manchuria in 1904, tearing control of the line from the Russians. After the Bolshevik Revolution, thousands of White Russians (supporters of the Tsar, and Cossack troops) poured across the border into China, fleeing the Red Army. They established Harbin as a city of Russian refugees, although under the control of the Japanese, overseeing their puppet state of Manchukuo, with the hapless Pu Yi as emperor. Soviet troops helped the Chinese Kuomintang to boot the Japanese out in 1945, but there was still much bitter fighting to be done before Mao Zedong gained his victory over Chiang Kaishek, and was able to proclaim the People's Republic in Beijing in 1949. The Soviets decided that it would be safer all around to construct a new branch of the railway, giving northern China a miss altogether, but the border remained a dicey one.

The Chinese restaurant car opened for dinner, to great acclaim. Everyone poured in, crowding the tables and ordering everything on the menu. You had to admit, they knew how to cook, even in the cramped confines of a tiny kitchen. We feasted on roast chicken, stewed greens with pork, mushroom soup and rice. The tablecloths had been thoughtfully pre-stained before the restaurant car opened, the plastic flowers were in their proper place by the windows, and the Chinese waiters had just the right amount of swagger and teeth-sucking to make us feel right at home. They overcharged us by Y50, then argued about it, but they were just being friendly.

We rolled into Beijing Station about two o'clock in the afternoon, either six or 30 hours late, depending on how you interpreted the tangled Chinese timetable. Carsten and I found a taxi, we all got in, and spent the next two hours trying to argue our way into a succession of cheap hotels, most of which refused us on sight. We found one eventually, a comfortable, somewhat cavernous place a few kilometres out of the centre. We had a series of long, lovely baths, then went out to dinner in a local restaurant, where the stunned proprietor did his best to understand us, then provided an excellent meal.

The next day, we explored Beijing. It was enormous. What looked like a few minutes' walk on our map turned out to be kilometres away, and we were forced to elbow our way on to buses in order to reach Tiananmen Square. The crowds were very thick, although foreign faces were still surprisingly rare. Carsten and I set off on a long hunt for somewhere to change travellers' cheques on a Sunday. We walked miles, but eventually stumbled into the elegant lobby of the Beijing Hotel, dodging uniformed bellhops and shrill tour guides. The cashier gave us crisp new FEC notes, which we were loathe to spend until we had converted them to Renminbi at a better rate. A quiet negotiation at the bicycle hire shop sorted this out, and I set off on a squeaky machine for Beijing Railway Station, to see about tickets for the Shanghai train, while Carsten went to the Forbidden City.

The foreigners' ticket office was surprisingly well-organised, and I was able to come away with five tickets within an hour. On the way back to the hotel, I stopped into one of Beijing's famous duck restaurants, the *Qianmen Quanjude Kaoyadian* (more colourful in translation as 'The Big Duck'), where the lunch rush had died down enough for me to get a table. I sat in the fast-service café, where duck was more or less the only thing on the menu, and sipped a cold beer while the waitress went to fetch me a plate. The preparation of Peking Duck has become a familiar subject in western food magazines, but most of them I'd read seemed to miss the point—there isn't any recipe for this dish. Like Cantonese roast pork, it's simply a roasted meat. Whether it's any good or not has much more to do with technique than with ingredients. Even in Beijing, there's argument over how it should be done, and the 'open oven'/'closed oven' schools would probably come to blows if they didn't each have their own restaurants to retire to.

The ducks, of course, are specially chosen for the dish. Beijing cooks insist on the local breed, which has a high fat content and a stubby body. The unfortunate birds live a short but happy life, fed constantly with a mixture of grain and honey. Things do get a little ugly in the last few weeks, when the birds are force-fed to pile on the kilos, but it's over quickly, and the duck is sent to market. They are plucked and singed, inflated and lacquered with sugar syrup, all to ensure a particularly crisp skin when they're roasted. This is done in a wood-fired oven, and I was able to get a quick look through the kitchen door, where a dozen cooks monitored the progress of racks of hanging ducks in square brick ovens. They were watching the rate of browning, turning and adjusting the racks with long poles to ensure everything went along evenly. Their faces, lit by the glow of the ovens, were nearly as brown as their ducks.

I had read, in translation, a Chinese instruction book for professional duck roasters. It referred to 'early spring, cloudy day' syrups, quite different from 'late winter, cold sunshine' syrups, either of which might be required for coating the duck. The sorghum stalk used to seal the duck's backside had to be chosen from just such a part of the plant, so that it might be the right shape to form an efficient plug. There was a good deal of advice on the proper pouring of the traditional three ladles of boiling water to seal the skin. Shades of oven temperature were discussed without reference to a thermometer, according to whether they were 'rising wet heat' or 'falling dry heat'.

Roasting time was determined by the weight of the duck, time of the year, quality of the heat and shape of the oven. To achieve the perfect red-copper colour, it was permissible to lean parts of the carcass closer to the fire, but this was regarded, disdainfully, as an apprentice's trick. A skilled duck roaster should have no need of it.

The results were very good. The sliced meat and skin were served on a plate with a dollop of hoisin sauce. Another plate came with the chewy little pancakes in which you wrap your duck. Around me, about 50 people were chewing and slurping noisily. I did the same. The waitress brought a bowl of cloudy soup, made from the bones of the recently roasted.

The hotel was well out of the centre and we were content to hang around in our pleasant, leafy neighbourhood a few kilometres south of Tiananmen. The city centre crowds were best avoided. Our district was well supplied with small restaurants and the hotel rooms were comfortable. Just across the street, an all-purpose shop served cold beer, children's sweets and bottles of yogurt delivered fresh each morning. There was a set of rickety tables and chairs on the pavement, so we could sit quietly and watch the amazing Beijing bicycle traffic go by. Aside from taxis, and a few lorries, most of the transport was human or horse-powered. Tricycles were common, adult versions with a little seat on the back. These were used to convey spare parts, sides of pork, bushels of oranges, frail grandmothers or over-dressed children, according to need. We bought lichees and tangerines for the kids, and watched the local children bring their pet ducks out to feed in the evening. I was surprised by the easy friendliness we met; I'd been expecting something more severe from Beijing, and it had turned out to be a charmer.

Isobel had promised to show us lunch in the big city, so we met her the next day in town. We all squeezed into a taxi, and drove around the western side of the Forbidden City. (We would have gone in to see it, but the government had hiked the foreigner's admission price up to 80 times the Chinese rate, which made it roughly equivalent to charging Chinese visitors $500 each to have a look inside the Sydney Opera House.) We met up with Carsten and went into a sort of restaurant arcade, made up of a dozen little specialist shops. Isobel was enthusiastic, explaining each Beijing delicacy as we came to it. First, she said, we had to try the famous Ship's Head soup. We filed into a tiny place and took our seats next to a pair of bubbling vats, from which white-coated women were dishing out bowls of steaming soup. Carsten was a vegetarian, but a very polite one, so he didn't complain when Isobel presented him with brimming bowl full of tubes, membranes, organs and spongy things floating around in dark brown liquid.

'Why is it called Ship's Head soup?' I asked, struggling manfully with my bowlful of by-products.

'Because that's what it made from. Ship's Head.'

The penny dropped.

'You mean sheep as in baa-baa sheep?'

'Yes. What did you think?'

We slurped and chewed for a while. Carsten was looking a little ill, but still game.

'How did you do that?' I whispered. 'You've eaten half the bowl.'

'I kept telling myself it was tofu.'

'Brave man.'

We went to the next shop for more 'Beijing flavour' goodies. This was the noodle stall, where Isobel introduced us to *jia jou mien*, a dish that is, to a native Beijinger, what a slice of Sicilian pizza is to a New Yorker, a *croque monsieur* to a Parisian or a pie floater to someone from Adelaide. We were given bowls of thick, chewy noodles topped with spoonfuls of braised pork in soya sauce. The practice was to add to this from a platter of raw ingredients, including cucumber, radish, raw soya beans and bean sprouts. Isobel urged us to douse the whole thing in vinegar and wolf it down.

We stopped for a plate of 'King Chao's dumplings', a sort of fried triangle filled with diced beef tendon and vegetables. They were delicious. The highlight of our lunch, Isobel said, would be 'watching the dragon spit'. Carsten grinned weakly. He was approaching his limit, I could tell, for exotic Beijing specialties, and was not keen to find out what 'dragon's spit' might be. Isobel marched us firmly into another tiny shop, and explained the procedure.

You chose a base ingredient (one of three: toasted rice flour, fine semolina or almond meal) then indicated your favourite flavourings (pistachios, sweet spices, loaf sugar or cinnamon) and let the man grind and mix them for you in a china bowl. Isobel translated and advised.

'Now, see, the dragon spits!'

The enormous metal urn in the window, it seemed, was not just for decoration. In the shape of a fat-bellied dragon, ornately decorated with gold leaf and enamelwork, it was in fact a giant kettle, mounted on gimbals, so that it could be tipped. Boiling water shot out of the dragon's mouth, and the dry ingredients were whisked together quickly to make a sort of pudding, garnished with sweet coconut milk. The children were delighted, and insisted on seeing the dragon spit again.

We caught the express train to Shanghai, a remarkably modern, sleek Chinese equivalent of the French TGV. There were hostesses in airline-style uniforms, air-conditioning and special plastic souvenir coat-hangers. We would travel the 1500 kilometres to Shanghai, we were told, in less than sixteen hours—an unheard-of velocity for a Chinese train. We were not the only foreigners on board. We met a Dutch couple, a pair of Germans, two Israeli girls and a New Zealander. We were soon talking, sharing China stories and comparing notes.

At the old Pujiang Hotel in Shanghai, business was brisk. Tour groups of Japanese, Korean and overseas Chinese were being led through the lobby by shrill tour guides. The hotel dormitories were full of individual travellers, some of them students who had been studying in Beijing, now on their spring break. The atmosphere was lively and party-like, with many stories swapped over bottles of Seagull beer. I met a Swiss photo-journalist who had been living with nomads in Mongolia for six months, and a Japanese Shinto monk who had made a pilgrimage to Dunhuang. The Swiss fellow told me that he had indulged a passion for fly fishing on remote Mongolian lakes, but that his hosts refused to eat any of the fat brown trout and Arctic char he pulled out of the water.

'Why not?' I asked.

'You have seen the Mongolian national symbol?'

'No, what is it?'

'Two fish, you know, like Pisces, like yin-yang.'

'So?'

'So the Mongolians believe, in their mythology, that they are descended from two fish. It wouldn't be polite to eat your grandparents, you see?'

'Fair enough.'

Shanghai was bristling with people and with building sites. Dr Peng took us on an informal tour of the new Pudong Development Area, where his wife was directing yet another engineering project. There were cranes everywhere, and the concrete pumping machinery was operating full blast at 10.00 pm. New apartment blocks, bridges, factories and offices were going up in a fury of redevelopment. I asked Peng where all the money was coming from. He explained the government had encouraged hundreds of 'joint-venture' companies with Hong

Kong, Taiwanese and European partners supplying the cash, gambling on the enormous emerging markets in China. It made sense: Coca-Cola had only to sell one bottle to every Chinese person for their birthday each year, and they'd be shifting 1000 million bottles a year.

We enjoyed Shanghai, and grew much bolder about striding into strange restaurants to see what was on offer. We found the pastry-shops for which the city is famous, a curious left-over from the heyday of the Sassoons and the Jardine Mathiesons, when skilled pastrycooks from France and Austria had been imported to prepare the strudels, *mille-feuilles* and custard tarts demanded by their European clientele. These had in turn trained local cooks to make puff pastry, fondant icing and other exotic foreign foods. The Europeans had departed, but the Shanghainese had by that time developed their own taste for European pastries, much in the same way that the rest of the world had taken to Chinese spring rolls and fried rice. So the local pastrycooks continued the tradition, training their own apprentices, to keep up the supply of almond croissants and chocolate eclairs in the busy shops along Beijing Donglu. Most of the good young chefs and pastrycooks, I was told, were now being scooped up by the new hotels. The French Sofitel, Japanese Nikko and American Sheraton chains all had large properties in Shanghai, and were offering top wages for the best people.

Dorcas and I went for a walk through an early-morning market in the Hongkou district, for a look at the fresh seafood and live poultry, the tiny bakeries and roast-meat shops. I stopped to watch a barrel-chested cook in a white apron make the Shanghainese *jiao-tse*, rolling them nimbly with his fingers and setting them to fry on an oiled griddle. He waved us in grandly to his little shop, insisting that we take a seat to enjoy a plate of his best dumplings and a hearty bowl of soup. The dumplings were delicious, but Dorcas was regarding the soup suspiciously.

'What's the matter?' I said. 'It's lovely broth, isn't it?'

'Fine. But what are these brown cubes floating around in it?'

'You don't really want to know. Just eat them.'

'Out with it. What is this stuff?'

'Well, blood, actually. Chicken's blood. They pour it in these trays, you see, and then steam it until it's set, then . . . '

'That's enough.'

'It's really interesting, they use . . . '

'Please. Enough. You can finish mine.'

Outside the shop, our chef had lost no time taking advantage of this unexpected opportunity to drum up a little business. He had gathered a small crowd, and was addressing them at the top of his voice, pointing frequently at us, no doubt telling them that we had flown all the way from Australia for the pleasure of eating his dumplings. We paid the bill and left, not without feeling we ought to be signing autographs, or at least waving.

Along the road at the delicatessen, a crowd of women were queuing up for half-kilos of pork sausage and for chicken feet, which came either boiled in soya or plain. There were slices of deep-fried fish, platters of spiced pork and beef, and a tray of tiny creatures which I could not at first identify. They seemed to have four legs, and they'd certainly been deep-fried. But for the absence of tails, I'd have said they were mice. I learned later that they were 'rice sparrows', tiny birds that live in the paddy fields. They're caught in nets, and make a popular, if bony little snack.

We found the Shanghai Art Museum, which had an interesting admissions policy: Chinese people, 40 cents; foreigners, US$20. I told them our own museums didn't charge that much, but I was wasting my breath. I was convinced that they sat in board meetings somewhere, telling each other wilder and wilder stories about how much foreign tourists would pay for things. Thanks to the package-tour companies, they were probably right. We crossed the street to the charmingly decrepit Shanghai Natural History Museum, Admission: Y2 for everybody. Inside, there was a good anthropology display, a couple of huge, dusty dinosaur skeletons, and four floors of a magpie collection of dusty bottles and bad taxidermy. It was comically neglected; half the exhibits were invisible because the light bulbs had gone out and no one had bothered to change them. In each exhibit hall, there was a small school desk and chair, occupied by a semi-comatose guard. In the last one, the little wooden desk had simply fallen apart. There was nothing but a few bits of crumbling wood and peeling paint in a heap on the floor. I wondered for a moment if the bones of the guard were in there, too.

TWENTY

We were conscious now that the trip was coming to an end. Not for a couple of weeks yet, but soon. It would be hard to readjust to the life we led at home, with appointments to be kept, deadlines to be met and the telephone bill to be paid. It is one of the real luxuries of long-distance travel that you can devote time and thought to how you are going to spend a particular day. It must be like that for people with inherited wealth (perhaps not, I really don't know many): the ability to go to another city on an impulse, to linger in a place because you like the view, to hire a boat on a whim. We'd enjoyed that sort of luxury as we twice crossed the width of Asia. It was at times a battle, of course, but then it would have been boring otherwise. To travel, with all your days planned and all your tickets arranged, seems a pointless exercise, for how then do you find the chance meeting, the odd restaurant, the unexpected kindness? And if there are none of those, why go?

Dr Peng and his wife asked all of us to their house for dinner, a few days before we were due to leave for Hong Kong. Hospitality, especially in the realms of food and drink, can be ruinously expensive in Chinese society, because of the notion of face. To entertain someone, and retain face, it's necessary to be almost criminally irresponsible with money, choosing the most expensive restaurant and the most expensive foods. To provide is not enough; one must be seen to waste, with profligacy and carelessness. Dr Peng had told me on our last visit that it was a serious problem, and led easily to corruption, as one government official sought to outdo another with the magnificence of the meals provided for their cronies. Even in relatively poor families, he said, it was not unusual to spend Y1000 on a large family dinner at a restaurant, if face was to be maintained by the head of the family. This would equate to four months' wages, say $A10 000, for an Australian worker on an average wage.

This matter of face, and of gift-giving, is a subtle business among the Chinese, and we were conscious of blundering mightily when it came to returning favours. When we had seen them last, the Pengs had showered gifts on us, from toys for the children to a beautiful jade chop with my name carved in it. To visit their house, we carried a bottle of cognac, a porcelain tea set and a set of *matrushka* dolls bought in Russia, for their daughter. Whether these were the right scale or type of gifts, we didn't know, but we hoped for the best. That we had received the invitation at all, I thought, was a mark of friendship that went beyond mere curiosity and interest in foreign visitors.

The Pengs lived in a block of flats on the south side of the city. There were three rooms and a tiny balcony. The largest room held a high, Chinese-style bed and the dinner table, with a new Japanese television set in pride of place. The kitchen-cum-laundry was next to that, then a second bedroom where their daughter slept. It was, by Shanghai standards, a spacious flat. Mrs Peng had been working all day on the food, it seemed, because the table was already laden with ten or twelve cold dishes when we arrived. We sat to dinner straight away, and Mrs Peng went to the kitchen. Steamed prawns, fried eel, steamed pomfret and braised chicken appeared, followed by roast chicken, congee with fresh herbs, spiced beef and tomato soup. We ate ourselves to a standstill, while Dr Peng insisted we take another morsel, another bowlful. Mrs Peng joined us only at the end of the meal, to pick at a few mouthfuls, before jumping up, putting on her coat, and bidding us goodnight.

She had to go to work, Dr Peng explained. The Pudong development plan was going on just as quickly in the night as in the day, so she would be working overnight, and this after spending all day preparing a feast! Even in socialist, egalitarian China, a woman was expected to hold down a professional job, raise a child, cook and wash for the whole family, and in her spare time, presumably, attend political consciousness-raising classes.

We talked for a long time, about the changes China was going through, and Peng's plans for the future. He was considering getting out of public practice, he said, and devoting his time to setting up a private dental clinic with a few partners (this from a leading neuro surgeon, who in any western country would be counting his BMWs), because there was more money in it. Peng was no opportunist; he came across as a dedicated Party man, but there was no way he could remain human and not want some part of the new wealth being created all around him. There were a lot of highly skilled people in the same boat, I thought: technicians, doctors, engineers and scientists who were now earning less than bicycle repairmen.

We breakfasted at the Peace Hotel, admiring the extraordinary Art Deco interiors—stained glass and wrought iron, illuminated panels and brass chandeliers. The buffet was an eclectic mix of western and Chinese foods; steamed *wan tuns* sat oddly next to Danish pastries, *chow ho fan* rubbed chafing dishes with poached eggs on toast. The girls were delighted to find that the Peace Hotel chefs considered strawberry layer cake and chocolate eclairs to be part of a nutritionally balanced breakfast.

We spent the last day shopping, marching up and down Beijing Donglu in search of a dozen small gifts for friends. In the evening, we took ourselves off to see the Shanghai Acrobatic Circus, an amazing troupe of jugglers, contortionists, acrobats and musicians who held the five of us entranced for three hours. We dragged the Swiss journalist and a Canadian acquaintance off to a last meal of Shanghainese special cooking. The Swiss got the point immediately, and was delighted to discover the special Shanghai fried spinach, the chicken in wine lees sauce, the braised eel with green onions; but it was lost on the Canadian, who couldn't understand why you would want to spend $5 on a meal when you could get one for 50 cents.

We'd booked tickets on the MV Hai Xing, a small liner which plied the route between Shanghai and Hong Kong, taking two and a half days to complete the trip. The service was run by the Chinese government shipping line, and was rumoured to be quite the most luxurious thing they had afloat. Most of our fellow passengers, who turned up in the morning to pass Customs and Emigration control, were Hong Kongers returning home after visiting relatives in China, but there were a few Europeans and Australians, too. We boarded the ship in the late morning, and found our cabins easily. We had two of them, handsomely fitted out with portholes, writing desks, comfortable berths and private showers. We couldn't believe our luck.

The girls flew off to investigate the rest of the ship, racing back at intervals to report the discovery of a library, a games lounge, a spacious restaurant and deck chairs. The swimming pool, unfortunately, was a cracked square hole on the upper deck, bereft of water. When I asked the purser whether it would be filled, I got a curt 'mei you'. We weren't out of China yet.

Promptly on schedule, the ship blew its horn, and we had a last look at the Shanghai Bund, before turning for the trip down river, passing under the framework of a second massive suspension bridge being built across the river. In a few hours, we would turn south, heading for the Formosa Strait, and the South China Sea.

The passage was easy and uneventful, mostly spent reading or chatting with a mixed group of other travellers, over cold beers in the upstairs bar. We were all on our way out of China, and it was almost the only topic of conversation. All of us had grim stories to tell, of bureaucratic malevolence, over-charging, greed and incompetence, but when we'd all vented our spleens, we all agreed sheepishly that we would probably go back. It was the Chinese people themselves who stayed in our minds, and it wasn't fair to judge them by the habits of a regime only 45 years old when their culture stretched back 4500 years and more. As a people, the Chinese certainly had their faults. They were horribly messy with their waste products, they could not look at a rare animal without wanting to eat it, they were racist to the core, and certainly imperialists (to which the Tibetans, Mongols and the Uighurs could testify). On the other hand, they were incredibly industrious, they valued learning and respected old age, they were patient, enduring and persistent. The Chinese students and cadres we'd met were very interested in the outside world, and were eager to see their country join the wider community of nations. Whether the present system of government could survive the enormous strains being put upon it, none of us could tell; but that the Chinese people would survive it, and would probably be running the world within a few decades, none of us doubted.

The Hong Kongers were holed up in the forward lounge, deep into a continuous mah-jong contest that would last the rest of the trip. The room was thick with cigarette smoke, there was tinny Cantonese music coming from the speakers, and hefty piles of money lay on the tables. The players emerged three times a day for meals, which were served all at once in the restaurant. The food was reasonable, but unremarkable.

On the second night, the sea was full of lights. We were passing through the Formosa Strait, and the busy sea lanes were full of tankers, containers ships and tugs. By morning, the wind had blown up, and we had a fine porthole view of deep blue rollers and wind-torn spray. We were somewhere off Xiamen, the old city of Amoy, from which most of the great waves of emigration had come in the 19th century. It was here that Chiang Kaishek had made his last stand, before fleeing to Taiwan with the greater part of China's imperial treasury and a priceless collection of art.

We approached Hong Kong very early in the morning. The early risers were already up, practicing *tai chi chuan* on the ship's wide teak decks. The sun rose from a bank of clouds the colour of orange juice, and I could feel its heat on my face. I noticed the high-tech communications equipment on the tiny islands on either side: radar dishes and microwave repeaters, transmission masts and clusters of aerials. We moved slowly through a glassy sea, past dozens of ocean-going ships and hundreds of busy junks. The astonishing buildings appeared next, vertical white towers rising up out of the green cliffs. Then, we were in the harbour. The bizarre grey exoskeleton of the Hong Kong & Shanghai Bank stood close by on the port side, and the Star Ferry boats were clanking back and forth from Central to Kowloon. The MV *Hai Xing* anchored, and the crew formed up to wave at us as we boarded the ferry that would take us into Kowloon. We'd come full circle.

The land mass that forms a continuous continent from the China Sea to the English Channel is the largest on earth. We may call it China or India or Russia or Europe, but of course, from space, it's all one piece. From its mountains and hidden valleys, its deserts and oases and inland seas, come all the stories and legends that have formed our western civilisation. This is the land that knew the Sumerians and the Greeks, the Persians and the Han, the Celts, the Huns, the Romans, the T'ang emperors, the Sassanids, the Arabs and the Seljuk Turks. Once, an obscure Mongol chieftain named Temujin rose to conquer nearly all of it and rule an empire that stretched from the Korean peninsula to the plains of Hungary. The Mongols re-opened and made passable the ancient trade route we call the Silk Road and thus ushered in the modern era. All of our history is here, much of it still visible on the ground, or imprinted on the faces of the people, or remembered in the foods they eat. If we can find traces of our tangled history in language and architecture, myth and religion, then we can also find them in the traditional foods prepared by people who still live close to the land that produced them.

I watched bakers in Xinjiang prepare flatbreads in the same way they might have been made in the ancient cities of Ur and Kish 5000 years ago, and reflected on the fact that wheat was unknown in China before about 3000 BC. Someone had brought it there from Asia Minor. The chickens that ran about in the villages outside Xi'an had come originally from India, as had the ginger and the sugar-cane we saw in the markets at Lanzhou. Buddhism, which was to become one of the state religions of China, came that way too, but I had an idea the chickens got there first. In the Gobi Desert, I ate delicious apricots and melon grown with the aid of an irrigation system which was invented in Persia, and indeed, may still be seen working in Afghanistan and modern Iraq. Maize and chillies, staple crops all over China, were New World natives, and since there is no record of the Chinese crossing the Pacific, they had to come from Europe sometime after the end of the 15th century.

Of course, the trade had travelled in both directions and silk was not the only thing carried from China to the markets at Samarkand, Baghdad and Damascus. The English would have gone without chestnuts, the French without peaches, and the Poles without their plum brandy if the seeds had not come from China sometime after the fall of Rome. The steak tartare so popular in Moscow had arrived under the saddle of some Mongol soldier (although I had to admit the Russians had refined the dish somewhat), and if mutton was the meat of choice in Ürümqi, it was because the flame of Islam had come across the mountains and made it so.

The route we travelled had seen many pass before us. The T'ang capital at Chang'an (modern Xi'an) was once the largest city on earth, the beginning and the end of a road that carried Phoenician glass and Indian spices, Chinese silk and Persian art. The caravans had traversed the dead wastes of the Gobi Desert, the frozen Karakorum passes into India, and the lonely Dzungarian Gate that led to Central Asia.

To make our journey, we relied upon the vast spider web of long-distance railways that spans these enormous distances, from Siberia to Gibraltar. We were fascinated by the idea that this tenuous ribbon of steel physically connects remote Malaysian hill stations with the frozen ports of the Arctic Ocean, the rice paddies of Vietnam with the tulip fields of Holland. To take a train is the most romantic form of travel, and the same time the most prosaic. Railways go through places, not over them. You do not have exclusive use; anyone who wants to can get on your train or off it. You may share a compartment with a Mongolian farmer, a Kashgari merchant or a party of French schoolgirls, and there's absolutely no predicting who might get on next. Your train will transport you through densely packed city slums or across barren desert wastes with equal reliability and despatch. It will even stop occasionally, so that you may breathe the local air, watch a sparrow on a tiled roof or buy a packet of biscuits in a language you've never heard before. It is the last great public transport: there is nothing to stop you getting on in one place and simply staying on until you reach the other side of the world.

By the time we reached Hong Kong, each of the girls had celebrated a birthday somewhere on the road, and so would return home officially one year older. For nearly five months they had put up with eating whatever there was to eat and sleeping whenever they got the chance. They did not complain or demand to go home. They did adapt quite happily to any sort of travel, and never once got seriously lost. They asked a lot of questions, listened to many long-winded explanations, and looked at everything with the calm, open eyes of children. We had lived in each other's pockets, spent weeks at a time in cramped train compartments and had eaten almost every meal *en famille*. This is a great deal more togetherness than the average Australian family is accustomed to putting up with, and I'm pleased to report that we enjoyed it very much. The sense of looking after each other, forgiving each other's little eccentricities, and a common eagerness to see what was around the next bend made bonds that are still with us today.